LEFT BEHIND

**a study of
mental handicap**

PSYCHIATRIC TOPICS for community workers
General Editor: Alistair Munro
Psychiatrist-in-Chief, University of Toronto

Signs of Stress: the social problems of psychiatric illness
J. Wallace McCulloch, University of Bradford
Herschel A. Prins, University of Leicester

Insanity: a study of major psychiatric disorders
Professor R. G. Priest, St. Mary's Hospital Medical School, London
Dr. J. Steinert, Springfield Hospital, London

Alcoholism and Addiction
Dr. R. Swinson, Toronto General Hospital
Dr. Derek Eaves, Western Regional Medical Centre, British Columbia

Growing Pains: a study of teenage distress
Dr. Edna M. Irwin, Hollymoor Hospital, Birmingham

LEFT BEHIND
a study of
mental handicap

W. Alan Heaton-Ward

Consultant Psychiatrist, Stoke Park Group of Hospitals,
Clinical Teacher in Mental Health, University of Bristol

MACDONALD AND EVANS

MACDONALD & EVANS LTD.
Estover, Plymouth PL6 7PZ

First published 1977

© W. Alan Heaton-Ward 1977

ISBN: 0 7121 1236 7

Text set in 11/12 pt Photon Times, printed by photolithography.
and bound in Great Britain at The Pitman Press, Bath

This book would have been impossible without the help of a great many people to whom the author wishes to express his very sincere thanks—Professor Alistair Munro, the editor of the series and Mr. David Sutherland, now of Messrs. Macdonald and Evans Ltd., for their advice and encouragement; Dr. J. E. M. Glancy, and Mr. K. Pennington, Professor A. K. M. Macrae and Dr. B. G. Scally for their advice on consequential amendments to the Mental Health Acts of 1959, 1960 and 1961 respectively; Dr. R. Wilkins and Mr. D. Cridge for providing statistics; all the authors who have sent reprints of their papers, Mrs. Stella Waller for help with the references, and Mrs. Joy Fearnley-Taylor for her patience and skill in deciphering the author's handwriting and typing the manuscript.

The author owes a very special expression of thanks to his friend and colleague, Dr. Joźe Jancar, for suggesting the title of this book.

Chapter 10 is reproduced from *Mental Subnormality* by W. Alan Heaton-Ward by kind permission of the publishers, Messrs. John Wright & Sons, Ltd., Bristol.

W. A. H-W.

To my wife Christine for putting up with the very unsocial hours which it meant!

Contents

'The problem of mental subnormality will never be solved by pretending it doesn't exist.'

Heaton-Ward, 1958

List of Tables

Editor's Foreword

When the series to which this book belongs was conceived, the primary aim was to provide authoritative accounts of a number of important topics in the complex and rapidly-developing field of psychiatric disorder, presented in such a way as to be of interest and value to those involved in social work, using this term in its widest sense. It was hoped that the series would also be of help to the interested layman who wished an accurate, but not over-technical description of modern developments in mental health practice. The authors in the series have been asked to present their specialties from their own standpoints, setting them forth as they themselves view them. By adopting this method, it was felt that the reader would benefit from a more accurate and informed picture of present-day psychiatry than would be the case if an artificial 'social worker's approach' was adopted.

Information which would only be of interest to a medical readership has not necessarily been excluded, but where it is present it is because of some particular relevance and it has been given the proper emphasis for the present context. We believe that, by presenting the subject as it exists, it comes across with all the more immediacy and accuracy.

Dr. Heaton-Ward has followed these editorial precepts to the letter and the present volume does exactly what was asked of it.

However, in addition he has produced a compact, readable text on Mental Handicap which I can recommend as highly suitable to the medical student who wishes a brief but comprehensive account, and even to the medical postgraduate who may need an introductory primer on the subject. At the present time, when increasing interdisciplinary effort is being sought to help with the problems of the mentally handicapped, a book which can appeal to such a varied background must be, among other things, a valuable influence towards shared learning and professional co-operation.

Mental deficiency—now virtually an obsolete term—mental subnormality—the title still used by many medical experts in the field—and mental handicap—seen by an increasing number of people as having possibly less derogatory overtones—all describe the same area of endeavour. In this country, for many years, much of the responsibility for the care of the mentally handicapped has been given to medical practitioners and, traditionally, mental subnormality has been a subspecialty of psychiatry. Until lately, psychiatry was one of the most underprivileged of the medical specialties, and even now it still lags gravely behind in terms of investment, resources and staff as compared with much of modern medicine. As may be imagined, subnormality trailed even further behind and it is only now that the voices of those working in this subject are beginning to be heard. Unhappily, they are too often listened to because of the scandals which have come to light in an undermanned and underequipped service. The great majority of workers in the subnormality service, whatever their profession, display dedication, skill and resourcefulness in circumstances that are usually difficult and sometimes appalling. It would be rather easy to be carried away at the present time on a wave of sentiment and emotion and to say that because some things are bad, everything in the field of mental subnormality should be swept out and a totally fresh start made.

How wrong this would be! Dr. Heaton-Ward gives an excellent account of the way in which his specialty has slowly developed over the years. As he shows, it has not always been a 'Cinderella' subject and there have been many valuable contributions to its body of knowledge and expertise. At the present time, we know of many ways to help the mentally handicapped individual to realise his fullest potential and to aid his family in dealing with the extra burden inevitably thrust upon them, but lack of resources so often prevents these methods from being put to adequate use. Here we have a discipline with great potential: obviously there is room for much innovation, for contributions from many sources, for a diversity of skills. But having read this book, I hope you will be convinced as I am that it would be totally against reason to throw away all the knowledge that has already been gained with such effort. Unfortunately, there *are* some zealots who adopt such an illogical attitude. Their efforts, and undoubted sincerity, would best be spent in trying to develop the combination of expertise which is so self-evidently required.

Every handicapped individual has his own particular needs. Very often, mental and physical disability are inseparably intertwined, and in some tragic cases, actual mental and physical disease are superadded. Families may or may not be able to cope within their own resources; usually great or lesser degrees of help are required. A closely-integrated team approach is necessary to deal with such situations comprehensively. At present, something of an ideological battle is being fought over the question of who should make up the membership of such a team and who its leader should be. Dr. Heaton-Ward admittedly adopts a polemical approach in this conflict and argues for medical leadership; certainly not all the readers of this book will agree with him on this point. Indeed, a great deal of soul-searching is taking place among the group of doctors concerned with this specialty on this very issue. They are increasingly entering into dialogue with other professional colleagues and a good deal of experimentation in methods and realignment in functions is beginning to take place as a result.

At the end of the day, there is little doubt that this will be to the patient's great benefit. In the meantime, there is a danger that his welfare may be partly overlooked as the experts jockey for position and status-problems become of predominant importance. No one is arguing for the retention of some absolute *status quo*: no field of health-care needs so many advances so quickly as does this one. But there is already a large body of expertise which is potentially available to help the handicapped. Dr. Heaton-Ward brings some of this to our attention, he proposes ways of deploying it effectively, and he indicates where he thinks advances ought to take place. He is a leading expert on subnormality with a wealth of practical experience behind him. Without sentiment, but with great compassion, he describes this subject as it is today, introducing theory where it is appropriate but never letting it ride roughshod over practical realities.

This specialty is a fascinating meeting ground for so many fields of study and of effort—genetics, obstetrics, paediatrics, psychiatry, psychology, education, social work, and several of the therapeutic professions, among others. But essentially these are all subordinated to the need to help a handicapped and underprivileged child who increasingly, with advances in modern medicine, will survive into adulthood. I hope that the practical usefulness of this book will be self-evident to those of the helping professions who read it. To relatives of the mentally handicapped who may find it of value, I trust it will convey a sense of professional commitment and of therapeutic hopefulness. To the general reader, I think that it must emphasise the enormous need for investment of time, talent and resources. Much is being achieved, but so much is still to be done. Many of our present-day subnormality institutions are blasphemies by current standards, not because the staff want them to be so but because the State and the public at large chose until recently to regard psychiatry as a relatively unimportant and unpromising field of endeavour. With proper support, it could rapidly become one of the most productive areas of preventive medicine and of rationally designed therapy. The better informed the public is about the situation and the fewer the taboos surrounding the subject, the more rapidly are advances likely to occur.

Alistair Munro
Toronto, 1977

1 The concept of mental subnormality

In England, the law first recognised a distinction between mental illness and mental defect in the fourteenth century, during the reign of Edward II. At that time the *Statute de Praerogativa Regis* drew a distinction between a 'lunatic' or 'person of unsound mind' (*non compos mentis* in the Statute) on the one hand, and an 'idiot' or 'natural fool' on the other. It asserted that the wardship of lunatics and idiots was to be a prerogative of the Crown and that the property of a lunatic must be preserved intact and returned to him on recovery, subject only to his maintenance and that of his family meanwhile out of his estate, whereas the profits of the property of an idiot, beyond what was spent on his maintenance, might be appropriated for the enjoyment of the Crown or of the person entrusted with the custody of the idiot.

Unfortunately, subsequent legislation, up to and including the *Mental Health Act* 1959, has tended to blur this distinction and it is not surprising, therefore, that the general public reveal obvious confusion in their use of the terms mental illness and mental handicap. Thus the *Lunatics Act* 1845 defined 'lunatics' as meaning 'every insane person being an idiot or lunatic of unsound mind'. The situation was temporarily clarified by the *Idiots Act* 1886, which stated that 'idiots or imbeciles does not include lunatics . . .' and 'lunatic does not mean or include idiot or imbecile'. However, the *Lunacy*

Act 1890 again defined 'lunatics' as meaning 'an idiot or person of unsound mind'.

The *Mental Deficiency Act* 1913 as amended by the *Mental Deficiency (Amending) Act* 1927, defined mental deficiency as 'a condition of arrested or incomplete development of mind occurring before the age of eighteen years, whether due to inherent causes or induced by injury or disease'. It defined four classes of mental defectives—idiots, imbeciles, feeble minded and moral imbeciles.

In the case of idiots, the mental defect was so severe that they were unable to guard themselves against common physical dangers; in the case of imbeciles, it was less severe but sufficient to render them incapable of managing themselves or their affairs, or, in the case of children, of being taught to do so, and, in the case of the feeble minded, the mental defect was less severe again, but was still so pronounced that they required care, supervision and control for their own protection or for the protection of others and, in the case of children, that they appeared to be permanently incapable by reason of such defectiveness of receiving proper benefit from the instruction of an ordinary school. The criterion in the fourth class—the moral imbeciles—was that their mental defectiveness was coupled with strongly vicious and criminal propensities for which they required care, supervision and control for the protection of others. The term 'moral imbecile' was amended to 'moral defective' in the *Mental Deficiency (Amending) Act* 1927 in recognition of the fact that the basic intelligence of persons in that category was often higher than the term imbecile would imply.

The *Mental Health Act* 1959 (which applies to England and Wales only) abolished the term mental defective and its four subdivisions, and substituted the terms 'severe subnormality' and 'subnormality', which it defined as follows: 'severe subnormality means a state of arrested or incomplete development of mind, which includes subnormality of intelligence and is of such a nature or degree that the patient is incapable of living an independent life or of guarding himself against serious exploitation, or will be so incapable when of an age to do so', and 'subnormality means a state of arrested or incomplete development of mind (not amounting to severe subnormality) which includes subnormality of intelligence and is of a nature or degree which requires or is susceptible to medical treatment or other special care or training of the patient'. It will be seen that the criterion of severe subnormality is primarily one of social incapacity, whereas that of subnormality is primarily one of therapeutic need. The terms subnormality and severe subnormality are much less precise than those they replaced, severe subnormality embracing both the former categories of idiocy and imbecility and covering a correspondingly wide range of ability. The imprecision is intensified by the widespread tendency to use 'subnormal' as an omnibus term to refer to all degrees of mental subnormality, rather than to confine its use more correctly to refer to the less severe of its two categories.

The 1959 Act also introduced the term 'psychopathic disorder', which it defined as meaning 'a persistent disorder or disability of mind (whether or not including subnormality of intelligence) which results in abnormally aggressive or seriously irresponsible conduct on the part of the patient, and requires or is susceptible to medical treatment'. It will be seen that it is possible to include in this category those of defective intelligence previously classified as moral defectives, as well as those of normal or superior intelligence showing the propensities stated in the definition, provided that they have a therapeutic requirement or susceptibility, and are not merely in need of care, supervision or control for their own protection or that of others, as the *Mental Deficiency Act* required them to be.

The *Mental Health Act* 1959 makes no attempt to define the subnormality of intelligence which is a requirement for the diagnosis of both subnormality and severe subnormality. It is tempting to equate intelligence with the intelligence quotient or I.Q. obtained by an individual on an intelligence test. However, as Sir Cyril Burt (1958) pointed out, it is important to distinguish between *genetic* intelligence, which sets the potential limits of intelligence and *observed* or *measured* intelligence, which is the result of the interaction of genetic intelligence with environmental factors, which determine whether the potential limits are reached or not. There is no general agreement as to the proportion of measured intelligence which is dependent on environmental stimulation. Sir Cyril Burt believed environmental factors to be responsible for about twelve per cent, whereas others have estimated their contribution at up to about thirty-three per cent. An I.Q. represents the measured intelligence of an individual at that particular time of testing, and testing on subsequent occasions may produce lower or higher I.Q.s

within the individual's genetically determined potential, as a result
of adverse or favourable influences during the intervening period.
The I.Q. should not, therefore, be regarded as fixed and immutable.
An intelligence test which has been standardised for use with one
cultural or racial group is not necessarily suitable for application to
a different cultural or racial group and this fact should always be
considered when comparing test results on different individuals.

There is no sharp dividing line in terms of I.Q. between normal
and subnormal intelligence and, indeed, this may vary according to
the particular intelligence test used. Thus, the World Health
Organisation's definition of its term 'mental retardation', as
applying to persons having intelligence quotients more than two
standard deviations below the mean, sets the arbitrary limit at an
I.Q. of 70, but only for a test having a mean of 100 and a standard
deviation of 15. For tests with a greater standard deviation, the
arbitrary I.Q. limit will be correspondingly lower. Kerracher and
Scott (1966) have pointed out that, in practice, medical and legal
diagnoses of subnormality appear to correspond with an upper I.Q.
cut-off point of 80 on the Wechsler Adult Intelligence Scale
(W.A.I.S.) rather than with the traditionally recommended 70.
Again, there is no sharp dividing line in terms of I.Q. between subnormality and severe subnormality, although many psychologists
appear to have adopted the arbitrary figure of 50 as the upper limit
of the latter. In practice, there are many patients with I.Q.s above
this figure who can quite properly be classified as severely subnormal when first seen, by virtue of their social incapacity at that time.

The *Mental Health (Scotland) Act* 1960 and the *Mental Health
Act (Northern Ireland)* 1961, did not adopt the terminology of the
Mental Health Act 1959. The Scottish Act has retained the term
'mental deficiency', which it does not define directly, but which for
the purpose of the Act has to be such as to render an individual incapable of living an independent life or of guarding himself against
serious exploitation (*cf.* severe subnormality). The Scottish Act
does not use the term 'psychopathic disorder', but includes
'. . . mental disorder being a mental illness which is a persistent disorder manifested only by abnormally aggressive or seriously
irresponsible conduct'.

The *Mental Health Act (Northern Ireland)* 1961 uses the term
'person requiring special care', which it defines as 'a person

suffering from arrested or incomplete development of mind (whether arising from inherent causes or induced by disease or injury) which renders him socially inefficient to such an extent that he requires supervision, training or control in his own interest or in the interests of other persons'. The Act goes on to define social inefficiency as 'being incapable of guarding oneself against common physical dangers, managing one's affairs, or, being a child, of being taught to do so or having been found unsuitable for education at school or being in need of care for the protection of other persons'. It will be seen that this definition includes those in the severely subnormal category in the *Mental Health Act* 1959 and, according to one's interpretation of 'arrested or incomplete development of mind', many of those in the psychopathic disorder category.

Quite apart from the confusion to the general public caused by the differing terminology used in the various parts of the British Isles already referred to, confusion between mental illness and mental subnormality is potentiated by the apparent attempt in each of the three Mental Health Acts to deal with the two very different problems on the same legal basis.

Since the *Mental Health Act* 1959, in deference to the wishes of a former Secretary of State, the Department of Health and Social Security has adopted the terms 'mental handicap' and 'severe mental handicap' in place of 'subnormality' and 'severe subnormality' and publishes all its statistics under these headings, although there are no legal definitions of them. The confusion is increased by the requirement that all admissions to psychiatric hospitals are classified in accordance with the General Register Office's *Glossary of Mental Disorders*, which defines mental retardation on the basis of I.Q.s ranging from 85 to under 20, as follows:

Borderline mental retardation	I.Q. 68–85
Mild mental retardation	I.Q. 52–67
Moderate mental retardation	I.Q. 36–51
Severe mental retardation	I.Q. 20–35
Profound mental retardation	I.Q. under 20

As has been pointed out by others, on that basis at least sixteen per cent of the general population would be considered mentally retarded!

REFERENCES

The concept of mental subnormality

Burt, Sir Cyril, *The Backward Child*. University of London Press, 1958.

General Register Office, *Studies on medical and population subjects No. 22. A Glossary of Medical Disorders*, H.M.S.O., London.

Kerracher, D. W. and Scott, J. 'I.Q. Scores and the Problem of Classification'. Brit. J. Psychiat., 1966, *112*, No. 487, pp. 537–541.

Mental Health Act 1959. 7 & 8 ELIZ. 2 Ch. 72, H.M.S.O., London.

Mental Health Act (Northern Ireland) 1961, (1961, Ch. 15), H.M.S.O., Belfast.

Mental Health (Scotland) Act 1960, 8 & 9 ELIZ. 2 Ch. 61, H.M.S.O., London.

World Health Organisation, *Organisation of Services for the Mentally Retarded*. W.H.O. Tech. Rep. Ser. No. 392, p. 11.

2 The causes of mental subnormality

As explained earlier, subnormality was a term introduced by the *Mental Health Act* 1959 and it is, therefore, a legal and not a scientific concept. However, underlying both subnormality and severe subnormality is the condition of *amentia*—literally, lack of mind. The causes of amentia fall into two broad divisions, the pathological and the subcultural. The pathological causes are in general responsible for the more severe degrees of amentia, in which there are demonstrable abnormalities of development or functioning of the brain.

PATHOLOGICAL CAUSES

These may be subdivided into the genetic and the environmental. In the genetic group there are abnormalities of the chromosomes or the genes, which are present from the moment of conception. In the environmental group are a number of conditions which can interfere with development at any time after conception, up to the age of about 15 or 16, by which time the basis for full mental development is normally considered to be complete. In some cases, both genetic and environmental factors are responsible.

Genetic causes
The development of a foetus depends upon the operation of many

thousands of genes, which are carried on chromosomes. It is not at present possible to identify individual genes under the microscope and their presence or absence can only be inferred from the effects they produce. Chromosomes can, however, be seen under the microscope and counted. Humans normally have a total of 46 chromosomes, half being contributed by each parent at the moment of conception. Of these 46 chromosomes, 44 are known as *autosomal* chromosomes, and the remaining 2 as *sex* chromosomes. A normal male has a large X and a small Y chromosome (XY), and a normal female a pair of large X chromosomes (XX). Chromosomes are carried in the nuclei of every cell in the body, and it is possible to culture them and to examine them under the microscope and to arrange them in pairs—22 pairs of similar size and shape in the case of autosomal chromosomes and, either one pair of similar X chromosomes, in the case of a normal XX female, or a pair of dissimilar size in the case of a normal XY male. The accurate identification of members of chromosome pairs is nowadays facilitated by staining chromosomes with a dye such as quinacrine mustard, which produces fluorescent banding patterns in the body of each chromosome, which are characteristic of each member of a particular pair. For purposes of reference, two methods of numbering chromosome pairs are used—in the Denver classification, the autosomal chromosome pairs are numbered from 1 to 22 in decreasing order of size; in the other, the pairs are arranged in a similar way but are, in this case, identified by the letters A to G, applied to groups of chromosome pairs of approximately similar size and shape as follows in Figure 1:

1-2-3	4-5	6-7-8-9-10-11-12	13-14-15	16-17-18	19-20	21-22
Group A	B	C	D	E	F	G

Fig. 1.

Autosomal chromosome abnormalities

The absence of a whole autosomal chromosome ('monosomy') is a lethal condition and the foetus fails to develop, but abnormal physical development and amentia may be associated with the absence of part of a chromosome (a *deletion*) or with the presence of additional chromosome material. The presence of a whole extra autosomal chromosome in any pair is known as a 'trisomy'. Sometimes two members of different chromosome pairs become stuck together. This is called a *translocation* and is of particular importance, as the abnormality may be passed on to later generations. In other cases, the ends of a chromosome may become damaged and join together to produce 'ring forms'. All these abnormalities have been regularly reported in cases of amentia with constant physical abnormalities.

Like monosomy, trisomy of the larger chromosome pairs appears to be a lethal condition, and it is not until we reach pairs 13–15 that the foetus survives to term. Even then, children with trisomy 13–15 (D Group trisomy or Patau's Syndrome) are grossly deformed and fortunately do not survive beyond the first year of life and do not, therefore, contribute materially to the total number of cases of amentia. The same may be said of children with trisomy 17–18 (E Group trisomy or Edward's Syndrome) in whom the congenital deformities are only a little less severe.

By far the most important of the trisomies as a cause of amentia is trisomy 21 (or G Group trisomy), which was demonstrated in 1959 by Lejeune, Gautier and Turpin in the condition of mongolism or Down's Syndrome, which accounts for a third of all cases of severe subnormality. The presence of the extra chromosome is due to a fault during the division of the mother's sex cells prior to conception, but the reasons for this fault are not yet known with certainty, although there is some evidence that it may be caused by maternal infections, such as infectious hepatitis nine months previously, or by hormonal changes in the mother as she gets older. The overall risk of a woman having a mongol baby is 1 in 600, but it increases from about 1 in 2,000 births in young mothers to about 1 in 50 births at the end of the child-bearing period. However, in absolute terms, the majority of mongols are born to younger mothers because, of course, the overall birth rate is higher in them than in older women. Nevertheless, when a woman gives birth to a mongol early in her reproductive life, it is important to ascertain whether she or her husband is the carrier of a translocation, which links one of their 21 chromosomes with a member of another chromosome pair, and involves a greatly increased risk of having another mongol child. In fact, translocations are responsible for only a small percentage of all mongol births, but there is a small number of cases on record of a translocated mongol girl herself giving birth to a mongol baby with a similar translocation.

The physical signs of Down's Syndrome are present at birth and are most obvious in the head and face and in the hands. The head is round, the eyes slope downwards and inwards towards the bridge of the nose, which is poorly developed. The upper eyelid may overlap the lower in an 'epicanthic fold'. The eyes themselves may show various abnormalities—white speckling (Brushfield Spots) of the iris surrounding the pupil, and there may be a squint or other disorders of co-ordination of eye movements. The pattern of the ears is simpler than normal, the tongue often has transverse fissures, the neck is short and thick, the limbs are characteristically 'floppy' and the shape of the hands is also characteristic—the palm is square and often the two main transverse skin creases are fused to form a 'simian' or single transverse palmar crease; the thumb and fifth finger are shorter than normal and the latter curves inwards towards the fourth finger. Apart from the simian crease, there are other features of the palmar and finger prints which are characteristic of mongols. The patterns of the skin ridges on the palms and fingers, and on the soles and toes are determined by genetic factors, but may be modified by environmental factors operating after conception early in intra-uterine life. The study of these patterns is known as *dermatoglyphics*, and some patterns are so constant in different syndromes associated with amentia as to provide useful confirmatory evidence of the presence of these syndromes in cases in which the general physical features are inconclusive (Cummins, 1926).

The abdomen of the mongol is typically protuberant, due to the generalised poor muscle tone, and there may be an umbilical hernia. When fully grown, mongols are short in stature. The lips and extremities of mongols are frequently blue due to their poor peripheral circulation, often caused by congenital abnormalities of the heart, and because of this they are very prone to develop chilblains.

Owing to a deficiency of their defence mechanism against infection, mongols are very prone to develop infections of the eyelid and they frequently have chronic nasal infections. They are, typically, mouth-breathers and are thus very liable to develop respiratory infections, from which they used to die at a very early age before the days of antibiotics. Mongols may also have congenital abnormalities of their gastrointestinal tracts.

Although all mongols look superficially very similar, individual cases, in fact, show different physical features and a wide range of abilities within the severely subnormal category. At one extreme, they are very severely mentally handicapped and very dependent on other people; at the other, they may be able to read and write or, as in the case of Nigel Hunt, to learn to type and to write a book. Mongols often give the impression of being much more intelligent than they really are, due to their great powers of mimicry and their tendency to repeat what other people have said without any real understanding of the meaning. In fact mongols usually do much better on the practical parts of intelligence tests than on those involving reasoning and abstract ideas. Most mongols are more easily habit-trained than other subnormals of a similar degree of mental handicap, and as a group they are cheerful, with a strong sense of humour, a well developed sense of rhythm and fondness for music. Although they are frequently mischievous and inclined to be stubborn, they are usually easily managed. However, as in their physical features, they may show wide individual variations of personality and temperament.

In some cases, only half the cells in the body contain the extra 21 chromosome and the remainder have a normal chromosome count. People with this abnormality are known as 'mosaic mongols' and have only partial physical and mental features of true mongols. Thus, they are usually of more average height and are of higher intelligence, falling within the subnormal rather than the severely subnormal category.

As has been stated earlier, cases of Down's Syndrome account for about one-third of all cases of severe subnormality and about thirty-five per cent of mongols are born to women over the age of thirty-five. Prevention of all mongol births to women in this age group would, therefore, significantly reduce the incidence of severe subnormality as a whole. This possibility was brought much nearer by the development of the techniques of *amniocentesis*, in which a sample of amniotic fluid surrounding the foetus in the mother's womb is drawn off through a needle passed through her abdominal

wall at about the fourteenth week of pregnancy. Examination of
chromosome cultures from cells in the amniotic samples enables
the presence or absence of trisomy 21 in the foetus to be stated with
a very high degree of accuracy in all single pregnancies. Where
evidence of trisomy 21 is found, the pregnancy may be terminated
at the mother's discretion. Amniocentesis is not yet completely
without risk to a normal foetus, but the risk is so small compared
with the risk of a woman over the age of thirty-five having a
mongol baby that she may feel that it is well worth taking. In
multiple pregnancies, the accuracy of the diagnosis will depend on
the possibility of withdrawing amniotic fluid from the amniotic sac
surrounding each foetus separately and, where a positive diagnosis
of trisomy 21 is made, the difficult choice for the mother may be
between termination of all her pregnancies and the acceptance of
the birth of a mongol child as well as one or more normal children.

Deletions have been demonstrated in a number of chromosome
groups and have been associated with constant developmental abnormalities in syndromes in which amentia occurs. One of the best
known is the deletion of the short arm of one of the fifth pair of
chromosomes, which occurs in the *Cri du chat* Syndrome, which is
so called because affected babies have a curious mewing cry
resembling that of an injured kitten. This cry is due to abnormal
development of the organs of speech; there may be abnormalities of
the face, but these are not constant. The cry becomes more normal
as the child grows older, but he will grow up usually severely subnormal (Lejeune *et al.*, 1963).

Sex chromosome abnormalities
Absence of a whole sex chromosome is not incompatible either
with life or the development of normal intelligence, but is usually
associated with physical abnormalities, as in Turner's Syndrome
(Turner, 1938). In this condition, affected individuals have only one
X chromosome and are described as having an XO chromosome
complement. They are short in stature and their general bodily configuration is female, but their genitalia are hypoplastic (underdeveloped), their secondary sexual characteristics are poorly
developed and they are sterile. An obvious feature is the webbing of
the neck muscles. In spite of their rather odd appearance, which
suggests subnormal intelligence, people with Turner's Syndrome

are usually of normal intelligence.

The presence of additional X chromosomes, on the other hand, carries with it the increased probability of subnormality of intelligence. In fact, the more X chromosomes a person has than the normal—1 in a male and 2 in a female—the more physically abnormal and the more severely mentally handicapped he is likely to be. In the simplest form in females there is an XXX sex chromosome complement (trisomy X) (Jacobs et al., 1959). Because of their endowment with an extra female chromosome, such women were at first referred to as 'super females', until it was realised that, in spite of their near normal physical appearance and ability to reproduce they were, in fact, subnormal in intelligence. In the simplest form in males there is an XXY sex chromosome complement (trisomy XXY: Klinefelter's Syndrome) (Klinefelter et al., 1942). Affected individuals have male external genitalia, but these are underdeveloped and they are usually sterile. Their male secondary sexual characteristics—beard and pubic hair—are poorly developed and their general bodily configuration may tend towards the female. Their degree of mental subnormality is usually mild, but they are often emotionally unstable and prone to super-imposed mental illness (Forssman, 1970). Klinefelter's Syndrome may occur in patients with Down's Syndrome, who then have a total chromosome count of 48, rather than the 47 expected in trisomy 21.

Up to 3 extra X chromosomes have been reported in both females (XXXX Syndrome) (Kessaree et al., 1963) and males ($XXXXY$ Syndrome) (Fraccaro et al., 1960), associated in each case with gross physical abnormalities and severe subnormality.

In recent years, interest has centred on the presence of an extra Y chromosome in males (XYY Syndrome), since this was first reported among the residents in the special hospitals for patients with criminal or antisocial tendencies (Jacobs et al., 1965). Affected males were all over 6 ft. (183 cm) tall and were normal in their general physical and sexual development. They were usually mildly subnormal in intelligence. Subsequent reports suggest that XYY males have difficulty in making friends and that they tend to be impulsive, hot-tempered and easily provoked into acts of violence. However, their convictions, which have often begun in childhood, are usually for offences against property rather than against persons. As might be expected, a causal relationship was suggested between the presence of an extra *Y* chromosome and the antisocial behaviour described in affected patients, but it now seems likely that there are a number of males with an extra *Y* chromosome living quite normally in the community and showing no antisocial tendencies.

As in the case of autosomal chromosomes, the absence of whole sex chromosomes or the presence of extra sex chromosomes may occur in only a proportion of the cells of the body and this then gives rise to sex chromosome mosaics.

Abnormalities of genes

To understand the relationship of genes to some cases of amentia it is essential to know a little about the principles of human genetics. Genetically determined characteristics may be inherited in a dominant, recessive or *X*-linked manner. A recessively inherited condition can occur only when the individual inherits the same gene responsible for that condition from both parents at the time of conception. A dominantly inherited condition, on the other hand, occurs when only one parent carries the relevant gene, due to its ability to overcome the influence of that inherited from the other parent. When a person with a recessively inherited condition has children by a person with a dominantly inherited condition, they will all develop the dominant condition, although each will carry the gene for the recessive condition. This is because in each of the four possible pairings of the genes at the time of conception a dominant gene (*D*) will be found with a recessive gene (*R*) to give a *DR* combination (*see* Figure 2).

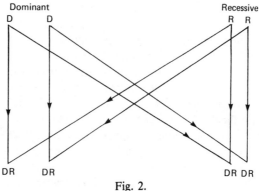

Fig. 2.

However, if two people who are each carriers of the gene for the same recessive condition mate, at every conception there is a 1 in 4 chance of a child being born with that condition (*RR*) and a 3 in 4 chance of his being born with the dominant condition *DD* or *DR* (*see* Figure 3).

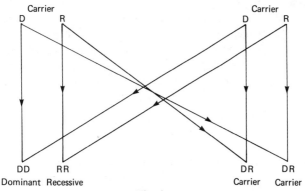

Fig. 3.

Some genes are not completely dominant and are able to express themselves fully only under ideal circumstances. Where these circumstances are not present a child may have only partial features of the dominant condition.

A small number of conditions are inherited in a sex-linked or *X*-linked manner, being carried by women who do not themselves have the condition, but may transmit it to their male but not to their female offspring (*see* Figure 4).

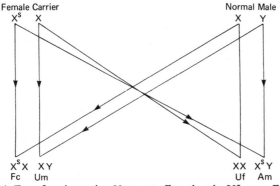

Fig. 4. Fc = female carrier, Um = unaffected male, Uf = unaffected female, Am = affected male, s = X-linked gene.

The X-linked condition can occur only when the X^s chromosome is not paired with a normal X chromosome at conception. It will be seen from Figure 3 that the chance of this happening in the offspring of a female carrier and a normal male is 1 in 4 at each conception (i.e. only in the X^sY male).

A number of syndromes exist which are due to abnormalities of genes and in which amentia is associated with constant physical abnormalities, by which they can be recognised. One of the most common is *microcephaly*, which is inherited in a recessive manner. The syndrome derives its name from the small head, usually with a receding forehead and chin. There is a striking disproportion between the face of near normal size and the tiny vault of the skull. The stature is usually short and there may be neurological abnormalities and epilepsy may occur. The degree of mental subnormality is usually severe, but those affected are usually pleasant in manner and well behaved. Of the other, rarer syndromes, only those will be described in which there are very obvious facial abnormalities which suggest the diagnosis.

The most obvious features of Apert's Syndrome (Apert, 1906) are the protuberant eyes and greatly increased height of the skull above the eyebrows, and gross abnormalities of the hands and feet, the fingers and toes being entirely absent or fused together. The abnormal facial appearance is due to premature fusion of the bones at the base of the skull, including the orbits. The brain and skull then continue to develop vertically; the degree of mental subnormality in this condition varies.

Apert's Syndrome is an example of a condition in which the mode of inheritance is inherited in an incompletely dominant manner. This is true also of a related condition—Crouzon's Syndrome (Crouzon, 1912)—in which the cranial and facial abnormalities are similar, but in which the limb abnormalities do not occur and in which mental subnormality is present in only about 20 per cent of cases. Greig's Syndrome (Greig, 1924), or *hypertelorism*, on the other hand, appears to be inherited in an incompletely dominant manner in some families and in an recessive manner in others. The most striking feature of this condition is the very wide spacing of the eyes and the broad, flattened bridge of the nose. Most cases are severely subnormal, but some are subnormal and, in rare cases, of normal intelligence. Hypertelorism may occur also as a feature of other genetically determined syndromes associated with mental subnormality.

The obvious feature of *epiloia* is the so-called 'butterfly rash' on the cheeks, which spreads out on either side of the nose like the wings of a butterfly. This is associated with severe subnormality and epilepsy, both of which are associated with tubero-sclerosis or nodular thickening of the brain. There may also be pigmented or depigmented areas of the skin elsewhere on the body.

In this condition, too, the mode of inheritance is incompletely dominant, and, as a result, relatives of normal intelligence may show partial features of the condition. The presence of the cutaneous signs in either parent of a child with epiloia indicates that that parent is a carrier of the gene causing this condition and runs a greatly increased risk of having another child similarly afflicted.

Most cases of *hydrocephalus* are due to environmental factors, which will be referred to later, but they can also occur as an X-linked disorder, causing obstruction to the circulation of the cerebrospinal fluid, which normally surrounds the brain and spinal cord, and resulting in its accumulation in the natural spaces within the brain. As a result, the brain and surrounding skull become progressively distended and thinned in a globular fashion so that the head has the appearance of an inverted pear, as the face is of normal size. Because of the brain damage, deafness and blindness may occur and the limbs may be spastic. The prognosis and treatment of hydrocephalus will be referred to under environmental causes.

A number of syndromes associated with amentia exist in which the cause is at present unknown but the easily recognised physical abnormalities suggest that this may be genetic. For convenience, two of the best known will be described here.

In the de Lange Syndrome (de Lange, 1933), the most obvious feature is the facial appearance—the eyebrows are bushy and meet across the midline, and the eye lashes are long and curved. The hairline is low on the forehead and the face is excessively hairy. The bridge of the nose is depressed and the nostrils are tilted forwards. The upper lip is elongated vertically and the corners of the mouth turn down; the ears are low set and the trunk is excessively hairy. The hands are said to have the appearance of a lobster's claw due to the fingers being held half-bent, close to the thumb. The degree of mental subnormality associated with this syndrome is usually severe and compulsive self-mutilative behaviour may occur.

In *naevoid amentia* (Sturge Weber Syndrome) (Sturge, 1879; Weber, 1922) one half of the face, neck and upper part of the chest is covered by a 'port wine stain'. This is, in fact, a naevus or area of dilated skin capillaries. It is associated with a similar vascular abnormality in the covering of the brain on the same side of the body which causes various degrees of spasticity and paralysis in the limbs on the opposite side of the body, and epileptic fits. The facial appearance is asymmetrical, with overdevelopment on the side of the naevus, so that the eyeball is larger than that on the opposite side. The degree of mental subnormality is usually severe and may be accompanied by disturbed behaviour, but this syndrome has been reported in people of normal intelligence.

At present, there is no known way of changing a person's genetic constitution in the conditions so far described, or of preventing the associated amentia, except by genetic counselling or termination of affected pregnancies. However, in the next group of disorders of genetic origin to be described—the inborn errors of metabolism—although the genetic constitution may not be changed, there is a good prospect in some cases of preventing, or at least reducing the ultimate degree of amentia, by early diagnosis and treatment of the condition.

The inborn errors of metabolism
The normal functioning of the body depends on the intake of food and its breakdown within the body into its component parts and their recombination to form the tissues of the body and to provide it with energy. These metabolic processes are dependent on the presence of enzymes, which act as catalysts at successive stages in each process. In their absence, there is an accumulation in the body of normal breakdown products in abnormal quantities, which can cause brain damage directly or by interfering with other normal metabolic processes.

The inborn errors of metabolism are each associated with a deficiency or absence of one or more enzymes and are mostly inherited in a recessive manner, although a small number are known to be X-linked. To date, about 80 inborn errors have been shown to cause amentia and more of these disorders continue to be identified, but at present some appear to be very rare. Only a few of the best known will be described here.

Phenylketonuria This condition was first described by Fölling in 1934, and is by far the best known and most widely investigated and treated of the inborn metabolic errors causing amentia. It is inherited in a recessive manner and occurs in this country in about 1 in 12,000 live births.

Phenylketonuria is a disorder of the metabolism of the aminoacid phenylalanine, which accumulates in the blood and is excreted in the urine as phenylpyruvic acid. Because of the absence of an enzyme, phenylalanine is not converted into the pigment melanin, which gives the hair, skin and eyes their varying degrees of dark colouring, and, as a result, people with phenylketonuria have lighter colouring than unaffected members of their families.

The degree of mental subnormality in untreated cases varies according to the severity of the metabolic disorder. About half the affected children never learn to talk and about a third never learn to walk. They sometimes show signs of autism: as babies they resist being cuddled and, as they grow older, they fail to relate to other people and become unusually attached to small objects, such as a tin or piece of string, or develop mannerisms, and may spend hours rocking backwards and forwards. Between a quarter and a third of children with phenylketonuria develop epilepsy, but this tends to disappear as they grow up.

Phenylketonuria can be diagnosed by tests on the baby's urine or by the Guthrie test on a drop of blood, usually obtained by pricking the baby's heel. The Guthrie test is more accurate as it provides a quantitative estimation of the level of phenylalanine in the baby's blood. When subsequent tests confirm the diagnosis, it is important that treatment is begun without delay if brain damage is to be avoided. Treatment consists of restricting the quantity of phenylalanine in the diet, so as to keep its level in the blood between acceptable limits—too little phenylalanine may be as harmful as too much. There is some evidence that, by the age of 3 years, the brain may be able to withstand the harmful effects of raised levels of phenylalanine in the blood and that a return to an unrestricted diet may be made after that age. However, successfully treated phenylketonuric women may have to return to their diets during pregnancy if damage to the brain of a non-phenylketonuric foetus is to be avoided. Similarly, women who do not themselves suffer from phenylketonuria, but who are carriers of the gene concerned, may have blood levels of phenylalanine which are raised sufficiently to damage a normal foetus, and they may also require phenylalanine-restricted diets during pregnancy.

Homocystinuria This was not first reported until 28 years after phenylketonuria (Field *et al.*, 1962), but now appears to be the second most common inborn error of aminoacid metabolism known to cause amentia. It occurs about a quarter as frequently as phenylketonuria and, like that condition, is inherited in a recessive manner. As a result of the missing enzyme, the aminoacid homocystine accumulates in the blood and is excreted in the urine, in which it may be detected by the cyanide-nitroprusside test.

People with homocystinuria are fair-haired and have fair skin, with a characteristic flush of the cheeks, and dislocation of the lenses of the eyes. Their joints are enlarged and they are knock-kneed and have a shuffling gait. They have a poor peripheral circulation and are very prone to develop thrombosis and embolisms. However, these signs of homocystinuria are not obvious at birth, but become more marked as the child becomes older, when his bones may become decalcified and atrophic. Epileptic fits are frequent.

The child's early mental development is usually normal, and mental deterioration may not become obvious until the child starts at school and, in the mildest cases, the intelligence in adult life may be normal. In the most severe cases, however, gross mental deterioration may occur in the first year of life.

As in phenylketonuria, mental subnormality may be prevented, or its severity reduced by dietary means, in the case of homocystinuria by restricting the amount of methionine—an aminoacid which is converted in the body into homocystine. A proportion of cases of homocystinuria respond to the administration of pyridoxine without any dietary restrictions.

Galactosaemia Irreversible brain damage and early death may result from this condition if it is not treated shortly after birth. This condition, which is inherited in a recessive manner, is a disorder of carbohydrate metabolism in which the enzyme deficiency leads to an accumulation in the blood of galactose derived from the mother's milk. Affected children start to vomit within the first 2 weeks of life and become increasingly lethargic and reluctant to feed, lose weight and become jaundiced. If they are untreated permanent liver damage occurs and they develop cataracts in the eyes.

Treatment consists of giving a galactose-free diet, and if this is started early enough the cataracts disappear and the liver function returns to normal and the degree of amentia may be reduced if not entirely prevented.

Idiopathic hypoglycaemia As damaging to the brain as an excess of galactose in the blood is a deficiency of another carbohydrate—glucose—in the condition of *hypoglycemosis* or idiopathic hypoglycaemia, which is inherited in a dominant manner. Affected children are abnormally sensitive to the aminoacid leucine, which causes a prolonged fall in the level of glucose in their blood and consequent convulsions, irreversible brain damage and amentia if this is not quickly restored to normal. Treatment consists of restricting leucine in the diet and giving extra glucose between feeds. Fortunately, the leucine sensitivity disappears as the child grows older, and by the age of 5 years it may be possible for the child to return to a normal unrestricted diet without any risk. Hypoglycaemia at birth may be caused by environmental factors and will be referred to later.

Tay-Sachs' disease Fat metabolism may be disturbed in a number of inborn errors associated with amentia. The best known of these is *Tay-Sachs' disease* (Tay, 1881; Sachs, 1887), which is inherited in a recessive manner and occurs most frequently in Ashkenazi Jews, 1 in 25 of whom may be a carrier for that condition.

The enzyme deficiency leads to an accumulation of fatty material in the tissues, which causes progressive mental deterioration, blindness, convulsions and spastic paralysis from about the third month onwards and death within 2 years.

There is, unfortunately, no known treatment for this condition, but it may be detected by amniocentesis in suspected carriers and the possibility of prevention by termination offered to them.

Gargoylism One of the most easily recognised conditions due to inborn metabolic errors is *gargoylism*, so called because of the distinctive facial appearance, which is said to resemble that of a gargoyle. This condition is inherited in both recessive (Hurler, 1919) and X-linked forms (Hunter, 1917).

As a result of an enzyme deficiency, large quantities of mucopolysaccharide substances are deposited throughout the body and appear in the urine.

The typical physical features are not present at birth, but during the first year of life the head becomes large and generally mis-shapen and thickened with prominent bony ridges above the eyebrows, which are coarse and bushy. The bridge of the nose is depressed, the ears are low-set and the tongue is large and fissured and is constantly protruded. The teeth appear late and are irregular. Opacities in the cornea of the eye are common in the recessive form but do not occur in the X-linked form.

The neck is short and thick and the forward curve of the back is increased, due to abnormal development of the vertebrae. The growth of the limbs is stunted, but less so in the X-linked form, and the joints cannot be fully extended. The abdomen is very protuberant due to great enlargement of the liver and spleen.

There is no known treatment and progressive mental and physical deterioration occurs and the child dies soon after he is 10 years old. Mental deterioration is less rapid in the X-linked form, but deafness is more common.

Cretinism A number of different inborn errors of metabolism may result in a deficiency of thyroxine, which is excreted by the thyroid gland. The exact mode of inheritance is not known in all cases, but in at least 3 it is in a recessive manner. Deficiency of thyroxine causes the condition of *cretinism*, which usually does not begin to become obvious until after the child is about 3 months old, by which time irreparable brain damage may have occurred, with the inevitability of some degree of amentia. When fully developed, the condition is easily recognised. The skin has a yellowish colour and is loose, wrinkled and puffy. There is thickening of the eyelids, nostrils, lips, hands, feet and back of the neck, which is short and thick. The hair of the head and eyebrows is scanty. Growth is stunted and the abdomen is protuberant, and sexual development may be delayed or incomplete. The pulse is slow and the temperature is subnormal. The baby's cry is described as 'leathery' and speech may not appear until the child is 7 or 8 years old and walking also is much delayed. If treatment with thyroxine is started after the age of 3 months, subsequent physical development may occur normally, but there is little chance of normal mental development. In untreated cases, severe subnormality is inevitable.

Infantile Hyperuricaemia One of the most distressing of the in-born metabolic disorders is *infantile hyperuricaemia* (juvenile gout or the Lesch-Nyhan Syndrome) (Lesch-Nyhan, 1964). This is inherited in an *X*-linked manner and is characterised by the tendency to extreme self-mutilation among affected males, who chew their lips and bite their fingers down to the bone, in spite of causing themselves obvious pain. While they are doing this they appear to be terrified and are obviously very relieved when they are restrained. Those affected develop increasing spasticity and undergo progressive mental deterioration and usually die before puberty. Unfortunately there is no known way of preventing the brain damage, but the condition can be detected during pregnancy and the latter's termination considered.

ENVIRONMENTAL CAUSES

Oxygen deficiency

Where the genetic constitution is normal at the time of conception, the subsequent development of the foetus will depend upon its receiving adequate nutrition and an adequate supply of oxygen from its mother through the placenta, by which it is attached to her womb. Therefore, any structural or functional abnormality of the placenta or its partial separation due, for example, to a haemorrhage, will obviously affect development. Not only will the baby be small but its brain may be abnormally developed. There is some evidence that smoking during pregnancy may adversely affect the development of the foetus—possibly by restricting the blood flow through the placenta—and be associated with retarded mental development after birth, but it has not been proved that this is irreversible and sufficient to cause amentia (Butler *et al.*, 1969). Brain damage may be caused if the baby's brain is deprived of oxygen by interference with the circulation during an unduly prolonged second stage of labour, or if its breathing is interfered with immediately after birth by heavy maternal sedation during labour. Severe respiratory infections during the first two years of a baby's life may also cause brain damage and amentia.

Nutritional deficiency
Normal foetal brain development may be prevented by serious lack of protein in the mother's diet during pregnancy or in the child's own diet during the first two years of life (Dobbing *et al.*, 1970). Such a deficiency is rare in Western civilisations during peace time. However, even in such relatively affluent societies, similar results may follow a maternal diet deficient in vitamin B_{12} upon which the foetus makes heavy demands for its normal development. Brain damage may also result from lowering of the blood sugar in the foetus by treatment of diabetes in the mother. Babies of nondiabetic mothers who are small at birth are also very likely to have low blood sugar and to develop irreversible brain damage and amentia if the condition is not treated (Cornblath *et al.*, 1966).

Exposure to radiation
In the past, the brain of the foetus was sometimes damaged by excessive diagnostic radiography during pregnancy, but this is unlikely to occur now that its dangers are well recognised and apparently safer methods such as diagnostic ultra-sound (Taylor *et al.*, 1972) may be used to provide the same information. However, foetal brain damage may be caused by exposure to excessive random radiation during pregnancy as in the case of pregnant women who survived the Hiroshima bomb blast and gave birth to microcephalic children (Miller, 1956). Other survivors were found to have persistent chromosome abnormalities and it is possible that 'mutations' or permanent changes in their genes may have been caused in others, which may produce abnormalities in later generations.

Direct violence
Direct violence to the foetus is unlikely to cause amentia, because the foetus is so well protected by the mother's abdominal wall, womb and amniotic fluid. However, amentia may arise from severe brain damage caused by a too-rapid second stage of labour, in which the blood vessels are torn and cerebral haemorrhage occurs. In such cases severe subnormality is accompanied by spasticity of the limbs. Severe brain damage may also be caused by violence to the skull during childhood, either deliberate, as in battered babies, or accidental, often as the result of collision with a motor vehicle.

Such accidents account for some of the most tragic of all cases of amentia, as they so often seem to involve children of previously above-normal intelligence who are reduced to the most severely subnormal and dependent level by the accident.

Rhesus factor incompatibility

The brain of the foetus may be damaged as the result of *Rhesus factor incompatibility*, i.e. when a woman who does not have the Rhesus factor in her blood (Rhesus negative) conceives by a man whose blood does have this factor (Rhesus positive). As the Rhesus factor is inherited in a dominant manner, any children will be Rhesus positive. At the time of the birth of the first child, some of its Rhesus positive cells enter its mother's circulation and provoke the development of antibodies whose purpose is to destroy all such cells. Usually the first child is itself unaffected by the incompatibility, but by the time of any later pregnancies, the level of maternal antibodies has risen sufficiently to pass through the placenta and to destroy the Rhesus positive blood cells in the foetus, which is born jaundiced and may be severely brain damaged. Typically, such a child develops *athetosis*, with spasticity affecting the muscles of speech and limbs. As a result, the speech is very indistinct and there are involuntary, serpentine movements of the arms and hands. The odd appearance of these patients, and their difficulty in making themselves understood, gives them an appearance of being much more seriously mentally handicapped than is often the case. Undoubtedly, in the past, a number of people with this affliction and of at least normal intelligence, have been wrongly diagnosed as mentally subnormal. Where a woman is found to be Rhesus negative, it is now possible to immunise her against the development of antibodies during her first pregnancy and so prevent damage to later children (Finn, 1960). Where the condition is not diagnosed until maternal antibodies have developed, brain damage may be prevented by carrying out a transfusion to replace the damaged foetal blood by healthy Rhesus positive blood, while the foetus is still in the uterus (Liley, 1963) or immediately the baby is born.

Infectious diseases

Infectious diseases are responsible for a number of cases of amentia, causing brain damage during both pregnancy and childhood.

The best known of the causes during pregnancy is *rubella* or German measles. If a woman contracts this disease during the first three months of pregnancy, she runs a great risk of giving birth to a child who may be deaf and blind and with congenital heart disease and various degrees of amentia. The earlier in pregnancy the infection occurs, the greater the risk of these abnormalities, which may be considered to justify termination of the pregnancy.

Cytomegalovirus infection Evidence is accumulating that *cytomegalovirus infection* during pregnancy may cause more cases of amentia than maternal rubella (Stern *et al.*, 1969), and that the foetus may be seriously affected when the maternal infection is contracted late in pregnancy. In contrast to maternal rubella, the infection may be very mild and may be unrecognised in the mother.

Amentia has been reported also in the offspring of women who have had a number of other virus infections during pregnancy. In the past, maternal syphilis was a frequent cause of amentia in the offspring, but fortunately it is now a rare cause.

Toxoplasmosis On the other hand, maternal *toxoplasmosis*—an infection contracted from farm and domestic animals and often causing only a mild infection in adults—has been shown to be a far more frequent cause of foetal brain damage and amentia than was previously realised. Like cytomegalovirus infection it can produce its harmful effects when contracted late in pregnancy and may result in a child who is either microcephalic or hydrocephalic, with abnormal eyes, spasticity, convulsions and various degrees of amentia.

Encephalitis Amentia may result from brain damage caused by *encephalitis* arising as a rare complication of the common virus infections of childhood, such as measles or mumps, and may be accompanied by spasticity and convulsions. The degree of amentia is variable. In some cases, the effect on intelligence is relatively mild compared with the marked damage to the personality. Children who, before the infection were stable and well-behaved, may become very disturbed in their behaviour and start lying, stealing and being sexually inhibited.

Post-encephalitic Parkinsonism Encephalitis may also occur as a primary infection of the brain, rather than as a complication of a more generalised childhood infection, and may be followed years after by the development of *post-encephalitic Parkinsonism*, with

its easily recognised [ ]ymptoms. Affected people have a
fixed facial express[ ]n dribble excessively. They may
have 'oculogyric cri[ ]l involuntary spasms of the external muscles of the e[ ]them to turn upwards, so that only
the whites of the ey[ ]The movements of the body as a
whole are slowed d[ ]lised muscular rigidity. When they
walk, they tend to l[ ]s and do not swing their arms in a
normal way. They [ ]nave a fine tremor of their hands,
which gives the app[ ]olling a pill between the thumb and
first finger. Their a[ ]nd slow responses suggest a more
severe degree of ar[ ]is often, in fact, the case and this
should always be [ ]nd when talking in front of them.
They, too, may unc[ ]onality change as a result of the infection. The physic[ ]of this disease may be beneficially
modified by drugs [ ]e cases, by brain surgery.

In fortunately ve[ ]very tragic cases, a child may suffer
effects similar to [ ]encephalitis, and become severely
physically and men[ ]capped, as the result of immunisation
against the comm[ ]ns of childhood, due to his own
hypersensitivity to [ ]al used (Malmgren et al., 1960).
Meningitis The [ ]ay also be damaged by *meningitis*
(inflammation of i[ ]rings), causing amentia in a previously
normal child, who may subsequently be paralysed, deaf and blind
in the most severe cases, or may show only mild impairment of intelligence and the personality changes previously described as
following encephalitis, in others.

Hydrocephalus Sometimes the circulation of the cerebrospinal
fluid becomes blocked, and it accumulates within the brain to cause
hydrocephalus, in which the most obvious feature is the disproportion between the face of normal size and the gross, globular
enlargement of the skull, giving the head the appearance of an inverted pear as already described. By the time the condition has
developed to this stage, marked irreversible brain damage will have
occurred and severe amentia will be inevitable. However, where the
condition is recognised early, it is now possible to prevent further
damage and to reduce the degree of amentia by bypassing the site
of the obstruction by the insertion of a Pudenz or Spitz Holter
valve, through which the cerebrospinal fluid is returned to the normal circulation through the veins of the neck.

Other Any illness, such as gastroenteritis, which causes dehydration during early childhood, may result in brain damage sufficient to cause amentia, which may be accompanied by spasticity and epilepsy.

Drugs

The proved connection between limb deformities in children and thalidomide taken by their mothers during pregnancy has intensified the interest in drugs which may cause foetal brain damage when taken at that time. In general, these are drugs which interfere with folic acid metabolism and include some drugs used in the treatment of epilepsy, and others whose primary use is in the treatment of skin disorders, but which also have a reputation as abortifacients (Milunsky *et al.*, 1968).

Metallic substances

A number of poisonous metallic substances may produce damage to the developing brain during the early years of childhood. The best known is lead, which was a more common cause in the past, when it was a basic constituent of paint, than now, when most paints do not contain lead. It is most frequently seen nowadays in children who live in poor accommodation, and who chew lead-containing paint flaking from the walls of old houses. It may possibly be seen to an increasing extent in future as the result of atmospheric pollution with lead from the exhausts of motor vehicles. Affected children are typically hyperactive in their behaviour (David *et al.*, 1972). Early diagnosis may enable the degree of brain damage to be reduced by administering drugs to facilitate excretion of lead from the body. Recent experience in Japan has shown that environmental pollution with mercury may cause brain damage and consequential abnormalities.

SUBCULTURAL CAUSES

The mind, like the body, needs adequate stimulation to ensure its full development and this may be prevented by anything which isolates an individual from his environment. The most obvious examples are complete deafness and blindness, but unfortunately, in the past, milder degrees of these disabilities have not been recognised and have led to children being labelled mentally subnormal when they had no primary defect of intelligence. A child may be deaf only to higher frequencies, but his inability to appreciate these in normal speech makes it unintelligible to him and prevents his own development of language.

However, even when there is no such sensory defect, enforced isolation for long periods in childhood may result in permanent disability amounting to mental subnormality, as in the case of Kasper Hauser, who, it was claimed, was kept in isolation in a small, dark cell for the first sixteen years of his life and who, after his release, was eventually found murdered in mysterious circumstances. Far more common are the less extreme forms of isolation associated with subcultural amentia, in which the degree of mental handicap is mild and which are seen most frequently in children from the poorer socio-economic groups. In a survey in Aberdeen, Birch *et al.* found that the prevalence of mild mental handicap was roughly nine times greater amongst the children of unskilled urban manual workers than amongst the children of those in non-manual occupations. Although the genetic constitution such children inherit may give them the potential for near normal intelligence, the environment which they inherit, possibly with parents whose intelligence is less than their own, may deprive them of the stimulation, affection and security which they require for their normal mental development. If their deprivation is recognised early enough and steps are taken to remedy it, such children obviously stand a much better chance of improving in intelligence than children whose mental handicap is due to brain damage (Clarke & Clarke, 1954).

It is sometimes claimed that parental rejection may cause the more severe degrees of amentia. In the author's experience, the latter always have an underlying organic pathology and parental rejection is not the primary cause, but may arise secondarily when for example the mother realises the severity of the child's handicap and he fails to respond to her in spite of all the care and affection she shows him.

Although we are now able to list nearly 200 known causes of amentia, it is possible to ascribe a definite cause in only just under sixty per cent of individual cases. The late Professor L. S. Penrose estimated in 1966 that about thirty-seven per cent of cases with a known cause were of genetic origin and that about twenty per cent were of environmental, non-genetic origin.

THE DIAGNOSIS OF MENTAL SUBNORMALITY

There are very few cases in which mental subnormality can be predicted with certainty at the time a baby is born. Such cases include those with such gross physical abnormalities of genetic origin that the baby is unlikely to live more than one or two years, and which, therefore, account for only a tiny proportion of the total prevalence of mental subnormality. In Down's Syndrome, however, the presence of the typical physical signs enables the diagnosis to be made as soon as the baby is born, with the certainty that the child will be mentally subnormal if he survives.

In the vast majority of cases, a diagnosis of mental subnormality can be made with certainty only after a comprehensive assessment, often over a prolonged period and involving observations and investigations by a multi-disciplinary team, consisting of members of a number of different professions. The more severe cases will usually be suspected early due to their lateness in achieving the 'milestones'—the average ages at which children reach the various stages of their development which are necessary for their eventual independent existence, such as sitting, standing, walking, talking, feeding, dressing and caring for their personal hygiene. Although it may be suspected earlier, the retardation in such cases is likely to become most apparent between the ages of about two and three, the period during which the development of the normal child is making rapid progress. The investigations in such cases will usually be undertaken by a paediatrician who, with the help of an audiometrician and ophthalmologist, will take great care to ensure that the child's retarded development is not due to a sensory defect masquerading as a mental defect, and with the help of a psychologist and perhaps a child psychiatrist, will assess the importance of any emotional disturbance which may be masquerading in the same way. With the help of geneticists and biochemists he will search for genetic or biochemical abnormalities known to cause mental subnormality, and for evidence of their occurrence in other members of the child's family.

The less severe degrees of mental subnormality are likely to reveal themselves progressively later; some on starting school, with the child's failing to keep pace with other children of the same age and perhaps playing truant or becoming disturbed in his behaviour;

others on leaving the protection of school and having to compete with others for employment and often showing their limitations by their irresponsibility, poor time-keeping and frequent changes of jobs for trivial reasons. Some such cases do not come to light until they are brought before the courts, often on a relatively minor charge, or even after they have been sent to prison, although this is rare nowadays since the psychological examination of offenders has become a more general practice.

Diagnosis of mental subnormality after early childhood is just as much a multidisciplinary exercise as that undertaken earlier and may be initiated by specialists working primarily in the child psychiatric or mental subnormality field, who are greatly helped in their assessment by the valuable social histories supplied by local authority social service staff.

It is essential, once a definite diagnosis of mental subnormality has been made, that the implications of this diagnosis should be explained to relatives and that they should be informed of the services which are available to help the mentally handicapped and their families. A number of surveys have shown that most parents prefer to be told as soon as a definite diagnosis has been made.

It is probable that parents of mentally subnormal children will seek advice on the probability of later children being similarly affected, and it is important that the advice given should have a scientific basis and preferably be given by a specialist in human genetics, after a full investigation of all relevant aspects of the case. It is important, too, that the assessment of mental subnormality should be an ongoing process as long as supervision is necessary, and not a once-for-all exercise as it has too often been in the past.

REFERENCES

The causes of mental subnormality

Pathological causes

Apert, E. 'De l'acrocephalosyndactyly.' Bull. Soc. Med. Hop. Paris, 1906, *23*, 1310.

Crouzon, O. 'Hereditary craniofacial dystostosis'. Bull. Soc. Med. Hop. Paris, 1912, *33*, 545.

Cummins, H. 'Epidermal ridge configurations in development defects.' Am. J. Anat. 1926, *38*, 89.

32   LEFT BEHIND

Down, J. L. H. L. 'Observations on an Ethnic Classification of Idiots.' Lond. Hosp. Clin. Rep. 1866, *iii*, 259.

Edwards, J. H., Harnden, D. G., Cameron, A. H., Crosse, V. M., and Wolff, O. H. 'A new trisomic syndrome.' Lancet, 1960, *1*, 787.

Field, C. M. B., Carson, N. A. J., Cusworth, D. C., Dent, C. E., and Neil, D. W. Abstr. Tenth Internat. Congr. Paed. Lisbon, 1962, p. 274.

Fölling, A. Z. 'Uber Ausscheidung von Phenylbrenztraub ensaure in den harn als Stoffwechselanomalie in verbindung mit imbezillitat.' Hoppe-Seylers Z. physiol. Chem. 1934, *227*, 169.

Forssman, H. 'The mental implications of sex chromosome aberrations.' Brit. J. Psychiat., 1970, *117*, No. 359, 353–363.

Fraccaro, M., Kaijser, K. and Lindsten, J. 'A child with 49 chromosomes.' Lancet, 1960, *2*, 899.

Greig, D. M. 'Hypertelorism.' Ed. med. J., 1924, *31*, 560.

Hunt, N. *The World of Nigel Hunt*. Darwen Finlayson, Beaconsfield.

Hunter, C. 'A rare disease in two brothers.' Proc. R. Soc. Med. 1917, *10*, 104.

Hurler, G. 'Uber einen Typ. multipler Abartungen. Vorwiegend am Skellettsystem.' Z. Kinderheilk. 1919, *24*, 220.

Jacobs, P. A., Baikie, A. G., Court Brown, W. M., MacGregor, T. N. and Harnde, D. G. 'Evidence for the existence of the human superfemale.' Lancet, 1959, *2*, 423.

Jacobs, P. A., Brunton, M., Melville, M. M., Brittain, R. P. and McClemont, W. F. 'Aggressive behaviour, mental subnormality and the XYY male.' Nature (Lond.) 1965, *208*, 1351.

Kessaree, N. and Woolley, P. V. 'A phenotypic female with 49 chromosomes, presumably XXXXX.' J. Pediat., 1963, *63*, 1099.

Klinefelter, H. R., Reifienstein, E. C. and Albright, F. 'Syndrome characterised by gynaecomastia, asperogenesis without A-leydigism and increased excretion of follicle stimulating hormone.' J. Clin. Edocrinol. 1942, *2*, 615–627.

de Lange, C. 'Sur un type nouveau de degeneration (Typus Amstelodamensis).' Arch. med. des Enfants, 1933, *36*, 713.

Lejeune, J., Lafourcade, J., Berger, R., Vialatte, J., Boeswillwald, M., Seringe, P. and Turpin, R. 'Trois cas de délétion du bras court d'un chromosome 5.' C.R. Acad. Sci. Paris, 1963, *257*, 3098–3102.

Lejeune, J., Turpin, R. and Gautier, M. 'Le Mongolisme, Premier exemple d'aberration autosomique humane.' Ann. Genet. 1959, *1*, 2, 41.

Lesch, M. and Nyhan, W. L. 'A Familial Disorder or Uric Acid Metabolism and Central Nervous System; Hyperuricemia and Brain Disorder in Children.' Amer. J. Med. 1964, *36*, 561.

Patau, K., Smith, D. W., Therman, E., Inhorn, S. L. and Wagner, H. P. 'Multiple Congenital Anomaly caused by an Extra Chromosome.' Lancet, 1960, *1*, 790.

Sachs, B. 'On Arrested Cerebral Development, with special reference to its Cortical Pathology.' J. nerv. ment. Dis. 1887, *14*, 541.

Sturge, W. A. 'A Cause of Partial Epilepsy, apparently due to a lesion of one of the Vasomotor Centres of the Brain.' Tr. Clin. Soc. London, 1879, *12*, 162.

Tay, W. 'Symmetrical Changes in the Region of the Yellow Spot in each Eye of an Infant.' Trans. ophthal. Soc. U.K. 1881, *2*, 55.

Turner, H. H. 'A Syndrome of Infantilism, Congenital Webbed Neck, and Cubitus Valgus.' Endocrinology, 1938, *23*, 566.

Weber, F. P. 'Right-sided Hemi-hypotrophy resulting from right-sided Congenital Spastic Hemiplegia with a Morbid Condition of the Left Side of the Brain revealed by Radiographs.' J. Neurol. Psychopath., London. 1922, *37*, 301.

Environmental causes

Birch, H. G., Richardson, S. A., Baird, D., Harobin, G. and Illesley, R. *Mental Subnormality in the Community.* Williams and Wilkins, Baltimore. 1970.

Butler, N. R. and Alberman, E. D. *Perinatal Problems.* Livingstone, Edinburgh. 1969.

Clarke, A. D. B. and Clarke, A. M. 'Congnitive Changes in the feeble-minded.' Brit. J. Psychol. 1954, *45*, 173.

Cornblath, M. and Schwartz, R. *Disorders of Carbohydrate Metabolism in Infancy.* Philadelphia, 1966.

David, O., Clarke, J. and Voeller, K. 'Lead and Hyperactivity.' Lancet, 1972, *ii*, 900.

Dobbing, J. and Sands, J. 'Timing of neuroblast multiplication in the developing brain.' Nature, 1970, *226*, 639.

Finn, R. Speaking at Liverpool Medical Institute Symposium on '*Role of inheritance in common diseases.*' Lancet 1960, *i*, 526.

Gregg, N. 'Congenital cataract following German measles in the mother.' Trans. ophthal. Soc. Aust. 1941. *3.35.*

Liley, A. W. 'Intrauterine transfusion of foetus in haemolytic disease.' Brit. med. J. 1963, *2*, 1107.

Malmgren, B., Vahlquist, B. and Zetterstrom, R. 'Complications of immunisation.' Brit. med. J. 1960, *2*, 1800.

Miller, R. W. 'Delayed effects occurring within the first decade after exposure of young individuals to the Hiroshima atomic bomb.' Pediatrics, 1956, *18*, 1.

Milunsky, A., Graef, J. W. and Gaylor, M. F. 'Methotrexate induced congenital malformations.' J. Ped. 1968, *72*, 790.

Penrose, L. S. 'Heredity, environment and mental subnormality.' J. ment. Subnormality, 1966, *12*, 55.

Stern, H., Booth, J. C., Elek, S. D. and Fleck, D. G. 'The Role of prenatal infections with cytomegalovius, rubella virus and toxoplasma.' Lancet, 1969, *ii*, 443.

Studies in Hydrocephalus and Spina Bifida. Devel. Med. Child. Neurol. 1970, 12, supple. 22, London.

Taylor, K. J. W. and Dyson, M. 'Possible hazards of diagnostic ultrasound.' Brit. J. hosp. med. 1972, *8*, No. 5, 577.

3 The abilities and behaviour of the mentally subnormal

There may be a wide variation in the abilities and behaviour of mentally subnormal people, even when they are superficially similar in appearance and of apparently similar I.Q. Those with the most profound degrees of amentia remain completely dependent throughout their lives, lying in bed and showing no obvious awareness of their environment and no purposeful activity. They never speak and show no sign of understanding what is said to them and make little response to attempts to stimulate them. They have to be washed, dressed and fed and never acquire any control of their bowels or bladder. With less severe degrees of amentia, spontaneous activity and understanding increase, as do the response to training and the ability for self-care. In those with moderate degrees of amentia, academic abilities are limited and although their rote memory may be good and they may be able to count and read in a mechanical manner, they are usually unable to do any but the simplest calculations and do not have the reasoning ability necessary for leading an independent life. However, they may show surprising islands of above-average ability, for example in music and art, or, as in several well known cases, in arithmetical ability (the so-called *idiots savants*), completely out of keeping with their otherwise obvious mental subnormality. With training, those with moderate degrees of amentia should be capable of carrying out simple repetitive tasks, at which they will continue for long periods at a steady pace. Those with still less severe degrees of amentia are likely to be capable of unskilled or semi-skilled employment, although they may need constant supervision because of their poor powers of concentration and their greater capacity for being distracted by events around them. On the other hand, many people with a mild mental handicap are able to hold down regular jobs in the community in competition with people of higher intelligence.

Just as there is a wide variation in the abilities of mentally subnormal people, so there is a wide variation in their behaviour and stability. Stable behaviour may be seen throughout the range of amentia, and unstable and antisocial behaviour may accompany all degrees, except the most profound, in which, as has been described, existence is almost completely passive. The instability may take the form of temper outbursts, aggressive behaviour, both verbal and physical, towards other people, window-smashing, clothes-tearing or other destructive behaviour, and self-mutilation, such as tearing or biting the skin, head-banging, or pulling out the hair or rubbing it thin, as well as smearing themselves or their surroundings with faeces. Some of this unstable behaviour is unpredictable and difficult to explain except as a manifestation of brain damage, but it is always desirable to search for a cause rather than to attribute it to an unavoidable accompaniment of mental handicap. Possible causes include disappointment at the failure of a relative or friend to visit or write or to keep a promise, jealousy of other members of the family or others in the same residential care, a thoughtless remark by someone in their environment, or frustration at their inability to make themselves understood or to succeed in something they are trying to do. Sometimes such behaviour represents an attention-seeking device, particularly in those who are emotionally deprived. Some mentally subnormal females become unstable about the time of menstruation and, in both male and female epileptics, in whom the fits are well controlled by drugs, periodic unstable behaviour may occur at the time when fits would be occurring if it were not for the effect of the drugs.

Various tranquillising drugs have been tried in an attempt to modify disturbed behaviour in the mentally subnormal without affecting their level of consciousness. None has yet proved to be effective in every case, but the most commonly used include chlorpromazine (Largactil) and haloperidol (Serenace).

One of the greatest problems is posed by hyperkinetic children, whose intense and continuous purposeless overactivity is usually associated with brain damage. Such children are often able to sustain their overactivity by night as well as by day without showing signs of fatigue long after those caring for them are exhausted. They may show remarkable ability at climbing or squeezing through narrow spaces, such as partly-opened windows. They are unable to concentrate on any particular activity for more than a short period and they are very distractible. They may be vicious towards other children, unable to play constructively and are often destructive. They frequently suffer from epileptic fits, but unfortunately phenobarbitone, commonly used to control epilepsy, may increase the child's overactivity. However, some respond to amphetamine (a drug normally used in others to stimulate activity) which, for a reason not yet fully understood, has a sedative action in some hyperkinetic children, who can tolerate abnormally high doses of the drug (Eisenberg, 1966).

Many mentally subnormal people are capable of showing great affection to other people, but unfortunately, as children, they have few friends among those of the same age and of normal intelligence, who tend to become impatient with them. As a result, any friends of normal intelligence are usually younger than themselves. In general, the more severe the degree of amentia the weaker the heterosexual urge is likely to be, but even very severely mentally subnormal people may masturbate quite openly and cause embarrassment to others. Less severely handicapped people may indulge in mutual masturbation, or more serious homosexual deviations, particularly when they are deprived of the company of members of the opposite sex. The most serious sexual problems are likely to arise in mildly mentally-handicapped women who have a strong sexual drive, but impaired self-control. Such women are obviously at great risk of sexual exploitation and of conceiving unwanted children, as they are unlikely to heed contraceptive advice. The question of marriage of mentally-handicapped people will be considered in a later chapter.

Unfortunately, on occasions, mentally subnormal females make unfounded allegations of sexual interference against members of the opposite sex who are unattainable love objects or, conversely objects of their disfavour. Such allegations are distressing to those against whom they are made and may be very difficult to disprove in the absence of any independent refuting evidence. Where they are found to be untrue and concern the patient's employer, great care has to be taken in arranging any future employment with a member of the opposite sex.

Offences committed by moderately mentally subnormal people are usually minor, such as petty thieving, including shop-lifting of articles of little value. The mildly mentally subnormal may, on occasions, commit acts of arson or be used by others of higher intelligence to commit more serious thefts on their behalf. Crimes of violence are rare among the mentally subnormal, but the latter may be provoked, by the unsympathetic attitude of others, to react aggressively in the way that normal children may do under similar circumstances. There is some evidence that parents of battered babies are excessively likely to be of subnormal intelligence.

REFERENCES

The abilities and behaviour of the mentally subnormal
Eisenberg, L. 'Management of the Hyperkinetic Child.' Devel. med. and child. neurol. 1966, 8, 593.

4 Epilepsy in the mentally subnormal

Epilepsy is a group of disorders, which are a manifestation of cerebral dysrhythmia (or disturbance of the normal electrophysiological activity of the brain), which may be recorded on an electroencephalogram (E.E.G.) This disturbance may be caused by abnormal development or damage of the brain, or interference with its function by inherited or acquired disorders of the chemistry of the body.

The manifestations of epilepsy include both obvious convulsions and transitory interruptions of consciousness. The best known is major epilepsy, or *grand mal*, in which the attack follows a set sequence—the affected person falls to the ground and becomes rigid and blue as breathing stops. The rigidity gives way to violent jerking of the limbs and jaw. During this stage urine may be passed, joints may become dislocated or bones broken, and the tongue may be badly lacerated if trapped between the teeth. Saliva may be whipped into a froth and give the typical appearance of foaming at the mouth. During this stage, too, normal breathing is gradually restored and the colour returns to normal. As the convulsions pass off, the epileptic usually goes to sleep for a period and, on waking, may complain of headache. Epileptic people show varying degrees of confusion after a fit and some may act in a completely automatic manner, with no subsequent recollection of their actions during this time. Major epileptic fits are more likely to occur when the susceptible person becomes constipated or during feverish illnesses. Most major fits can be prevented or reduced in frequency by anticonvulsant drugs, such as phenobarbitone, primidone (Mysoline) or phenytoin (Epanutin), alone or in combination. It is important that people liable to major epileptic fits should take their anticonvulsants regularly. If the drugs are suddenly withdrawn, *status epilepticus* may occur, in which one major fit succeeds another in quick succession and which may lead to death in some cases.

In *petit mal*, convulsions do not occur, but consciousness is interrupted briefly by the attack so that an affected individual may suddenly stop talking in the middle of a sentence and then start talking again as soon as the attack passes. Ethosuximide (Zarontin) has a specific effect in controlling *petit mal* attacks.

What appear to be typical *grand mal* or *petit mal* attacks may, in fact, be manifestations of temporal lobe epilepsy (Aird, 1970) due to lesions in the temporal lobe of the brain and, in such cases, those affected may learn to recognise the aura, or warning of the imminence of an attack, such as a particular taste or smell, and know to take appropriate steps to avoid injury. Drugs used to control temporal lobe epilepsy include sulthiame (Ospolot) and carbamazepine (Tegretol).

In *myoclonic* epilepsy, the convulsions may be confined to a single limb and do not involve the whole body as in *grand mal*. Drugs used to control myoclonic epilepsy include troxidone (Tridione) and paramethadione (Paradione).

A particular form of epilepsy of grave prognostic significance is the so-called *salaam spasm*, occurring in a child in the first year of life and associated with a diagnostic pattern in the E.E.G. The salaam attacks are so-called because the affected child suddenly falls forwards and prostrates himself in an attitude of obeisance. Unless the condition is recognised and treated early, irreversible brain damage and severe mental subnormality will be inevitable and, even though treatment with cortisone may restore the E.E.G. pattern to normal and stop the salaam spasms, it does not prevent mental deterioration in all cases.

REFERENCES

Epilepsy in the mentally subnormal
Aird, R. B. 'Drug treatment of epilepsy.' Mod. Med. Feb. 1970, 149.

5 Mental illness in the mentally subnormal

Mentally subnormal people are liable to the full range of mental illnesses which occur in people of normal intelligence, but the incidence of different mental illnesses varies according to the degree of mental handicap, *e.g.* the manic-depressive type of psychosis occurs only in the least severely handicapped, whereas the schizophrenic group of psychoses occur through a much wider range of intelligence (Reid, 1972). However, when a case is first seen several years after the onset of a schizophrenic deterioration, it is very difficult to be sure what the level of intelligence was before the onset of the psychosis. In juvenile schizophrenia, the psychosis starts before mental development is complete and is itself a cause of both mental subnormality and subsequent mental deterioration.

In manic-depressive psychosis, there are alternating periods of abnormal elation, garrulousness and intense overactivity to the neglect of food and sleep, and of extreme depression, withdrawal and slowing of thought, speech and movement, and loss of appetite; early-morning waking frequently and delusions of guilt and unworthiness sometimes occur. In less extreme states of depressive withdrawal, agitation and restlessness may be the prominent features, with a higher risk of successful or attempted suicide.

The manic phases are usually controlled with tranquillising drugs such as chlorpromazine (Largactil) or haloperidol (Serenace), and the depressive phases with antidepressant drugs such as imipramine (Tofranil) or amitriptyline (Tryptizol). However, it may be necessary on occasions to treat depression with electroconvulsive therapy (E.C.T.). It is now possible to prevent the manic-depressive swings or to modify their intensity in susceptible individuals by the regular administration of lithium carbonate.

Schizophrenia is not a single entity, but consists of a group of disorders in which the most obvious disturbance is of thinking rather than of feeling, although the emotion expressed may be quite inappropriate to the idea being expressed at the time. The most common form—*hebephrenic schizophrenia*—usually occurs in the late teens or early twenties, typically in introverted personalities, and manifests itself as a progressive withdrawal from contact with other people, both inside and outside their own family, often with an abnormal preoccupation with religious or pseudo-philosophical matters. At the same time, bizarre or eccentric behaviour may develop, with neglect of personal hygiene and appearance. Conversation with others becomes increasingly difficult, due to the loss of the normal associative links by which logical thinking ordinarily proceeds, so that thought processes appear quite inconsequential to an observer. Hallucinations—usually of voices—and delusions —often persecutory—occur, and may prompt violent retaliatory acts. If untreated, progressive, irreversible mental deterioration occurs.

Other schizophrenic disorders are of later onset, and are usually accompanied by less marked withdrawal from social contact and less severe deterioration of the personality. In *catatonic schizophrenia*, periods of extreme stupor and withdrawal, during which the patient can maintain bizarre postures for long periods, may alternate with periods of the most extreme excitement known in psychiatry, with a return to periods of quite normal behaviour in between.

Schizophrenia is usually treated by phenothiazine drugs such as chlorpromazine (Largactil) or trifluoperazine (Stelazine), or fluphenazine (Moditen) may be given by injection in its long-acting form, fluphenazine decanoate (Modecate), which requires administration only at intervals of up to 40 days. Such drug therapy may be combined with E.C.T. Because of the mixed nature of mental illness in the mentally subnormal, it is often necessary in their treatment to use a combination of the drugs usually prescribed specifically for the treatment of manic-depressive or schizophrenic psychoses.

Both subnormal and severely subnormal people may develop short-lived acute anxiety states as an immediate response to stress, but prolonged, chronic anxiety states due to an unresolved conflict are confined to the subnormal and those at the upper end of the severely subnormal range of handicap. In the same way, depression caused, for example, by bereavement is likely to be of shorter duration in severely subnormal than in subnormal people. Obsessional ruminations may occur in both anxious and depressed mentally subnormal people, and are likely to disappear with the underlying condition, which may be treated with the tranquillisers or antidepressant drugs already referred to, either alone or in combination.

Because of their smaller reserve of brain cells, the signs of cell loss due to any cause are more likely to become obvious at an earlier age in the mentally subnormal than in those of higher intelligence. Thus, signs typical of *senile dementia* may first be recognised in middle age in the severely subnormal, but may, on the other hand, be considerably delayed in the mildly subnormal who have led sheltered lives in hospital. Acute episodes of confusion may occur in the mentally subnormal during high fevers, but more prolonged periods of confusion may occur, particularly in those with epilepsy, due to the effect of anticonvulsant drugs.

Because of the poor integration of personality in mentally subnormal people, mental illnesses do not often present among them in clear-cut, textbook forms, but rather in mixed forms in which there are both manic-depressive and schizophrenic features (Tredgold, 1947). For this reason, it is difficult to give an accurate estimate of the incidence of mental illness among mentally subnormal people generally. However, surveys of mental illness in the residents of mental subnormality hospitals have shown an incidence of about eight to ten per cent.

AUTISTIC CHILDREN

There is an unfortunate tendency to use the term 'autistic' as a euphemism for mental subnormality in all children who are unable to communicate, irrespective of their level of intelligence, with the implication that their prognosis is, somehow, better than in those to whom the term mentally subnormal is applied. As in the case of the similar use of the term 'spastic' in the past, it is inferred that with special treatment and education they may prove to be of normal intelligence.

Such a widespread use of the term autistic makes it meaningless and the term should be restricted to children who satisfy the following criteria:

1. A failure to develop normal interpersonal relationships, shown from an early age as a characteristic failure to cuddle and later, as a tendency to avoid direct eye-contact with those in his environment.
2. Difficulty in understanding spoken and gesture language and in developing his own verbal and gestural speech.
3. Rigid patterns of behaviour with strong resistance to change. The autistic child develops ritualistic patterns of behaviour, including mannerisms such as finger-flicking or grimacing and, typically, develops abnormal attachments to objects such as a tin lid or shoe-lace, and any attempt to alter his ritual or separate him from such objects may precipitate a violent temper outburst, during which he may inflict injuries upon himself (Wing, 1970).

Seventy per cent of autistic children have I.Q.s below 70, including forty per cent with I.Q.s below 50 (Rutter, 1972). There is evidence that the cause is a neurological abnormality, which may be inherited.

There is no specific treatment for autism, but the accompanying overactivity may be reduced by tranquillisers, and operant conditioning techniques may help some autistic children to develop some skills and to modify their disturbed behaviour (Lovaas, 1966). However, there is, in the author's view, unfortunately no evidence that, given an equal expenditure of manpower, time and money, the prognosis of autistic children is better than that in non-autistic mentally subnormal children of similar levels of intelligence.

REFERENCES

Mental illness in the mentally subnormal

Reid, A. H. 'Psychoses in Adult Mental Defectives. I. Manic-depressive Psychosis.' Brit. J. Psychiat. 1972, *120*, 205.

Reid, A. H. 'Psychoses in Adult Mental Defectives. II. Schizophrenia and Paranoid Psychoses.' Brit. J. Psych. 1972, *120*, 213.

Reid, A. H. and Aungle, P. G. 'Dementia in Ageing Mental Defectives. A Clinical Psychiatric Study.' J. ment. Depr. Res. 1974, *18*, 15.

Tredgold, A. F. *A Textbook of Mental Deficiency*, 7th Edition. Bailliere, Tindall & Cox, London 1947.

Autistic children

Lovaas, J. *in Early Childhood Autism*. Pergamon Press, Oxford. 1966, p. 115.

Rutter, M. L. 'Psychiatric disorder and intellectual impairment in childhood.' Brit. J. hosp. med. 1972, 137.

Wing, L. 'The syndrome of early childhood autism.' Brit. J. hosp. med. 1970, 381.

6. The development of care of the mentally subnormal

In 1933, Dr. E. D. Turner, who was then Medical Superintendent of the Royal Eastern Counties Institution, Colchester, chose Mental Deficiency as the subject for his Presidential address to the then Royal Medico-Psychological Association (now the Royal College of Psychiatrists). Dr. Turner suggested 'The Wheel Always Turns Full Circle' as an alternative title because, he said, 'Over and over again, in the case of defectives during the past hundred years, it has happened that methods and ideas thought out quite early in the movement and later discarded and forgotten have been rediscovered and treated as new ideas'. This statement is as true today as when Dr. Turner made it and at a time when the present pattern of care of the mentally handicapped is being questioned, often by people with only a recent and often minimal personal involvement with the problem, it is important to consider the lessons of the past and how the present system of care, with all its admitted deficiencies, has evolved before discarding it completely in favour of a 'new' system which has been shown to be unsatisfactory in the past.

THE PAST TO THE TWENTIETH CENTURY

Throughout the ages the mentally handicapped have been alternately reviled and revered. In ancient times, for example, mental defectives were believed to be cursed by the gods and were allowed to perish, or as in Sparta, directly exposed to danger of death. With the physically feeble, they were thrown into the river Eurotas. Attempts to maintain the physical and mental health of the race in this way still existed at the beginning of the present century among certain South Sea Islanders and among a tribe of American Indians, who were said to be distinguished for their intelligence, strength and physical beauty. Unsuccessful attempts to control the number of mental defectives by methods little less ruthless were made by Hitler and, using rather more sophisticated methods, this control is advocated by some to this day in the name of eugenics. Those, in ancient times, who by chance escaped death, were treated with ridicule and scorn and sometimes kept in the houses of the rich for diversion and amusement.

Things changed for the better with the dawn of the Christian era. About 300 A.D., in the Imperial reign of Constantine the Great, the Bishop of Myra was caring for mental defectives and, when she was only twelve, Euphrasia, of the imperial household of Theodosius, retired into the convent of Thebiad to do similar work.

During the Middle Ages mental defectives were often employed as court fools or jesters. At this time the house into which a mental defective was born was considered to be blessed of God. This sympathetic attitude towards defectives was not confined to Christians, but was encouraged in the Koran and in the writings of Confucius and Zoroaster. To quote the Koran, 'Give not unto those who are weak of understanding the substance which Allah hath appointed you to preserve for them; but maintain them thereout and clothe them and speak kindly unto them' (Macgillivray, 1962).

Unfortunately, by the time of the Reformation, the pendulum had swung back and defectives were once again persecuted and denounced by such religious leaders as Calvin as being 'filled with Satan', and by Martin Luther as being the illegitimate children of the devil. On one occasion Luther recommended that an imbecile boy of twelve be drowned (Macgillivray, 1962).

To France, in the middle of the seventeenth century, must be given the credit for the first organised effort to provide asylum for mental defectives at the Bicêtre near Paris, where St. Vincent de Paul and his Confrèrie de Charité (or Lazarites, as they were called) cared for defective children along with other homeless, outcast and physically feeble children from Paris and the provinces.

The eighteenth century saw the beginning of what came to be called 'physiologic education' of the mental defective. The method had its roots in the work of Jacob Rodrigues Pereire among the deaf and dumb. Having demonstrated that spoken speech consisted of two elements, the sound and the vibration which produced it, Pereire taught deaf patients, first to perceive the vibration and, later, to produce intelligible speech by imitating the appropriate vibration. The success of Pereire with the deaf-mute inspired Itard (himself physician to a school for deaf-mutes) and Seguin to attempt to educate mental defectives in France. It is interesting to note how many pioneers in the care of defectives at that time had previously been working in institutions for the deaf-mute.

In 1798, in the woods of Caune in the Department of Aveyron in France, a boy, aged between eleven and twelve years, looking for acorns and nuts, was caught by a party of sportsmen. He was described by Professor Bonaterre of the Chair of Natural History in the Central School of the Department of Aveyron as being unaccustomed to ordinary food and as selecting what he ate by his sense of smell. He lay flat on the ground and immersed his chin in the water to drink. He tore all sorts of garments, tried constantly to escape and often walked on all fours. He fought with his teeth, showed few signs of intelligence, had no articulate language and appeared devoid of natural speech. He was complaisant and pleased at receiving caresses (Bonaterre, 1799). The 'Savage of Aveyron', as he became known, was taken to Paris to become, under Itard's care, 'the first example recorded of an idiot reclaimed from the life of a mere animal to be trained to a human existence' (Barr, 1904).

Itard believed that all ideas were derived directly from the senses and that, by the repeated stimulation of different sensations, correspondingly different ideas could be produced and a given character formed. This was the basis of his training programme for the Savage of Aveyron, which continued for five years. At the end of this time Itard felt he had failed completely (Itard, 1801), but this view was not shared by the French Academy, who recognised how much he had achieved with a most difficult subject and the novelty and ingenuity of the teaching methods he had employed.

Itard's work inspired his pupil Edward Seguin to open a private school in Paris in 1837 for the education of the idiot and to elaborate a system of training, which led to his appointment in 1842 as Director of the school for idiots at the Bicêtre. At this point, to avoid any misunderstanding, it is important to stress that until the beginning of the twentieth century the term 'idiot' was used indiscriminately to cover all grades of mental defectives and not confined to the most severe grade as defined in the *Mental Deficiency Act* 1913.

Seguin realised that ideas were not derived directly from sensations as Itard had believed, but depended for their development on the presence of an intermediate, intelligent reflective power. Seguin's methods, based on this realisation, were discussed by him in his famous book *The Theory and Nature of the Education of Idiots* (Seguin, 1842, 1843). He stressed the importance of a careful physiological and psychological examination to ascertain the aptitudes, the faculties and the instinctive and moral tendencies of the individual, before planning a programme of education which was to end in every case with the choice of an occupation, which would 'keep in activity the muscular system as well as the mental faculties'. Seguin was obviously aware of the benefits of physiotherapy and stressed the importance of well ventilated accommodation 'accessible equally to natural and artificial heat' and with windows '. . . so placed that the children can, from the tables, enjoy the view of the gardens which have purposely been laid out'. Seguin stressed also the importance of singing and dancing and of having a large common assembly hall.

France herself was slow to follow the lead given her by Itard and Seguin in providing care for the mentally defective and, after only a few years at the Bicêtre, Seguin resigned his post of Director because of personal difficulties with the authorities, who made false accusations against him. However, 1842, the year of Seguin's appointment, had seen the almost simultaneous and independent development in three other countries—Switzerland, Germany and America—of institutions for the care of defectives by his methods. That in Switzerland—the Abendberg—was to become the model of care copied in many other countries. Its founder, a young physician named Guggenbuhl, had in 1836 been so moved by the sight of a poor, deformed cretin murmuring his prayers before a wayside cross, that he devoted his whole life to the study and treatment of that condition. The hospital was erected 100 feet from the summit of the 4,000 feet high Abendberg near Interlaken and soon cottages covered an area of about forty acres on the Southern slope. It was staffed by the Evangelical Sisters of Mercy—the Diakonissen. Guggenbuhl closely followed Seguin's methods, modified to suit the special needs of the cretin. The senses were continuously stimulated by methods which were frequently changed to avoid monotony. Exercise in the open air was encouraged and was supplemented by frequent baths and massage (Guggenbuhl, 1840).

News of the success of the Abendberg quickly spread abroad and it was visited by scientists, philanthropists and physicians from Europe and the U.S.A. who were inspired to start similar institutions on the colony plan for the care of the idiot in their own countries. Unfortunately, like Seguin in France, Guggenbuhl ran into difficulties with the authorities and he was condemned as a charlatan and the Abendberg was dissolved.

In Germany, in 1845, Saegert, Director of the Asylum for deaf-mutes in Berlin, opened a private institution for the treatment by physiological methods of twenty mental defectives in that city and in 1846 he published his monograph 'The Cure of Imbecility by Intellectual Means' (Saegert, 1846). Saegert advocated nursing by humane nurses and 'that the company of other children was desirable; that there should be careful exercises and special nurseries would be useful'.

It was these three, Seguin, Guggenbuhl and Saegert who put the theories of Pereire and Itard regarding the teaching and training of mental defectives on a practical basis. Of them, only Saegert lived to see these methods encouraged and spread in his native land and, in Germany, between 1846 and 1881 no fewer than thirty-two training schools for idiots were founded. Saxony became the first state in the world to make such training compulsory by law.

As a result of the visit of the King of Württemburg to the Abendberg, the disused Convent of Mariaberg was opened in 1847 as an educational institution for cretins, under the royal patronage of the Crown Princess Olga. However, as in so many institutions which followed, the need for a custodial or asylum department quickly became apparent and, in 1874, a farm of between 300 and 400 acres was added. At a time when it is being suggested by some paediatricians that we should abolish the distinction between physically and mentally handicapped children, at least nominally, and refer to them both as 'handicapped children', it is interesting to note that in the colonies which developed in Germany, a wide variety of children were accommodated—for example, in that at Alsterdorfer, founded in 1850, there were: a home for friendless normal children, an asylum for idiot and feeble-minded children, including epileptics, a home for crippled children of normal intelligence, a school for defectives of the wealthier classes, and hospital and isolation wards.

The Scandinavian countries were quick to follow the example of Switzerland and Germany in providing residential care and training for mental defectives, and Norway became the second country in Europe to make their education compulsory. Stress was placed on complete separation of the sexes, and small classes to permit individual attention. All these institutions in Norway were placed under state control in 1892, but the government made no special provision for untrainable defectives.

Visits of the Queen of the Netherlands and of the Austrian Ambassador to the Abendberg led to the establishment of institutions for defectives in Holland in 1855 and in Austria in 1864. For some reason, Belgium seems to have taken little part in this European movement to provide training for the mentally defective in the middle of the nineteenth century. A notable exception was a private institution for imbecile and backward children, established in 1896 at Rèves, Hainault, and conducted by Sisters of Charity. The children were divided into five grades according to intelligence and capacity. There was an average of eight pupils to one teacher and special cases were often assigned singly to one instructor. The daily programme consisted of the education of the senses, and physical, musical and manual training.

In Italy, in 1898, a National League for the Protection of Backward Children was founded, and concerned itself with the moral and intellectual education of mental defectives adjudged incurable. The League had the great benefit of the support of Signorina Montessori, who gave special lectures in the principal Italian towns. In 1899, the institution of Saint John Persiceto was founded with classrooms for special grades, workshops for the arts and trades, a farm for training in agriculture, a theatre, music- and drill-halls, a gymnasium and a section of hydrotherapeutics. There were separate sections for boys and girls, and for the rich and poor.

Before coming nearer to home, I must refer to the contribution of the U.S.A. where, as I have mentioned, the first institution for mental defectives was opened in 1842, the same year as those in Switzerland and Germany. Again, the needs of the mentally defective were recognised by someone working in an institution catering for the needs of those with another handicap—Dr. Samuel G. Howe, the Director of the Perkins Institution for the Blind. Dr. Howe's interest led to the establishment in 1850 of the Massachusetts School for Idiot and Feeble-Minded Children. Dr. Seguin, who had been caring for private pupils after his resignation from the Bicêtre school, agreed to help in its organisation. By 1900, the school had become a colony of nearly 1,700 acres, providing a permanent home for 800 children who had completed their training. In 1851, Seguin assisted in the foundation, at Syracuse in New York State, of the first institution in America catering specifically for the feeble-minded. Seguin also played a part in the organisation of training schools, in 1856 in Pennsylvania, and in 1857 in Ohio. By the beginning of the present century, twenty-one states across the United States were each providing at least one institution for mental defectives. In this connection it is of interest nowadays to note the comment of Barr—'The attention of the public is constantly aroused to the necessity for the segregation and permanent sequestration of these unfortunates, as conducive alike to their own and to the public welfare'. In Switzerland in 1899, Schenker, in a paper on the 'Etiology and Therapeutics of Idiocy', had recommended the legal prohibition of 'marriage between the weak-minded, epileptics and idiots . . . the diffusion of information, both by speeches and through the press, as to the causes of idiocy and the means of combating it; special classes and asylums for incurable idiots' as means of combating the increase in imbecility (Schenker, 1899).

In 1846 the Misses White opened their private school for mental defectives in Bath. In 1843, articles were published in England by Dr. William Twining, describing the achievements at the Abendberg and in 1847 by Mr. Gaskell, afterwards a Commissioner in Lunacy, and Dr. John Conolly, Superintendent of Hanwell Insane Asylum, describing work at the Bicêtre. As the result of the enthusiasm of the Rev. Andrew Reed about his visit to the Abendberg in 1847, and the support of Dr. Conolly, Park House, Highgate was opened the following year as a temporary home for twenty-seven children. In 1850, the patients were moved to another temporary, but larger, home at Essex Hall, near Colchester. In 1853, the cornerstone of Royal Earlswood was laid by the Prince Consort and in 1855 the patients from Essex Hall were transferred to this 500-bedded institution, and Essex Hall became the Royal Eastern Counties Institution for mental defectives.

The Royal Western Counties Institution and the Royal Albert Asylum, Lancaster, opened in 1864, and the Northern and Midland Counties Institution in 1866. By the end of the nineteenth century, these three institutions accommodated only 1,000 defectives between them. The first large institution in this country was the Metropolitan School of Darenth, Dartford, Kent, which catered for 1,000 patients.

Scotland was provided with its first institution (now Strathmartine Hospital) in 1852 by Sir John and Lady Jane Ogilvy on their estate at Baldovan, near Dundee, in gratitude for all that had been accomplished for their defective child at the Abendberg. In 1861, the Royal Scottish National Institution for the Education of Imbecile Children, at Larbert, Stirlingshire was founded, with accommodation for 200. It is interesting to note the objects of its forerunner, the Gayfield Square Institution, in Edinburgh, which were stated to be: 'Firstly, improvement in general health; secondly, the awakening and development of mental powers by those means which have already been found so effective in similar institutions. Thirdly, the employment of educational resources to meet the peculiarities of the pupils. Fourthly, in the case of the more advanced pupils, of providing some suitable occupation giving healthy employment, at once agreeable and profitable to all their powers, keeping in view such occupations as may fit the pupil for future usefulness and intercourse with society' (MacGillivray, 1962).

The first institution in Ireland was the Stewart Institution at Palmerston, Dublin, which was opened in 1869 with 43 pupils.

In 1886, the *Idiots Act* was passed in this country, and permitted the detention of mental defectives in idiot asylums run by voluntary bodies. These idiot asylums were not intended to provide life-long care for patients, but their aim was education and cure.

THE TWENTIETH CENTURY

In July 1900 Dr. Fletcher Beach, the first worker from the field of
Mental Deficiency to be elected President of the Medico-
Psychological Association, as it then was, pointed out in his
presidential address that whereas, at that time, the institutions in
Great Britain were chiefly supported by voluntary contributions,
those in the United States were maintained by funds supplied by the
different states and he commented—'much remains to be done in
this country if we are to provide asylums supported by the rates
only up to the standard of State-aided institutions now at work in
America' (Beach, 1900).

Dr. Fletcher Beach made an interesting reference to early industrial therapy when he spoke of the children at the school for
idiots at the Hague who were employed on cigar making. However,
perhaps his most interesting references were to the care of the
moral imbecile and the juvenile delinquent in this country and the
U.S.A. 'The moral imbeciles', he said, 'found their way into institutions for idiots and imbeciles. They were', he said, 'a difficult
class to deal with, for they are often intellectually sharp and clever,
but morally they are thieves, liars, full of cunning and sometimes
criminal in their tendencies. If remonstrated with, they will promise
amendment, but their promises are soon forgotten and a slight
cause produces a fresh outbreak. In some cases they possess good
manual skill and use it for bad purposes'. Acts of Parliament may
change names but they cannot change patients and many readers
will already have recognised in this description patients we would
now call psychopathic. Dr. Fletcher Beach quoted the novel view
of Dr. Kerlin, Superintendent of the Pennsylvania Institution for
Feeble-Minded Children, that moral imbeciles should not be
educated, as it increased their power for evil, but that they should
live in buildings apart from other children, in order not to infect
them with their bad tendencies. Dr. Fletcher Beach himself thought
they should be cared for in special institutions, as he did not consider them fit subjects for lunatic asylums, reformatories or prisons.

In 1904, the Royal Commission on the Care and Control of the
Feeble-Minded was set up and produced its report in 1908 which
resulted in the *Mental Deficiency Act* of 1913. Apart from
removing some of the confusion caused by the existing terminology

concerning mental defectives, this Act permitted local authorities for the first time to build their own institutions for the care of defectives and to contract with existing voluntary institutions to take their cases on payment. By the time that this Act was passed it had been realised that lifelong care would be necessary for many defectives.

One of the members of the Royal Commission was the Rev. Harold Burden, who, with his wife, had become interested in the plight of mentally defective children, through their work at Horfield Prison, Bristol, where he was chaplain, and among the families of prisoners. Their visits to Germany to study the colony system led to the opening in 1909 of Stoke Park Colony, which was to become the first institution in the British Isles to be certified under the *Mental Deficiency Act* of 1913, as an institution for mental defectives. The statement of the objects of the institution began: 'The institutions are for PERMANENT as distinct from temporary care and no case is knowingly received as a temporary measure', and ended: 'PERMANENT care and control is the only method of securing economical and humane treatment'. We have no reason to doubt the humanity of the treatment, and economical it certainly was, as shown in the accounts by the weekly 'all-in' cost per inmate of $10/8\frac{1}{4}$d (53.6p)!

Mr. Burden had always worked to encourage research, and following his death in 1939, research into neuro-pathological and psychological aspects of mental defect was carried on at Stoke Park through the generosity of the Burden Mental Research Trust until these departments were removed to Frenchay Hospital, Bristol, and Great Ormond Street Children's Hospital, London, respectively. At about the same time, a research department was established at the Royal Eastern Counties Institution to assess the relative roles of heredity and environment in the causation of mental defect.

Once the incurability and need for lifelong care of many defectives was recognised, there developed among the general public in England and the U.S.A. what Davies of New York called the 'Alarmist period', with the fear, to quote Dr. Turner, of 'the inevitable downfall of the human race and the swamping of the good stock and the average normal person by the defective and incompetent'. What had started as an educational movement and recognition by those caring for them of the defectives' own needs, quickly grew in the minds of the general public into the belief that the lifelong segregation of defectives in institutions was the only way of preventing their propagation. Francis Galton, the geneticist, maintained that a defective mother would not only have a defective child, but would also breed faster than a mother of normal intelligence. At the time of the 1910 Parliamentary election campaign, the National Association for the Care of the Feeble-Minded and the Eugenics Education Society were asking candidates to support measures 'that tend to discourage parenthood on the part of the feeble-minded and other degenerate types'. The fact, of course, was then as it is now, that most defectives are not the children of defectives. However, as a result of this belief, many mildly mentally handicapped people were compulsorily admitted to mental deficiency institutions for what we would now regard as totally inadequate reasons, such as giving birth to an illegitimate child while in receipt of poor relief, and some have remained there to this day, although no longer compulsorily detained.

Fortunately, not all those who cared for the mentally handicapped in institutions shared the general public's fears or regarded the institutions' role as being solely custodial. Turner, for example, believed that the great majority of defectives were very much improved by the training and stabilisation they received in institutions, so that many of them could be sent back into the world to earn their living, or with some supervision, to be cared for more simply and less expensively than in an institution. 'The wheel', as Turner said in 1933, 'had come full circle and there had been a return to the faith Seguin preached'. Turner spoke some very prophetic words when he said: 'The institution of the future should be a flowing lake constantly fed by incoming patients, but just as constantly passing back to the world in several directions and by several different methods, many other patients who have been trained and stabilised while under its care. Resocialisation is the aim. Spread the available jam of teaching and training over the greatest possible number'. He did, however, recognise that many patients would have to remain in institutions all their lives.

As intermediate steps in achieving this resocialisation, many of the larger institutions established branches, or what we would now call hostels, from which patients went out to work each day before proceeding to residential licence in lodgings. Turner felt that it was essential that, for resocialisation to be successful, all patients should remain on licence indefinitely from the institution, so that there should be no barrier to a patient's immediate return, should the need for this arise. He believed that, in addition to its resocialising role, a large institution for defectives should provide an outpatient consulting and diagnostic service and should undertake research and the training of teachers and nurses.

The *Health Service Act* of 1946 transferred all local authority mental deficiency institutions to the State, which also assumed responsibility for many other institutions, such as Stoke Park Colony, which had been privately administered previously. In view of this takeover, it was perhaps not surprising that local authorities were reluctant to open hostels, and that it was the hospital authorities who opened most of the fifteen or so hostels that started during the period between the *Health Service Act* and the *Mental Health Act* of 1959.

In 1954, another Royal Commission namely the 'Royal Commission on the Law Relating to Mental Illness and Mental Deficiency' was set up. Its report, published in 1957, suggested that the term 'mental defective' should be abolished and replaced by the terms 'severely subnormal' and 'psychopathic'. To quote the Royal Commission: 'Hospitals should provide in-patient and out-patient services for patients who need specialist medical treatment or continual nursing attention. This includes the care of helpless patients in the severely subnormal group who need continual nursing, if proper care cannot be provided at home. It also includes in-patient training designed to promote the mental or physical development of severely subnormal and psychopathic patients, if such training requires individual psychiatric supervision, by which we mean that the patient's individual progress needs to be watched and, if possible, controlled by a psychiatrist. The aim of treatment or training is to make the patient fit to live in the general community. No patient should be retained as a hospital in-patient when he has reached the stage at which he could return home if he had a reasonably good home to go to. At that stage the provision of residential care becomes the responsibility of the local authority'.

As has been stated in a previous chapter, the resulting *Mental Health Act* of 1959 abolished the term 'mental defective', but added 'subnormality' to the two categories suggested in its place by the Royal Commission; following the passing of the *Mental Health Act*, the cry 'Community care for the mentally subnormal' was raised, as though community care *per se* possessed some magic therapeutic power. However, the more cynical were tempted to regard it more as a means of shifting financial responsibility from central to local government.

Since that time, the role and organisation of the mental subnormality hospital has been reviewed by a number of individuals and groups, including nurses, paediatricians, psychologists, psychiatrists, the Department of Health and Social Security and, not least, by sociologists. A small number of such hospitals have been the subject of official government enquiries. The general tone of many of these reviews was such that the 1960s might well be regarded as the decade of the attack upon the mental subnormality hospital.

In 1960 Tizard, in an oft-quoted paper, discussed the results of what has come to be known as the 'Brooklands Experiment', which demonstrated the advantages, to children, of care in small family units with a high staff to patient ratio. Tizard asserted: 'It is clear, even now, that the mental deficiency hospital is no longer a necessary part of our health and education system as it was in the past'. However, in October of the same year, a leading article in the *British Medical Journal* said that hospitals for the mentally subnormal had suffered from neglect more than any other branch of medicine. It went on to say: 'there is danger that special knowledge and training in the care of the mentally subnormal will be dissipated if it is too hastily assumed that the problem can be handed over to the paediatric unit, the general mental hospital, or the public health authority without more ado. Hospital Boards', the article went on, 'should not feel that the problem is no longer their concern', and it recommended that they should plan a number of small residential nursery units of not more than twenty beds on the lines of the Brooklands experiment. The leading article made the important suggestion that mental subnormality hospitals should foster links with their neighbouring universities and that at least one unit might well be designated as a national centre for research into mental subnormality.

In a letter published in the same edition of the Journal, the present author described all that had been achieved in spite of financial restrictions and numerically inadequate establishments. He pointed out the dangers of the view that mental subnormality was not primarily a psychiatric problem (a theme to be discussed further at a later stage) and expressed the hope that psychiatrists, in their enthusiasm to welcome others into the therapeutic team, did not abandon their overall responsibility for ensuring that the team was working in the very best interests of each patient in hospital. At the Annual Conference of the National Association of Mental Health in March the following year, the author defined the types of mentally subnormal patients likely to require treatment in hospital. He stressed his view that the care of the mentally subnormal patient in hospital was essentially a team effort, to which a number of people contributed under medical leadership, and suggested ways in which the liaison between psychiatrists and paediatricians might be improved to the benefit of mentally subnormal children in hospital. He anticipated the setting up in mental subnormality hospitals of units of the Coldharbour Farm (Stoke Park Hospital) type for adolescents in the 70–90 I.Q. range, with very disturbed behaviour, who had tended to fall into a therapeutic vacuum. (Unfortunately, the Coldharbour Farm unit itself failed to achieve recognition by the South Western Regional Hospital Board and it had to cease its specialist function due to shortage of psychiatric staff.) The author stressed, too, the need for more realistic consultant establishments in mental subnormality hospitals.

In 1962, a working party set up by the Paediatric Society of the South East Metropolitan Region recommended the coordination of services for the residential and community care of mentally subnormal children. They said there was a need for expansion, not contraction, of residential accommodation, but said that the large insitution should be regarded as obsolete and that there was an urgent need for discussion, enquiry and experiment as to the best type of residential care. Somewhat patronisingly, they commented that there were some large institutions with enthusiastic medical staff. They suggested that paediatric hospitals and departments should be used for severely subnormal children who required nursing care and that consideration should be given to the idea of the long-stay annexe, attached to paediatric wards, for older children with multiple handicaps. Later the same year, Kirman said there was no place in the National Health Service for the old type of mental deficiency service behind the hospital wall and that the psychiatrist must take a lead in the community service with the provision for clinics for the infant, the schoolchild and the adolescent.

In November 1963, Pilkington, himself a consultant psychiatrist in a mental subnormality hospital, launched the heaviest broadside yet against the large hospital. 'They are large (1000–2000 beds)' he said, 'they are usually in remote parts of the country and for many years they have been permanently geared for custodial care. Many of the patients have additional "institutional neurosis", and so do some of their staff, who lived in closed colonies within the hospital, with whole families, whose way of life is centred on the pattern of the institution'. He went on: 'The hierarchical structure, with the medical superintendent as chief officer, is no longer supported by statutory requirement, but not much more has been done to introduce a modern outlook. Little of the present forward-looking research emanates from these institutions, which have a vested interest in retaining the past. Progress', asserted Pilkington, 'will be made only when the subject escapes from the clinical and therapeutic nihilism of the custodial institution'.

Pilkington's proposed solution was the establishment of units in general hospitals for investigation and early treatment and an intensive rehabilitation programme (including work, social therapy, special education and psychiatric treatment) lasting a year or two. He described the advantages of such a unit which was in operation at Offerton House, Stockport, under a general hospital management committee. His criticisms of hospitals for the mentally subnormal were echoed by O'Brien, the Supervisor of a comprehensive training centre in Essex, by Mittler, then Principal Psychologist at Borocourt Hospital and by Leys, the Chairman, and MacKeith, a member, of the working party of the Paediatric Society. Pilkington's attack, and that of the Paediatric Society, was answered by a number of writers, including Gibson, McKenzie, Payne, Sampson and Shapiro, who pointed out the threat to progress if the speciality of mental subnormality was allowed to become one of marginal interest to a number of specialists who were primarily concerned with other clinical problems, and the great danger that the existence of a few general hospital units would provide an excuse for neglecting the needs of existing hospitals and starving them even further of money and facilities. Gibson gave a beautiful description of the very full life lived by patients in St. Lawrence's Hospital, Caterham, which was organised like a village of 2,000 inhabitants. At about the same time, a letter from a Dutch child psychiatrist, Hoejenbos, stated that the mental subnormality hospital was still considered to have a useful place in his country, 'where much stress lies on the necessity of a medical-director, who has to be a psychiatrist-neurologist, or at least one who has much experience in this field of work'.

In 1964, Kushlick as a result of his Wessex survey, recommended the establishment of small residential units on the Tizard plan for severely subnormal children, situated near their own homes. This proposal appeared to be accepted quite uncritically by some Regional Hospital Boards, but it should be noted that Kushlick recognised that very little was known about the problems of running this type of unit and that experimental evaluation was needed.

The then Ministry of Health's 'Building Note No. 30', published in 1963, seemed to suggest that it was the Ministry's policy to limit the size of future mental subnormality hospitals to a maximum of 500 beds. The reasons for doubting the validity of the assumptions upon which this policy appeared to be based were voiced by McCoull, the then Chairman of the Mental Deficiency Section of the Royal Medico-Psychological Association (R.M.P.A.), who also expressed concern at the possible amalgamation of mental subnormality hospitals of this size with general or mixed groups; and by the Mental Deficiency Sub-Committee of the Psychiatric Advisory Committee of the North West Metropolitan Regional Hospital Board. The latter Committee pointed out the 'muddled thinking of the worst kind' which had led to the belief that institutions were bad because they were large and that units in the general community were much better because they were small. They defined the function of a mental subnormality hospital and the departments necessary to fulfil this and listed among the advantages of the large comprehensive mental subnormality hospital, made up of small homely residential units, its ability to provide special units for particular grades of patients, to provide medical ancillary departments, such as pathology, radiology, encephalography and audiology, and to provide a career structure for professional workers of high calibre, with the stimulus of research. The Committee concluded their report by commenting: 'Comprehensive schools are being introduced on the grounds that they allow flexibility of placement and transfer, the employment of a team of specialists for the maximum benefit of all, and wide social intercourse. In this climate of opinion, it seems paradoxical to us that mental deficiency hospitals are to be limited in size, with consequent loss of these very real advantages'.

Very similar views were expressed in 1965 by Kratter and, in June 1966, by Shapiro, in his inaugural address as Chairman of the Mental Deficiency Section of the R.M.P.A. when he spoke on the 'Role of the Mental Deficiency Hospital'. In December 1965, the circular H.M. (65) 104 'Improving the Effectiveness of the Hospital Service for the Mentally Subnormal' was published.

At the First Congress of the International Association for the Scientific Study of Mental Deficiency, held in Montpelier, France, in September 1967, Raynes and King reported on the use of their scale for measuring the extent to which a residential unit for children conformed to Goffman's model of a 'total institution' (Goffman, 1961) rather than catering for the needs of individual children. Applying that scale they were able to identify two extreme patterns of child management—the one in which the pattern was institutionally-oriented, and which they claimed was typical of long-stay hospital units for normal and subnormal children, and the other in which the pattern was inmate-oriented, said by them to be found in children's homes for normal children and in a number of local authority hostels for severely subnormal children. Raynes and King further claimed that institutionally-oriented patterns were more common where the head of the unit was trained as a nurse, whereas the head of inmate-oriented units tended to be trained in the care of normal or deprived children.

At the same Conference, Kushlick outlined the Wessex Regional Hospital Board's proposals for future residential care provision based on his own Wessex survey.

Instead of providing a new large, multi-purpose hospital for the mentally subnormal in the West of the Region, to serve (on traditional lines) a large catchment area, this Regional Board, on the basis of the research findings, proposed to set up:

(i) Six 25-place hostel-type units for children—two to serve catchment areas of 100,000 total population—four for populations of 200,000.

(ii) Twelve 25-place hostel-type units for severely subnormal adults—each to serve a catchment area of 100,000 total population.

These units were planned for the urban centres in which the residents' families lived and were to be intimately connected with the general medical, educational, psychological and social work services available to subnormal subjects living at home in those areas.

Ministry approval was given for the provision of two of the children's units, which have since been opened and are the subject of an experimental evaluation of that type of residential care, sponsored by the Medical Research Council. The progress of the children, the family problems, administrative problems and costs associated with the experimental units are being compared with those among a control group of children remaining in traditional hospitals and a second control group of matched children living at home. The original intention was to manage within these units the most difficult, overactive and incontinent children who normally required skilled nursing care, without any trained nursing staff on the establishment, but this has been modified to include some trained nursing staff.

In October 1968, the following Declaration of General and Special Rights of the Mentally Retarded was formulated in Jerusalem at the Fourth Congress of the International League of Societies for the Mentally Handicapped:

WHEREAS the universal declaration of human rights adopted by the United Nations, proclaims that all of the human family, without distinction of any kind, have equal and inalienable rights of human dignity and freedom:

WHEREAS the declaration of the right of the child, adopted by the United Nations, proclaims the right of the physically, mentally or socially handicapped child to special treatment, education and care required by his particular condition:

NOW THEREFORE

The International League of Societies for the Mentally Handicapped expresses the general and special rights of the mentally retarded as follows:

ARTICLE I
The mentally retarded person has the same basic rights as other citizens of the same country and same age.

ARTICLE II
The mentally retarded person has a right to proper medical care and physical restoration and to such education, training, habilitation and guidance as will enable him to develop his ability and potential to the fullest possible extent, no matter how severe his degree of disability. No mentally handicapped person should be deprived of such services by reason of the costs involved.

ARTICLE III
The mentally retarded person has a right to economic security and to a decent standard of living. He has a right to productive work or to other meaningful occupation.

ARTICLE IV
The mentally retarded person has a right to live with his own family or with foster parents; to participate in all aspects of community life, and to be provided with appropriate leisure time activities. If care in an institution becomes necessary, it should be in surroundings and under circumstances as close to normal living as possible.

ARTICLE V
The mentally retarded person has a right to a qualified guardian when this is required to protect his personal wellbeing and interest. No person rendering direct services to the mentally retarded should also serve as his guardian.

ARTICLE VI
The mentally retarded person has a right to protection from exploitation, abuse and degrading treatment. If accused, he has a right to a fair trial with full recognition being given to his degree of responsibility.

ARTICLE VII
Some mentally retarded persons may be unable, due to the severity of their handicap to exercise for themselves all of their rights in a meaningful way. For others, modification of some or all of these rights is appropriate. The procedure used for modification or denial of rights must contain proper legal safeguards against every form of abuse, must be based on an evaluation of the social capability of the mentally retarded person by qualified experts and must be subject to periodic reviews and to the right of appeal to higher authorities.

ABOVE ALL—THE MENTALLY RETARDED PERSON HAS THE RIGHT TO RESPECT.
October 24, 1968.

This Declaration was favourably reviewed by the Economic and Social Council of the United Nations and adopted by the United Nations' General Assembly as the 'Rights of Mentally Retarded Persons' in December 1971.

1968 and 1969 were particularly sad years for the staffs of mental subnormality hospitals as they saw, first the setting up, and then the publication of reports of Government Committees of Inquiry into allegations of ill-treatment of patients, and other irregularities, at Ely Hospital, Cardiff and Farleigh Hospital, Flax Bourton, Somerset. As a leading article in the *British Medical Journal* commented in August 1969: 'Running through all these reports, official and unofficial, is a tale of antique buildings, overcrowding and understaffing'. The leader further commented: 'Incontinence, faeces-smearing, together with a variety of degraded sexual practices, are seen against a cacophonous background of banging and screeching. It takes strong stomachs, cloth ears, insensitive noses, and, above all, dedication to their calling, for staff to be able to tolerate such continuing assaults on their senses and sensibilities. But with the diminution in the number of staff who can take their share of the burden, it is not surprising that at times tempers become frayed and patience exhausted. What may be accepted as a professional commitment in small doses can very easily become a disgusting chore in large'. Referring to the old aphorism: 'If mental hospitals are the Cinderella of the National Health Service then hospitals for the subnormal are her neglected, illegitimate child', the leader concluded 'Cinderella can be transformed, but to turn a kitchen slut into a princess costs a lot of money. The money can and must be found if a once-splendid service is itself to be rehabilitated'.

During 1969, reports financed by two major national voluntary organisations appeared. 'Put Away', a study of subnormality hospitals, was the result of a survey conducted by a team led by Dr. Pauline Morris of the Department of Sociology at Essex University for the National Society for Mentally Handicapped Children. 'Put Away' repeated many of the criticisms referred to in the Government reports already mentioned, and spoke also of low staff morale and poor communication and resentment between different disciplines. It is doubtful whether there was a single mental subnormality hospital in the country to which at least one of Dr.

Morris's criticisms did not apply. The survey suggested that one-third of the hospital patients could live in the community if facilities were available. The second report, 'Caring for the Severely Subnormal', by Anita Hunt, was financed by the Spastics Society, and took the form of a survey of the statistics and literature on mental subnormality hospitals and related services. Among other things, the survey recommended that some large, impersonal hospitals with 'rigid routines and geographical isolation' should be emptied as soon as possible and that building of new extensions of existing subnormality hospitals must stop immediately pending the forthcoming Ministry Policy, with the hope that money already set aside for these schemes can be channelled into a crash hostel building programme. The survey also recommended the establishment of 'non-medical patterns of care', and that children should not be admitted to subnormality hospitals 'except for medical treatment and periods of short term care, for example, for assessment and observation'. It was in favour of effective coordination between hospital and local authority and voluntary services for the mentally subnormal, which many professional workers in the field had been advocating for a number of years.

This incursion into the mental subnormality field represented a major change of policy on the part of the Spastics Society, who had previously appealed to the general public on the basis that all spastics were potentially normal if adequately treated, and had shown little interest in the mentally subnormal. However, in May 1968 Mr. James Loring, Director of the Spastics Society, admitted that the view 'that all spastics were of more or less average intelligence and that their functioning at home, at school and in the community was hindered only by physical handicap' was quite false, and that approximately half of all spastics suffered from some degree of intellectual impairment and that about 25 per cent of all spastics had a severe mental retardation. Following this, the Society published a document stating its Mental Subnormality Policy and committed itself to 'drawing attention to the deplorable conditions in some subnormality hospitals, and also to the lack of provision by some local authorities'.

Following these reports, it is perhaps not surprising that subsequent discussion about care for the mentally subnormal should, regrettably, have become polarised as a hospital-versus-community provision, as though it had to be an 'either-or' choice. This polarisation was reflected in 'Nowhere Else to Go', a report issued by CARE (Cottage and Rural Enterprises) on the provisions for the mentally handicapped. The report 'questions the whole basis of the present provision'. The stress of the report was almost entirely on local authority provision and asserted quite uncritically 'that the mental subnormality hospital is the wrong environment for over 60 per cent of the 60,000 mentally subnormal in hospitals today', and the added inference 'that they are well able to exist outside a hospital environment, and that they are only in mental subnormality hospitals for there is nowhere else to go'. However, as Ann Shearer, herself an ardent critic of hospital care, commented in writing on Pauline Morris's book, community care was 'in danger of becoming the woolliest panacea of our times', and as Dr. A. Shapiro, Medical Superintendent of Harperbury Hospital, St. Albans, and Chairman of the Mental Deficiency Section of the Royal Medico-Psychological Association, wrote, there was 'little if any hard scientific evidence that community care is of greater advantage to the handicapped than care in hospitals. Evidence from the little work that has been done is invalidated by the fact that small well-endowed and amply staffed projects on community care are compared with neglected, overworked and under-financed hospitals deprived of every facility. . . . One of the major failings of the existing schemes for community care is the very vague and naive concepts upon which they are founded. There has been no attempt to define what social and interpersonal needs are going to be met by community care, and as a consequence many people will be in danger of being more "institutionalised" in the community than in the hospital, where there are much greater facilities for social mobility and communication. There is a great and very urgent need for an intensive study into the problems of social psychology to identify the social needs of the handicapped and the structure of groups which would give them the maximum support and provide the most satisfactory interpersonal relationships'. Writing in reply to Shapiro, Dr. H. P. Burrowes, of the City of Bradford Mental Health Services, stressed the need to improve understanding between those individuals who worked in hospitals and those who worked in the community, pointing out that the latter were 'often pressed to receive into community care patients whom

we do not believe suitable: psychiatrists in hospitals for the
mentally subnormal do not always seem to appreciate that there
are certain forms of behaviour which the community will not
tolerate though the patients themselves may be inherently harmless'.

The hospitals' dilemma was well put by Spencer, who wrote:

> One day, hospitals for the subnormal are being pressed by local
> authorities to accept cases under the threat of being reported to the
> Regional Hospital Board if they do not. The next day the hospitals
> are accused of keeping in hospital patients who should not be there
> .... If patients receive medication they are being 'drugged', if they
> do not their relatives complain that they are not having any treat-
> ment. Where patients are busily working, the murmur is 'exploita-
> tion', where they sit and rest they are 'vegetating' (Spencer, 1969).

In November 1969, the National Association for Mental Health,
which for many years had concerned itself closely with the care of
the mentally handicapped and had pioneered training courses for
teachers of the mentally handicapped, published its memorandum
'First Priorities in Reaching a Policy for Hospitals for the Mentally
Subnormal'. This memorandum contrasted the 'great advances that
have been made in the diagnosis, care and training of the subnormal child' with 'the failure to turn the same concentration of attention ... on adult patients' whom the memorandum described as
presenting an 'unlovely spectacle' and who were 'to be found in
carefully scoured wards where any pretence of mental stimulation
has been abandoned' and who could 'sometimes still be seen in
"airing courts" within cage-like bars'. According to the memorandum, the handicaps of the child who came into hospital were usually very great and, in many cases, he was physically handicapped as
well. He was looked after in hospital with devotion 'but often in
heartbreakingly stark conditions complicated by lack of staff'. The
hospital adult population consisted of an increasing number of
long-stay, grossly-handicapped patients and 'adults over 20, often
admitted there for the first time for whom dynamic programmes
inside or outside hospitals should be available'.

The memorandum continued: 'The Government is now faced
with a growing outcry about conditions for the mentally handicapped, and a mounting discontent among doctors and nurses
directly involved who feel that the difficulty of their tasks has never
been properly appreciated: that, notwithstanding the undoubted ad-

vances that have been made, their task gets more difficult year by
year as they are asked to care for more cases of gross handicap and
to harbour and deal humanely with society's rejects—their protest
is, in fact, that they have been impoverished by the Government
and largely ignored by the main body of professional and lay
people'. It suggested that the Government's first priority in
attacking the problem should be 'without doubt in avoiding
admission to hospital, other than for short stay purposes, for
stable adults who need residential care for social reasons only',
and pointed out that this meant 'a proper estimation of the needs of
a given area and an end to internecine warfare between hospitals and
local authorities', which did 'not necessarily mean building hostels
instead of providing hospital beds', but 'should mean a variety of
residential provision all under one hand, some of it long stay, some
of it short stay, some of it community and some of it hospital
based' and it warned the Government to 'beware of exchanging
competent residential oversight in hospital for unskilled supervision
outside'. 'A thought-out recruitment and training programme' was
'virtually non-existent so far' and this should go 'hand in hand,
therefore, with any expansion in the provision of small units'. If
'crisis psychiatry' with 'reluctant hospitals (forced) into the role of
custodians where no treatment is needed' was to be avoided in
future, a realistic assessment should be made 'of people at risk and
of their probable needs from the cradle to the grave'. The
memorandum suggested that a 'corollary ought to be a firm refusal
to increase the number of hospital beds available', but pointed out
that this would be possible and acceptable only 'if a real drive were
made area by area to examine local authority support for mentally
handicapped adults'. On the other hand, 'no increase in the number
of hospital beds certainly must not mean no money for the
hospitals'. The National Association of Mental Health stated as its
second priority that 'the Government should declare that by a
specified date no hospital unit should house more than 30 adults'.
Its memorandum asked who knew what was the function of the
doctor in a subnormality hospital, what was the role of the nurse
and where did the psychologist and teacher have a function and
what should the training and status of each be. These are questions
which are still being hotly debated and to which reference will be
made later.

The need for the establishment of an integrated service for the mentally subnormal was stressed in the memorandum 'Future Patterns of Care for the Mentally Subnormal', which was published by the Royal Medico-Psychological Association following a Teach-In organised by its Mental Deficiency Section in December 1969. This memorandum stated: 'The coordination of the statutory and voluntary services for the mentally subnormal should be a fundamental step in planning future patterns of care. General practitioner, local health authority and hospital services should be integrated on an area basis so as to provide the maximum flexibility of service to the patient according to his requirements at different times. We expect that in such an area appointments would be made to the mental subnormality service as a whole and not to its hospital or local health authority divisions alone. We are aware of the possible difficulties in putting this into practice which may result from the transfer of local health authority junior training centres and hospital schools to the Department of Education and Science, and the implementation of the proposals of the Seebohm Report in its present form'.

During 1969 the Government established the Hospital Advisory Service (H.A.S.) with the following functions:

1. by constructive criticism and by propagating good practices and new ideas, to help to improve the management of patient care in individual hospitals (excluding matters of individual clinical judgment) and in the hospital service as a whole; and
2. to advise the Secretary of State for Social Services about conditions in hospitals in England, and the Secretary of State for Wales about conditions in hospitals in Wales.

The Hospital Advisory Service was to operate independently of the Department of Health and Social Security and the Welsh Office, and its Director was to report directly to the Secretary of State for Social Services in relation to England, and to the Secretary of State for Wales in relation to that country. The Director was to be assisted by a staff of professional advisers, who were to visit hospitals in teams which would normally consist of people drawn from the following professional groups:

1. A consultant
2. A senior nurse (Chief or Principal Nursing Officer, or equivalent grade)
3. A ward sister or charge nurse
4. A hospital administrator (Group Secretary or equivalent)
5. A social worker.

Dr. A. A. Baker was appointed Director and took up his appointment on the 1st November 1969. In his first Annual Report, published in 1971, Baker reported on the work of two teams which had commenced surveying the hospital services for the mentally handicapped in February 1970 and May 1970 respectively. It had not been possible to complete this survey during the first year of the Hospital Advisory Service's existence, but it was hoped to do this by Autumn, 1971. (This was, in fact, achieved by October of that year, and in December 1971 the two teams visiting hospitals for the mentally handicapped were replaced by a single team which commenced the process of revisiting).

In the Preface to his report, Baker said that: 'On the evidence of our visiting so far ... any evidence of deliberate cruelty or ill-treatment in hospitals is rare. On the other hand, however, a measure of neglect is common. This neglect is seldom the fault of staff working on the ward, but it is an inevitable result of a situation where too few staff are trying to care for far too many patients in badly equipped premises. In general, we have found that the warmth of heart and genuine concern of staff at ward level is very impressive and many ward staff, particularly nurses, give far more in terms of time, effort and emotional involvement than the immediate call of duty would dictate .... Visiting teams have all reported serious failures at all levels in the management and organisation of therapeutic resources. These failures occur both within the hospital service and between the hospital service and other parts of the Health Service. Within the hospital service, failures of coordination and planning between the doctors, nurses and other therapeutic staff, and administrators, are common. Similarly, at ward level, many patients are not receiving the benefit of a coordinated therapeutic team to which they are entitled. At meetings in hospitals, it has sometimes become obvious that those present, representing the professions within the hospital, had rarely met together to discuss their common problems and objectives'.

However, in contrast, the main body of the Report states: 'As would be expected, the consultant staff of a hospital often provide outstanding leadership and set the tone of all the therapeutic services. . . . In view of the fact that the amount of time a consultant can give to each individual patient is limited, the most effective services have often been those where the consultant takes particular care to see that he enables other therapeutic professional staff to play their full role. It is usually the consultants of the hospital who play a major role in developing schemes for rehabilitation'. The latter comment was echoed in Baker's Annual Report for 1971 which stated: 'The good services always seem to centre round an effective clinician who has developed a team around himself through whom his therapeutic policies can be implemented'. This Report stated that: 'The hallmarks of a good service seem to be the investment of considerable time and effort in out-patient counselling and early assessment. The second feature would be the full and frequent use of short term care and emphasis on the hospital's role in providing a treatment and training situation rather than simply a custodial and keeping situation . . . . A complete multi-disciplinary assessment of each patient, recorded in the notes and repeated at appropriate intervals, is the basis of accurate diagnosis and the provision of a suitable therapeutic programme.

Another hallmark of good services can be found where the remedial, teaching or occupational departments and their staff feel themselves totally integrated with the patient's life at ward level'.

Baker's Report for 1972 recorded the disbanding of the team which was making the second series of visits to the hospitals for the mentally handicapped. However, he was able to report that since their first visit there had been a significant reduction in overcrowding in hospitals revisited, 'sometimes by new building on the hospital site, but most commonly by increased discharges and a restricted admissions policy', but that 'despite the measures described, overcrowding continues, sometimes to a serious degree, and is still a major problem in many hospitals.' Upgrading was proceeding in all hospitals and, contrary to staff expectations, 'patients did not destroy or damage furnishings and fittings . . . but rather showed a marked improvement in social behaviour'. The Report commented also on the benefits to staff and patients in those hospitals where 'mixed (sex) wards' had been introduced. It noted the absence of a physiotherapist or speech therapist in many hospitals and commented on the lack of opportunity for patients 'to practise the ordinary skills of everyday living, such as travelling by public transport, using ordinary shops, managing escalators and eating in a café', which is the 'sort of skill which will often determine whether or not a patient survives on discharge to the community'. It was 'essential to define the nurse's role in patient care and training and to ensure that her skills are fully utilised'. It referred also to the difficulty some clinical psychologists were experiencing 'in relations with their medical colleagues in emerging from their traditional role as "assessors" to take a more active part in assessment and training programmes for neglected groups of patients.'

The Report claimed that the 'transfer of responsibility for education in hospitals from hospital to education authorities was taking place smoothly' and that 'in all hospitals visited there had been a resulting improvement in facilities for children, particularly the greater availability of services for the severely handicapped'. It pointed, however, to the 'marked absence of planned adult education in hospitals for the mentally handicapped. . . .

Concentration on out-patient services, including intensive treatment and parental instruction, has resulted in fewer requests for long-stay admissions. . . . The importance of an out-patient service for family support and counselling, out-patient treatment and follow up of rehabilitated patients cannot be over-stressed and should be accorded an equal priority to the improvement of in-patient facilities', and the Report suggested ways in which physiotherapists might be more effectively used in providing guidance for parents in patient handling in out-patient clinics, and in passing on 'ideas and skills to nursing staff so that the basic approach to everyday living becomes therapeutic'.

In conclusion, the Report claimed that there was 'inadequate diagnosis and treatment for deafness and hearing defects', and that there was an 'outstanding community need . . . for day care facilities for the adult severely subnormal and multiply handicapped patients living at home'. This group had been previously absorbed to some extent by the junior training centres, but the recent re-organisation had resulted in many such patients being thrown back on their families. There was a 'need to develop more satisfying and acceptable sheltered work and recreational facilities' for 'the borderline patient who frequently cannot fit either into normal society or comparably into the type of facilities provided by the typical adult training unit'.

In December 1969, in a talk to a Conference on 'Subnormality in the Seventies', organised by the National Society for Mentally Handicapped Children, Dr. Jack Bavin discussed 'Priority in Resources' and 'the priority which should be given to upgrading the present hospital services as opposed to developing the community-based service'. He dismissed as 'nonsense' the view that 'all extra resources should go to the latter . . . and that money must be taken from subnormality hospitals and given to community services'. Bavin suggested that it was 'a realistic moderate-term objective' to try to discharge half the 60,000 mentally handicapped people in hospitals, and calculated that a capital expenditure of about £120–£140 million would be required to provide a hostel place and adult training centre facilities for the 'discharged' 30,000, plus another 10,000 already needing sheltered accommodation. His experience at Leavesden Hospital indicated that capital expenditure of about £500.00 in each case would be needed to provide tolerable improvement for each of the remaining 30,000 hospital beds, 'making a round sum of £15 million'.

Bavin asked how top management—Regional Boards and the Department—had let the subnormality hospitals get in their present state and urged that they should introduce democratic management. He pointed out that there was 'no adviser in the Department from among consultants in subnormality' and continued: 'It appears that the Department forms its policy, goes through the motions of consulting workers in the hospitals and then showers us with paper directives, which, as they are seldom accompanied by the money necessary to execute them, only serve to exasperate and demoralise. The present state of subnormality hospitals is no accident'; Bavin claimed 'it is the inevitable end-result of a top-management policy to deprive them of resources'.

The Report of the Royal Commission on Local Authority and Allied Personal Social Services—the Seebohm Report—was published in 1969 and many of its recommendations were incorporated in the *Local Authority Social Services Act* 1970, which transferred several of the responsibilities imposed on local health authorities by the *Mental Health Act* 1959, to local authorities' social service departments. These transferred responsibilities included the supervision of the mentally handicapped living in the community, the running of adult training centres and the running of hostels for mentally handicapped people not in need of continuous psychiatric supervision. The specially trained and widely experienced mental welfare officers became part of the general social worker establishment of the local authorities, and, regrettably, a number of generally trained social workers, with inadequate training and experience in the field of mental handicap, were designated as mental welfare officers for the purposes of the *Mental Health Act* 1959. There is still a widespread view among psychiatrists in the mental handicap field that social worker services have deteriorated since the *Local Authority Social Services Act* 1970 came into force.

In November 1970, the Royal Medico-Psychological Association published the following Memorandum on Future Patterns of Care for the Mentally Subnormal, already referred to briefly:

1. The Royal Medico-Psychological Association feels obliged to express concern at the Department of Health's apparent lack of consultation in the past with practising clinicians in the mental subnormality field before formulating policy. The Association welcomes experimental schemes with regard to patient care, and considers that these schemes should be properly evaluated in various parts of the country before their acceptance or rejection as national policy.
2. The coordination of the statutory and voluntary services for the mentally subnormal should be a fundamental step in planning future patterns of care. General practitioner, local health authority and hospital services should be integrated on an area basis so as to provide the maximum flexibility of service to the patient according to his requirements at different times. We expect that in such an area appointments would be made to the mental subnormality service as a whole and not to its hospital or local health authority divisions alone. We are aware of the possible difficulties in putting this into practice which may result from the transfer of local health authority junior training centres and hospital schools to the Department of Education and Science, and the implementation of the proposals of the Seebohm Report in their present form.
3. The care of the mentally subnormal requires a team approach to which many different disciplines contribute. We believe that

the consultant psychiatrist is the most appropriate person to accept responsibility for coordinating the work of the team.

4. It is essential that there should be full assessment of every case of suspected mental subnormality on an out-patient and in-patient basis. Where in patient assessment is necessary, this could take place, in the case of children, in a paediatric hospital or in a paediatric unit in one of the proposed district general hospitals, with the specialist in mental subnormality as a member of the assessment team. However, we consider that in-patient assessment units for the mentally subnormal of all ages should also be further developed in the larger hospitals for the mentally subnormal, with the various disciplines working there as a team. The assessment should be an ongoing process, with regular review of the patient's progress, rather than a once for all exercise as it has sometimes been in the past. The development of assessment centres and the subsequent provision for the residential care of cases from them should be planned together.

5. There is a continuing need for the establishment of a number of hostels in the community to provide accommodation for patients on discharge from hospital. It will also be necessary to provide hostel accommodation for the mentally subnormal person who has been living with relatives for many years up to the time when they are no longer able to look after him, and who does not require hospital care.

6. The most urgent cases for admission on the waiting lists of most hospitals for the mentally subnormal are severely subnormal children, often doubly incontinent and with multiple handicaps or over-active and destructive behaviour, who impose an intolerable strain on their parents and often threaten the stability of the family unit. Such cases have usually already defeated the efforts of all other agencies (e.g. junior training centres, paediatric units and children's homes) to manage them, and it seems highly unlikely that any hostel-type unit would be able to do so unless it had the staff structure and facilities to make it, in effect, a small hospital. With the increased expectation of life, a high proportion of such children survive into adult life without becoming suitable for a hostel providing residential facilities only. Sooner or later, therefore, they must be transferred to hospital type care. The integrated area service should provide day-care for those patients who do not require residential care and who are unsuitable for attendance at junior and adult training centres or are special care problems.

7. Large hospitals for the mentally subnormal at present care for a number of stable adult patients who would not nowadays be considered to need hospital admission if they were being seen

for the first time. However, many of these patients have been in hospital for twenty or thirty years or more and have made the hospital their home. It is doubtful whether it would always be a kindness to transfer them to hostels in the community, if these were available. Further, humanitarian considerations apart, even if such a mass exodus were possible, the freed accommodation, often in large, multi-storey buildings, would be quite unsuitable, without very expensive adaptations, for the much more unstable and severely handicapped patients at present on hospital waiting lists. Rather, large unsuitable buildings should eventually be replaced by small, homely units, some located on existing hospital sites, some grouped to function as villages, some located singly in the community, and some within the curtilage of the district general hospital, and all providing for the educational, therapeutic, training, occupation and recreational needs of their residents, and allowing as full communication as possible with the surrounding community.

8. Existing waiting lists, and the 'hidden waiting list' of patients who are unknown until they are presented as urgent cases for hospital admission when an emergency occurs in their families, suggest that the present provisions are inadequate. We consider that a figure of 1·8 to 2·00 per 1,000 population is a fairly accurate estimate of the numbers of mentally subnormal persons likely to need residential care in local health authority and hospital accommodation.

9. Research into causation and methods of treatment and training of the mentally subnormal should be part of the function of the mental subnormality hospital. More links should be formed with neighbouring universities, and we would hope that Departments of Mental Subnormality would be established within the latter. Mental subnormality hospitals have an important role to play in the training of medical, nursing and other students at the undergraduate and postgraduate level.

10. We consider that the existing consultant psychiatrist establishments are inadequate to staff an integrated service for the mentally subnormal. The Association has recommended that one full-time consultant psychiatrist, with a supporting team, should serve a population of 200,000. The present population load is over twice this figure.

11. At present the output from the mental subnormality senior registrar grade is adequate to fill only one third of the consultant vacancies which occur in mental subnormality hospitals each year. There is an urgent need to increase the senior registrar establishment to meet the existing deficiencies and the needs of the increased consultant establishment referred to previously.

12. Nurses have a vital role to play in providing a twenty-four hour service for the mentally subnormal. We are gravely concerned at the present level of morale among nurses, and the shortage of nurses willing to make this specialty their permanent career. We recommend an urgent study of this problem.

1971 saw the birth of the Campaign for the Mentally Handicapped, an organisation which started 'from the basic assumption that the aim of any service for handicapped people must be to enable them to have as normal a life as possible', which corresponded closely to the Swedish principle of 'normalisation', which has been defined as 'making available to the mentally retarded patterns and conditions of every day life which are as close as possible to the norms and patterns of the mainstreams of society'. Unfortunately, this principle was misunderstood by many well-meaning people, who appeared to interpret it as advocating treating the mentally retarded as though they were, in fact, normal. The Campaign for the Mentally Handicapped itself contributed to this, in the author's view, unrealistic and unhelpful approach to the problems of the mentally handicapped in its document 'Future Services for the Mentally Handicapped' in which its authors, Sandra Francklin and Anne Shearer, claimed that 'if these (community) services were properly planned, every mentally handicapped person ... could have the right to live among the rest of us'. The authors preferred 'the Swedish emphasis on pushing the mentally handicapped as far into the normal, albeit imperfect, society as possible to the more protective attitudes of the Danish service which have led to large village-type institutions'. They did, however, state that any future services should offer a range of residential provision: children would live in family size groups with house parents, for adults there should be different degrees of supervision with sheltered housing, fostering schemes and group homes with support from a visiting social worker. The 'housing must be integrated into the local community, both geographically and emotionally' and 'must be truly domestic in appearance, layout and detail, differing simply in the degree of support given by staff'. The authors claimed that most of the hostels in the past had 'been too large and both physically and socially heavily protective: no more than institutions with all the well-documented vices'. They asserted that 'in future no home should be for more than 12 people and most for less. . . .'

Francklin and Shearer saw 'no place for the large specialist institution in future plans for the mentally handicapped', claiming that normalisation was 'not compatible with segregation from the community, with living in large groups or with living together with a large number of deviant people'. They rejected as 'a counsel of despair' the argument of 'supporters of the reformed hospital . . . that they could provide a richer life for residents than homes and hostels in the community', which, they said, 'assumes a hostile uncaring community, whereas we assume that an increasingly educated public will more and more welcome the handicapped among them and realise the valuable gifts that they bring'. They quoted Dr. Karl Grunewald, Director of the Swedish Service, as saying that we need the handicapped in our community to de-intellectualise and de-sophisticate us, and expressed their own support for this way of approaching future services for the mentally handicapped. They suggested that the present hospital population could be rehoused over a period of fifteen years by the adaptation of ordinary houses in the community and accused hospital staff who questioned the practicality of this, as regarding their proposals as constituting a threat to their jobs.

Having eliminated the specialist institution from their plans. Francklin and Shearer proceeded to exclude nurses from the future care of the mentally handicapped, claiming that Scandinavian experience had shown them to be unnecessary and suggesting that they should be replaced by 'a new breed of helper' whose 'generic training in care, which included a short introduction to mental handicap could be followed by periods of specialisation'. These sweeping assertions were made without any acknowledgment that mental subnormality nurses themselves had recognised the need for revising their training syllabus and had begun reorientating themselves towards an approach to the mentally handicapped which was more caring and less clinical and technical in the general nursing sense, long before Campaign for the Mentally Handicapped adopted its self-appointed messianic role.

Sandra Francklin later used the tragedy at Coldharbour Hospital, Sherborne, Dorset, in which severely mentally handicapped patients died in a fire in a recently upgraded *single-storey* building, as an excuse to castigate hospital authorities, whom she hoped would '. . . learn their lesson once and for all. . . .' She asserted that such upgrading was 'wasteful, misguided, can be dangerous and must stop'. She further asserted that 'Mentally handicapped people, even the heavily handicapped, are best off (*and, in this particular context, one must infer, safer—author*) living in the same way as the rest of us in ordinary houses. . . .' At about the same time, the present author wrote: 'I suggest that, on present evidence, the only place that most mentally subnormal people are likely to receive real *community* care in the foreseeable future is within the much criticised existing mental subnormality hospitals.

It was unfortunate in 1948 that, in their desire for improved status, mental deficiency colonies adopted the more prestigious term 'hospital' and laid themselves open to the justifiable charge of sociologists and others that many of their residents did not require *hospital* care. It does not follow, however, that they do not require care in a sheltered environment such as colonies provided, within which they can live a much fuller and freer life than may be possible in a hostel in an urban area in which they are, in effect, isolated by their own limitations from full participation in the life of the area.

I suggest that parents' support for village communities for the mentally handicapped, provided by non-statutory organisations, indicates that they recognise the benefits of this type of care for children and adults who are incapable of greater independence and that these benefits should be recognised by the Department of Health and Social Services also, by a return to the concept of the colony, embracing both the therapeutic and caring aspects referred to in your leading article' (*British Medical Journal*).

The Report of the Farleigh Hospital Committee of Inquiry was published in April 1971. Its fifteen recommendations included the following: the consideration by representatives of the psychiatric and nursing professions of 'a code of conduct for nurses in handling of violent and difficult patients' and the urgent appointment of a 'Health Commissioner, given the widest possible powers . . . to avert public anxiety about the investigation of complaints in the Health Service'. The Report contains an Appendix (5), dated April 1970, in which the nurses of Farleigh Hospital

respectfully and most urgently request your advice and guidance with special emphasis on:

1. Are we to restrain a patient who is self-mutilating?
2. Are we to restrain a patient making a violent attack on a weaker patient?
3. Are we allowed to protect ourselves when attacked by patients?

If the answers to the above are in the affirmative then we would like to know:

1. The degree of force which may be used to restrain a patient or to protect oneself before it is interpreted as ill-treatment.
2. What safeguards can be given to protect our professional integrity against reports as outlined above and perhaps not made for a period of some years after an incident'.

The National Association for Mental Health, whose General Secretary, Miss Mary Applebey, had been a member of the Committee of Inquiry, had, in fact, already published a consultative document—'Guidelines for the Care of Patients who Exhibit Violent Behaviour in Mental and Mental Subnormality Hospitals'. This was to become the basis for discussion by the Liaison Committee of the Royal College of Nursing and the Royal College of Psychiatrists, which prepared a Memorandum on 'The Care of the Violent Patient', at the request of the then Secretary of State for Social Services, Sir Keith Joseph, to whom it was sent in April 1972. This Memorandum, while giving practical guidance for dealing with violent episodes, recognised that the action suggested did not cover all eventualities. An incident in which a male assistant nurse sustained facial and head injuries while attempting to separate two male patients who were fighting in another hospital in the Bristol area, led nurses to claim that patient discipline had deteriorated since the Farleigh Inquiry, due to staffs' fear of assertions of ill-treatment of patients. It is to be hoped that the publication by the succeeding Government of its own guidelines in March 1976 on 'The Management of Violent or Potentially Violent Hospital Patients', HC(76)11 will have gone some way towards reassuring the staff concerned.

A Committee on Hospital Complaints Procedure was set up under the chairmanship of Sir Michael Davis, and Miss Mary Applebey was again a member. Its report was published in December 1973 and referred to incidents at Ely Hospital, Cardiff (1968), Farleigh Hospital, Bristol (1969) and at Whittingham Hospital, Preston (1970), where patients were ill-treated and where, the report claimed, the truth emerged only after 'prolonged attempts at suppression', and the reports on the inquiries at each of these hospitals showed 'the inadequacies of established machinery and its inability to deal properly with complaints as they arose'. The report recommended that in-patients should be given admission booklets laying down the complaints procedure and advising on a course of action if the complaints appeared to have been ignored. The current confusion in the mental subnormality field was reflected in a paper read to the Midland Society for the Study of Mental Subnormality in May 1971, by James Elliott, Associate Director of the King's Fund Hospital Centre in London. Elliott said that if he were a Cabinet Minister, with no knowledge about mental handicap, seeking concerted advice on how to spend the extra money everyone said was needed, and 'were to study the correspondence columns in the journals, or went to a whole series of conferences, national and international, or if I conducted a Gallup Poll among patients, I would be faced by such a conflicting set of opinions and, worse still, prejudices, that I would be justified in spending no extra money at all'. He went on to state his own Eight Propositions for Mental Handicap as follows:

Proposition 1. We need to organise a unified service for the Mentally Handicapped, even though parts of the service are provided by different agencies which are separately funded;
'. . . the service for an area ought to be headed by a director with powers of leadership and vision and with the special skills of coordinating a team. He could be of any of the concerned professions'. [In a letter to *The Times* in February 1966, in a paper presented to a meeting at the Hospital Centre, London, of 60 people representing 30 organisations, both statutory and voluntary, to discuss Coordination of Services for the Mentally Subnormal, and in a paper read at a Conference on Patterns of Care for the Subnormal at the University of Dundee in March 1970, the present author had referred to some of the problems arising from the existing division of responsibility for the care of the mentally subnormal between local authorities and hospitals, with different conditions of service for staff doing similar jobs in each. He had advocated the establishment of a 'truly integrated service for the care of the mentally subnormal' similar to those which had been introduced, until they were disbanded following the introduction of the National Health Service, as part of comprehensive Mental Health services in Portsmouth by Dr. T. B. Beaton (Freeman, 1962) and in Nottingham by Dr. D. Macmillan, and similar to that which had existed

in Northern Ireland since 1949 under the Northern Ireland Hospitals Authority for 'persons requiring special care', as the mentally subnormal are called in the *Mental Health Act (Northern Ireland)* 1961.]

Proposition 2. No single profession is uniquely qualified to direct the unified service for the mentally handicapped.

'... we are entitled to ask whether the hospital necessarily contains all or most of the experts in aspects of mental handicap. This would be a very difficult argument to sustain'.

Proposition 3. No single site is automatically the best one from which to coordinate the service.

Proposition 4. That hospitals redouble their efforts to help the mentally handicapped become part of the general community; and try to find out, pragmatically, the point at which the process has to stop in the interests of the mentally handicapped person. 'Let us assume that we work on a belief that the discharge from a large hospital to a community facility is a good thing for some of our patients, and that we will run our hospital on the basis that people are not admitted unless they need something special we can offer'.

Proposition 5. A hospital should be retained only if it has a particular job to do which cannot be done effectively any other way; and that job is likely to include:

(a) giving medical and nursing treatment to those who need this in a hospital setting
(b) detaining legally a small number in their own interests, and in the interests of the community
(c) increasing the level of competence of the mentally handicapped. 'I find that there are at least six points which are universally acknowledged. All agree that the life style of the mentally handicapped in hospital ought to include:

(a) privacy: territory
(b) small group living
(c) personal choice
(d) freedom to socialise
(e) absence of regimentation
(f) a chance to increase personal competence

... you will note that I have not uttered the word "normalisation" which seems to be suspect to some people'.

Proposition 6. A hospital must decide upon the life-style which it aims to encourage, and must bend all its activities, clinical or otherwise to that end.

'It is sometimes assumed that a large hospital is necessarily a bad one. Not so. Regimentation can appear in its worst form just as easily in a small unit as in a large one. . . . There is no doubt that in a big hospital you have to try a great deal harder, and guard against making the handicapped fit into the system instead of making the system fit the handicapped'.

Proposition 7. If the mentally handicapped are to enjoy the lifestyle embodied in the six points, a hospital must decentralise, to the level of the living unit, as much authority as is consistent with keeping the whole hospital on course towards its major operational objectives. 'Instead of building new wards, the hospital is likely to go in for hostels, or even group homes, as part of its service for the most handicapped quarter of the whole. These would be hostels or homes under fairly close supervision and advice, as opposed to the simple residential hostels likely to be provided by the Director of Social Services'.

Proposition 8. Wherever the mentally handicapped are, even at home, they should be aided by the same team of professionals: in whatever skills staff are trained, they should gain their experience throughout the whole service; no single profession has the automatic right to dominate post-qualification training in the field of mental handicap. 'Surely we can now avoid the intense polarisation of view, which means that you have to side with the extreme left or the extreme right; or that you have to say hospitals are wholly good or that they are wholly bad when neither statement is at all true. . . . We will make more progress if we stop defending carefully prepared professional positions and begin to look honestly at the needs of the mentally handicapped and the best way to meet those needs'.

In June 1971, the Government published its long awaited White Paper *Better Services for the Mentally Handicapped.* This stated the following general principles on which current thinking about mental handicap is based:

(i) A family with a handicapped member has the same needs for general social services as all other families. The family and the handicapped child or adult also need special additional help, which varies according to the severity of the handicap, whether there are associated physical handicaps or behaviour problems, the age of the handicapped person and his family situation.

(ii) Mentally handicapped children and adults should not be segregated unnecessarily from other people of similar age, nor from the general life of the local community.

(iii) Full use should be made of available knowledge which can help to prevent mental handicap or to reduce the severity of its effects.

(iv) There should be a comprehensive initial assessment and periodic reassessment of the needs of each handicapped person and his family.

(v) Each handicapped person needs stimulation, social training and education and purposeful occupation or employment in order to develop to his maximum capacity and to exercise all the skills he acquires, however limited they may be.

(vi) Each handicapped person should live with his own family as long as this does not impose an undue burden on them or him, and he and his family should receive full advice and support. If he has to leave home for a foster home, residential home or hospital, temporarily or permanently, links with his own family should normally be maintained.

(vii) The range of services in every area should be such that the family can be sure that their handicapped member will be properly cared for when it becomes necessary for him to leave the family home.

(viii) When a handicapped person has to leave his family home, temporarily or permanently, the substitute home should be as homelike as possible, even if it is also a hospital. It should provide sympathetic and constant human relationships.

(ix) There should be proper coordination in the application of relevant professional skills for the benefit of individual handicapped people and their families, and in the planning and administration of relevant services, whether or not these cross administrative frontiers.

(x) Local authority personal social services for the mentally handicapped should develop as an integral part of the services recently brought together under the *Local Authority Social Services Act* 1970.

(xi) There should be close collaboration between these services and those provided by other local authority departments (e.g. child health services and education), and with general practitioners, hospitals and other services for the disabled.

(xii) Hospital service for the mentally handicapped should be easily accessible to the population they serve. They should be associated with other hospital services, so that a full range of specialist skills is easily available when needed for assessment or treatment.

(xiii) Hospital and local authority services should be planned and operated in partnership; the Government's proposals for the reorganisation of the National Health Service will encourage the closest cooperation.

(xiv) Voluntary service can make a contribution to the welfare of mentally handicapped people and their families at all stages of their lives and wherever they are living.

(xv) Understanding and help from friends and neighbours and
from the community at large are needed to help the family to
maintain a normal social life and to give the handicapped
member as nearly normal a life as his handicap or handicaps
permit.

The White Paper stated that no new large specialised hospitals
for the mentally handicapped would be built, and that no hospital
of 500 beds or more would be enlarged. New building to relieve
overcrowding at hospitals with 500 or more patients on one site
would be located in areas of population elsewhere in the hospital's
catchment area, but such hospitals might occasionally be allowed
to provide 'one system-built unit' to allow existing wards to be
vacated for upgrading. Any new hospitals or units for the mentally
handicapped would contain not more than 100–200 beds as part of
a comprehensive range of in-patient, out-patient and day facilities
for the mentally handicapped in a district with a population not
exceeding 250,000. It was anticipated that they would have close
operational links with general hospitals serving the same district
and that about £100 million would be spent by the Government
during the four years 1971–2 to 1974–5 on improving the hospital
and local authority services for the mentally handicapped and
that capital expenditure on the hospital side during that period
would reach about £30 million. The White Paper set target figures
for local authority and hospital facilities, which it anticipated could
be reached over the next fifteen years by additional provisions
(see Table I).

The general principles in the White Paper were given a cautious
welcome by most professionals in the field, but there was considerable criticism of a number of its detailed proposals—James
Elliott regretted that 'a great chance of fundamental reform' to
produce one united and comprehensive service for the mentally
handicapped had been missed. However, he wondered whether the
recent legislative split of the mental handicap service into three
separately financed parts could not be overcome by setting up for
each area a board or directorate for the whole mental handicap service. He pointed out that 'To make a programme to provide 20,000
places in residential homes over a period of fifteen years is the
equivalent of making a programme to build 5,000 council houses

TABLE I

England and Wales

Additional places required beyond the 1969 provision to meet target figures in the White Paper *Better Services for the Mentally Handicapped.*

Type of Service	Children (age 0–15)	Adults (age 16+)	All ages
Day care or education for children under five	3,400		
Education for children of school age			
In the community			
1. for children with severe mental handicap living in the community	6,900		
2. for children coming by day from hospital			
In hospitals			
3. for in-patients	1,500		
4. for day patients			
Occupation and training for adults			
In the community			
1. for adults living in the community		39,200	
2. for adults coming by day from hospital		9,700	
In hospitals			
3. for day patients		4,700	
Residential care in the community (including short-stay)			
1. in local authority, voluntary or privately owned residential homes	3,100	25,100	28,200
2. foster homes, lodgings, etc.	900	6,850	7,750
Hospital treatment for day patients	2,700	4,400	7,100

over fifteen years for people who have in any case been queuing for most of their lives' (Elliott, 1971).

The Association of Hospital Management Committees (1972) considered the White Paper in the context of the proposals for reorganisation of the National Health Service and they, also, regretted the perpetuation of divisions of responsibility within the mental handicap service and envisaged 'additional difficulties in the recruitment of staff as two bodies, possibly offering different salary and conditions of service, will be competing for a limited amount of skilled and qualified labour'. The Association felt that 'life in hospital for a high proportion of patients provides the best prospect of progress and the happiest life . . .' but that '. . . mentally handicapped adults should not be looked after within the curtilage of the District General Hospital. . . .' It appeared to the Association '. . . that local authorities at present are still left far too much freedom as to whether they implement the provisions or not and it should be stressed that if they do not fulfil their obligations the hospitals cannot be held responsible for not undertaking the role for which they are designed'.

Dr. Alexander Shapiro was perhaps the most vocal of all consultant psychiatrists working in the mental handicap field in questioning 'all the facile assumptions that underlie the present planning of services for the mentally handicapped by the Department of Health and Social Security' in the White Paper. In challenging the idea that subnormal children were better cared for at home, he said he had no knowledge of any 'attempt at comparing the quality of community to hospital care under conditions which are comparable, that is, when the cost per head is the same'. Neither had 'the claims that hostels can take the same type of patients as hospitals' even been substantiated and 'patients who are settled, clean and happy, and giving little trouble in a hospital setting do break down if they are not given the skilled nursing care which they have in hospital'. Shapiro claimed that 'most of the plans for the services for the handicapped are based upon the emotional and social needs of young children and show a basic lack of understanding of adult needs'. The aspect of the hospital being a supportive community for adults as well as a place of treatment, care and training was 'so ignored at present', but 'our predecessors' awareness of the social needs of people in their charge was one of the reasons why many present hospitals all began as "colonies"'. Shapiro was concerned that 'the care of the mentally handicapped will become divided between a number of specialists such as paediatricians and general and child psychiatrists, to whom the care of the mentally handicapped will represent a fringe interest' (Shapiro, 1972).

In December 1971, the National Society for Mentally Handicapped Children published its policy statement on the Residential Needs of the Mentally Handicapped. The statement expressed the fear that 'the special needs of some retarded persons, who require care and training by specially trained personnel, might be overlooked, even to the point of apparent denial of handicap' by enthusiasts who were tempted to take the principle of normalisation too far and that 'the term "humanisation" might be found by many to be more appropriate than "normalisation"'. The National Society considered that the proposal to replace all subnormality hospitals over the next 10–15 years by a community based system of care was unrealistic 'in terms of the foreseeable future' and that there would always remain a number of severely or multiply handicapped people 'whose manifest need of medical and nursing care must best be provided within a hospital situation', and that some of the special needs of some overactive and behaviourly disturbed mentally handicapped people 'could not be met in the informal institutional environment of a hostel or the open community'. The statement observed that 'even in much quoted Sweden it is still found necessary to provide hospitals for special care cases'. However, it considered the multi-tiered hierarchical system in hospitals to be ill-suited to the long term needs of the mentally handicapped and favoured its replacement by 'a system calculated to engender a team spirit through staff consultation and involvement at all levels'. To avoid a purely medical orientation, which it regarded as holding back progress, the team should include 'administrators and the service departments, engineering and catering staff, etc.' as well as 'psychologists, educators, speech therapists, physiotherapists, etc.' The National Society was 'severely sceptical about the Government's intention to leave the initiative for the implementation of this laudable plan (for the Local Authority Social Service Departments to be responsible for the provision of "more appropriate residential alternatives to the hospital") to the authorities concerned'. There seemed little likelihood that action would be taken by local authorities at a pace which would match the urgency of the need without the practical encouragement of realistic Exchequer grant-aid. Moreover, the need to set up and improve local authority services should not be made an excuse for failure to spend what was necessary to improve the physical conditions in hospitals. The absence of a joint approach to the residential problems of the mentally handicapped over the years had been little short of disastrous.

The National Society made the following recommendations:

1. Strict adherence to the now officially declared principle that no mentally handicapped person of whatever age, who is otherwise uncomplicated by physical or behavioural conditions requiring medical, nursing and/or psychiatric care, should be permanently placed in hospital for social or custodial purposes only.
2. Chairmen and members of Hospital Management Committees and the appropriate committees of local authorities should be encouraged to acquaint themselves with new ideas and methods now being adopted in relation to the development of care of the mentally handicapped, through participation in seminars and conferences, and in professional tours to advanced institutions at home and abroad.
3. *Hospitals*. Large institutions, on the old model, with extensive wards, be replaced as quickly as possible by new hospitals, constructed in such a way as to conform with modern nursing and developmental care methods. Such hospitals might well be modelled on the Scandinavian pattern, with centralised small intensive care wards surrounded by small living units catering for the more able-bodied cases, with accommodation for 8–12 residents in single or double bedrooms, or the Wessex Region pattern of small locally-based hospital units linked to a main hospital providing intensive care.

   In the short term, the wards of existing hospitals should immediately be adapted so as to provide accommodation along modern lines for no more than 30 persons. Many of these hospitals could be greatly improved, at comparatively low cost, through the lowering of ceilings, by the colouring of walls and through the introduction of gaily coloured curtains and floor coverings, as has already been shown in a number of progressively minded hospitals.

   Every attempt should be made to personalise life for hospital residents, through the provision of individual lockers and where possible personal clothing. The current policy, all too common in many hospitals, of forbidding the 'defacing of walls' should be abandoned in favour of the introduction of colourful pictures, posters, tapestries, mobiles, etc. In children's villas perhaps one wall could be covered with a blackboard to encourage the children to express themselves by drawing with chalks—within the ward which is their home, and not just in the hospital school. The Society would welcome a readier acceptance on the part of Hospital Management Committees and nursing staff of the following innovations, which are proving so valuable.

(a) The abandonment of uniforms by nurses and other staff.
(b) Less regimentation and 'block treatment' in favour of greater personal stimulation of residents who should be allowed to retain their own toys and possessions.
(c) The mixing of the sexes throughout the daily life of the hospital and experimentation in the mixing of various age groups.
(d) Hospitals should strive to involve the outside community in their work through the greater use of voluntary workers. Where appropriate, a 'revolving door' policy should be adopted through the admission of patients on a one-to-two days basis, especially children in need of specialist services such as intensive therapy.

4. *Community Residential Care.* Residential provision, alternative to the hospital, be made available immediately by Local Authorities, acting in concert with Hospital Management Committees, for those at present in hospital or on waiting lists, whose condition is considered appropriate to this form of care, by way of hostels, group homes, sheltered housing, supervised apartments and fostering services.

In recognition of the need for experimentation in other forms of care, the claims of community settlement schemes might also be investigated. Such choice of residential provision should subsequently be made available to parents unable to continue to retain their children in the family home.

Parents caring for an adult handicapped person at home should automatically be given maximum support from Social Security and Supplementary Benefits.

5. *Staff.*
(a) Community Care. Since the success of residential provision in the community is inevitably dependent on the availability of personnel suitably equipped for their various tasks, officially recognised staff training schemes must be initiated without delay.
(b) Hospitals. In the short term, the care of the mentally handicapped in hospital should be undertaken by nurses equipped by further training, which would give emphasis to their patients' developmental and social needs. An oppor-

tunity must be provided for more advanced forms of training and ultimately for living outside the hospital.

It is also important that consideration be given to the natural needs of many nurses, especially those engaged over long periods of time in caring for the most grievously subnormal, to have the opportunity to transfer from time to time to less demanding work, on other wards or units for the mentally handicapped in different categories, without detriment to the need of the children for stable relationships with a mother substitute.

It might well prove beneficial to all concerned if a system were to be devised whereby nurses undertaking intensive care and other nursing work in hospitals for the subnormal might periodically interchange with those engaged in nursing in general hospitals.

6. *Joint planning and overall financing.* We believe that eventually one authority should be responsible for the planning and financing of the whole service.

In his Presidential address to the British Society for the Study of Mental Subnormality in April 1972 Professor Jack Tizard considered 'Science and Policy Issues of Research into Services for the Mentally Handicapped'. He stressed the importance of a technological approach to the social sciences, using properly controlled experiments similar to the controlled trials of different treatments in the field of clinical medicine, but he recognised the difficulty when investigating differences between different ways of running mental subnormality services of measuring the quality of those services. Demonstration projects which were 'successful' were those which were persuasively reported, and it was likely to be the quality of the reporting rather than the success of what actually went on in the project itself which led others to take up the ideas of a pioneer. It should be remembered, said Tizard, that 'Even the great pioneers in special education and mental retardation (with the exception of Itard), made claims about the success of their methods which simply aren't true. . . . And the power they exert is often that of a visionary or an enthusiast who is able to convey his enthusiasm to others. If this is true even of the greatest of our predecessors, how much more true is it not likely to be of the countless numbers of less gifted enthusiasts who are pressing their ill-considered and mutually contradictory notions upon the educators, administrators and planners of the world today'. There were not, Tizard thought, adequate models for research on complex organisations—all that existed were 'behavioural case studies of reforms, usually implemented by a good fairy from a business school or institute of human relations, and usually having a happy ending. These case studies never sound like real life to me'.

Tizard's view was that the major contribution to our knowledge of, and treatment for, the mentally handicapped over the next two or three decades would come through studies of institutions rather than through the further study of biological problems or analysis of psychological deficit or of learning processes.

On 1st April 1971, the education of all children, whatever their level of intelligence, became the responsibility of the Department of Education and Science as a result of the *Education (Handicapped Children) Act* 1970. This Act had been greeted by the cry 'No child is ineducable', which rivalled in its uncritical acceptance that of 'Community care for the mentally handicapped' which had followed the passing of the *Mental Health Act* 1959. The National Association for Mental Health, however, which had pioneered courses for teachers of the mentally handicapped in junior training centres and hospital schools, expressed great concern that 'the junior training centres which had become the darlings of the health service might become the cinderellas of the educational services'. Unfortunately, other apprehensions expressed at that time by the Association and others, including the author, have proved justified by subsequent events—in some parts of the country head teachers of special schools are attempting to impose the same standards on severely subnormal children as they expect of educationally subnormal children and they are far less tolerant of disturbed behaviour than were the staffs of junior training centres. As a result, there has been a tendency for them to reject the more difficult severely subnormal children, and we have been under pressure to admit to our hospital schools children who were previously managed in junior training centres, thus not only perpetuating, but accentuating the two-class provision for children which the Act was designed to abolish. The transfer of responsibility has also meant the introduction of long school holidays, inappropriate, in the author's view, for mentally handicapped children, without any general provision for staggering teachers' holidays to provide at least a partial service. As a result, except when voluntary helpers are available, the children have to remain in the wards for much of the day and add to the problems of already over-burdened nursing staff. There are obvious emotional advantages to parents who feel that their children are no longer considered unsuitable for education (however unrealistic this may be, in the narrower sense of the word as usually understood, as far as the most severely handicapped are concerned), but so far, apart from this, the advantages to the teachers of the transfer, in terms of increased status and improved conditions of service, have been more obvious than those to the majority of mentally handicapped children, at least those in hospital.

In December 1971, the National Association for Mental Health published its Mind Report No. 5—'Community Care Provisions for Mentally Handicapped Men and Women', which indicated a small improvement in local authority provisions for the mentally handicapped since the surveys on which the figures quoted in the Government's White Paper were based were carried out. Mind Report No. 5 showed also that only thirty-one per cent of local authorities were up to their establishment of social workers. At the Annual Conference of the National Association for Mental Health in 1972, Sir Keith Joseph, the then Secretary of State for Health and Social Services, in answer to a question from the author, expressed his confidence that local authorities would be able to provide the recommended facilities for the mentally handicapped by the target dates in the Government White Paper, even though the Tory Government (like their Labour predecessors) were committed to a policy of allowing local authorities independence in deciding their priorities of spending (Heaton-Ward, 1972). The Secretary of State gave a similar answer to the same question from the author at the 1973 Annual Conference, adding that the author was judging the future by the past. However, Mind Report No. 11, published in October 1973, reported that local authority provisions for the mentally handicapped still fell far short of the targets set in the White Paper and that '45 local authorities informed Mind that targets for the year 1973/74 had been refused loan sanction. MND is aware of 70 such capital projects deferred, amounting to more than £7½ million'. The MND Report believed it would be unfair to castigate local authorities whose plans had been seriously affected by situations beyond their control and questioned 'the intentions of the Department of Health and Social Security in setting guidelines and targets and then withholding the financial approval for their implementation'. It should be noted that Mind Report No. 11 was referring to a period some months before the introduction of the Government's economic 'freeze'.

The 'desperate situation', in which parents of mentally handicapped children found themselves as a result of the run-down of hospitals without the building of alternative accommodation, was referred to in May 1972 by Mr. George Lee, Secretary General of the National Society for Mentally Handicapped Children, who reported that some were 'breaking under the strain'. He supported Viscount Davidson's proposal for the establishment of a new Government Department to care specifically for the needs of the mentally subnormal, referred to earlier (Lee, 1972). The Community Care of the Handicapped was debated in the House of Lords a few days later on a motion moved by Lord Grenfell, Treasurer of the National Society for Mentally Handicapped Children, who said '... it would be disastrous to transfer patients from a large institution such as a hospital into a smaller one such as a hostel, without ensuring that there are proper facilities for employment, recreation and all the other requirements of life which we consider proper'. Lord Grenfell had come to the firm conclusion in his close association with the mentally handicapped 'that, whatever their age, they are more at home with those in the same category of understanding as themselves, rather than being permanently isolated with those of normal intelligence', and he believed 'that some form of village community should be considered, with ready access to the towns or cities, but with its own industrial unit and its own agricultural unit, and with residential facilities shared by both male and female. . . . I do not believe that dwellers in villages feel isolated; in fact many prefer it'. Subsequent speakers included Baroness Young, who anticipated that at the then current increase in local authority capital investment on services for the mentally handicapped 'many authorities would reach their target figure within 10 years'. The Lord Bishop of Coventry suggested that the subnormal person was 'yet another victim of the bifurcation of responsibility between hospital and local authority'. Lord Hayter said it was a curious thing 'that in the British Isles the one place where there is a truly integrated service for the mentally handicapped is Northern Ireland.

There, education, social and health services are combined in a Special Care Service'. Viscount Davidson, speaking in support of his proposal for the establishment of 'a separate authority responsible for the planning and financing of the whole service for the mentally handicapped' said he had 'certainly seen a happier community spirit inside a so-called institution than I have seen in the community outside', and that he was 'far from convinced that the solution lay in further integration into the reorganised National Health Service'. His experience in hospital management (as Chairman of the Royal Eastern Counties Hospital for the mentally handicapped) had taught him that the problems for the mentally handicapped were totally different from those of other types of hospital. In replying to the debate, Lord Aberdare, Minister of Health, said that in stimulating local authority activity, the Government relied on persuasion by 'means of circulars, Papers of various hues and personal visits by Ministers ...' and on providing 'more money to make their task easier, even though in the end it is the local authority who decide how their available resources shall be spent' (Hansard, 1972).

In November 1970, the Secretary of State for Social Services reaffirmed the policy of the previous Government of unifying the administration of the National Health Service and stated that legislation would bring the change into effect at the same time as alterations were made in the structure of local Government. However, in his foreword to the Government's Consultative Document on National Health Service Reorganisation, published in May 1971, the Secretary of State said that the Government had *not* proposed full administrative unification of the health and related personal social services, '... but as comprehensive care of the citizen depended on both sets of services, strong and binding links between them will be of fundamental importance'. With this in mind, the Royal Medico-Psychological Association invited representatives of the British Medical Association and of the Society of Medical Officers of Health to form a Tripartite Committee with the following terms of reference: 'To consider the reorganisation of the Mental Health Service in all its aspects in the light of plans to unify the National Health Service as a whole'. The Tripartite Committee published its Report—*The Mental Health Service After Unification*—in May 1972. This Report consisted of twelve chapters dealing both with the development of the mental health service as a whole and with the special services for mental illness, mental handicap and the child psychiatric services and those for persons suffering with personality disorders, including psychopathic personalities, drug addicts and alcoholics. There were separate chapters on the roles of the general practitioner, the nurse and the social worker in the mental health service and of the voluntary services in relation to mental health. The introduction to the Report stated: 'The conclusion of our committee which stands out above all other is the necessity for *compulsory* provision for liaison between the National Health Service and local authorities at all levels. We firmly believe that nothing short of this will ensure against unilateral action—or no action at all—and consequent waste of resources by one or other of the bodies concerned. . . . We strongly support the concept of community care, both for the mentally ill and the mentally subnormal, but it is still rudimentary in some local authorities: the task of providing it adequately will be immense. As it develops, so must it be evaluated and it is our opinion that only when it is a proved success will it be prudent to plan for curtailing or abolishing existing facilities'.

The Report included more detail in expressing opinions on the services for the mentally handicapped, because of their special importance at that time, than was the case in most chapters on other services. It expressed strong support for the Government's Command Paper *Better Services for the Mentally Handicapped*, but stressed that a unified National Health Service should not relinquish its role in community mental health for the handicapped. It regarded as essential to any form of unified planning the creation of standing joint advisory committees for the services for the mentally handicapped by the statutory mental health liaison committees, which it had recommended at all administrative levels of the reorganised National Health Service. The Report did not think that an 'all purpose' social worker was likely to provide a satisfactory service and thought that hospitals would have a continued need for their own social workers for at least some time to come. It urged that more resources should be given to existing hospitals for the subnormal which were 'gravely short of money and seriously understaffed'. The whole problem of hospital accommodation for the subnormal needed further study and, in spite of long term plans, the transitional modernisation of existing hospitals would be essential. Day hospitals were a necessity and specialised hospital units should be provided for socially deviant subnormal adolescents. Assessment clinics and out-patient services should be established immediately where they did not already exist. There should be an increase in consultant, senior registrar and registrar establishments and departments of mental handicap should be developed in universities.

Other important matters dealt with in the Report were the prevention of mental handicap, including the increasing possibility of antenatal diagnosis through amniocentesis, early post-natal detection, ongoing assessment and parent counselling, with support from a social worker.

The Government White Paper, Cmn. 5055, *National Health Service Reorganisation: England*, was presented to Parliament in August 1972. This stated that there were very strong arguments for bringing health and social services under a single administration and that this could be accomplished by putting the N.H.S. within local government, but that 'for reasons accepted and fully explained by the previous and the present Government, that is not attainable at least in the foreseeable future'. The day to day running of services was to be based on districts, which were to form the natural community for the planning and delivery of comprehensive health care. Each district was to have a population of between 200,000 and 500,000. However, the fundamental unit in planning district services was to be the Area Health Authority which, it was anticipated, was to be coterminous in each case with the corresponding new local government county or metropolitan district proposed in the Local Government Bill. Hospital Management Committees were to be abolished and there was to be no statutory authority with executive power below area level, but Community Health Councils were to be established 'to represent the consumer' and 'to represent to the A.H.A. the interests of the public in the health service in its district'. The responsibility for ensuring that plans and activities within the district were coordinated was to rest with a district management team (D.M.T.) consisting of a medical officer (community physician), a nursing officer, a finance officer and an administrator and two elected medical representatives—one from the specialists and one from the general practitioners. The

D.M.T. was to function as a 'consensus group', i.e. all its decisions would have to be unanimous—and it would have operational control of district services.

The Royal College of Psychiatrists, in its memorandum on the White Paper, published in March 1973, commented that '... the proposed management structure, geared to authority from above downwards, was counter to the tendency in many spheres towards less authoritative and more domestic structures—either already in operation or being urged by numerous bodies representing the rank and file'. The Royal College was uncertain how far mental health would be allowed to assume its rightful share of priorities in the proposed reorganisation. Past experience had shown that in open competition, mental health had a tendency to lose out, priority going to the somatic specialities. This had happened following the amalgamation of psychiatric and general hospital groups. The memorandum pointed out that a psychiatric hospital might be, not only outside the District it served, but outside the Area, and suggested that the arrangement could be changed by establishing a Regional Mental Health Service. Others, including the author, suggested that, because existing mental subnormality hospitals were not geographically sited to allow them to become part of a comprehensive service linked with a district general hospital, services for the mentally handicapped should be coordinated as an area service pending the provision of adequate residential accommodation on a district basis (Heaton-Ward, 1974). In the case of the Stoke Park Hospital Group, with which the author is connected, the 'shadow' Avon Area Health Authority decided that, when reorganisation would take effect on 1st April 1974, the Group would retain its identity and become part of the Frenchay District Health Service, although not all of the Group's residential units are within that district.

Speaking at the Annual Conference of Mind/National Association for Mental Health in March 1973, Professor Kathleen Jones, Head of the Department of Social Administration and Social Work at the University of York, said she thought it would be wrong to dismiss as merely reactionary the very real sense of disquiet which many mental health workers felt as they saw the achievements of the last twenty or thirty years disappearing into the melting pot of Seebohm and the coming Health Service reorganisation. A series of documents, from the Royal Commission Report of 1959 onwards, had assumed that small-group care was preferable to large-scale institutional care for many patients, yet very little research had been undertaken into the realities of hostel care. Somehow the 'magic figure' of twenty-five places had been arrived at as a suitable size, but Professor Jones knew of no study, empirical or theoretical, which suggested that homes for twenty-five people had an automatic social viability. Their studies at York on hostels for the mentally ill and mentally handicapped in the surrounding local authorities suggested that they varied enormously in policy goals, material provision, staffing and quality of social life; but that nearly all were very isolated, receiving little or nothing in the way of medical or social work support; and that while wardens were, on the whole, kind-hearted, homely people, their understanding of their work often stopped at the level of physical provision. 'The assumption,' said Professor Jones, 'that any reasonably humane person could turn twenty-five damaged and vulnerable people into something like a family group is not merely unjustified by the facts: it is positively dangerous'.

(A working party of the Central Council for Education and Training in Social Work (C.C.E.T.S.W.), which had been set up in 1972, recommended that there should be a single pattern of training for residential and field workers) (C.C.E.T.S.W., 1973).

Dr. Peter Sykes, a consultant psychiatrist then working in a service for the mentally handicapped based on Peterborough District Hospital (and now a consultant in the Merseyside Region), spoke at the same Conference on 'The Asylum Principle of Care for the Mentally Subnormal'. He felt that the need to discuss this principle was possibly greater than at any time previously, because we were in the process of starting to set up a service based largely on community care in a mainly non-caring community. Whilst many communities appeared to tolerate our clients, few really accepted them yet. It should not be beyond us in this day and age to construct a person-orientated type of residential unit in which the concepts of protection, combined with strengthening, could play a great part. Sykes said he came across able patients who had left hospital and were living at home, who told him that they were frequently not as happy as they were when they lived in a large, often highly-criticised hospital. He had been told on more than one occasion:

'Of course I was really happier in the hospital because I had my mates with me and now I haven't any real friends'. Sykes pointed out that quite a number of normal members of our society now opted out for a variety of reasons and asked whether we were to refuse the right of an individual to take this course of action because he had a handicap. Perhaps we should be a little more tolerant and let them exercise their rights if they really preferred a protected or asylum-type of environment.

In May 1974, the report of yet another committee of inquiry into allegations of ill-treatment at a mental subnormality hospital—this time South Ockendon Hospital in Essex—was published. This report criticised, not only the consultant who was clinically responsible for patients in three locked wards, but also the Physician Superintendent of the hospital for lack of leadership and for allowing the consultant to follow the criticised regime in the wards concerned. In this respect, this Committee of Inquiry showed the same unfairness and apparent unawareness of the difficult position of the Medical/Physician Superintendent since the *Mental Health Act* 1959, as their predecessors had done. Prior to that Act, the Medical Superintendent had had overall responsibility for the care of every patient in the hospital and, although some medical superintendents were criticised by other consultants in their hospitals for interfering with the treatment of patients under the latters' care, many of the superintendents delegated clinical authority to the hospitals' consultants and administrative authority to the heads of other departments of the hospitals, while themselves remaining legally responsible for the whole hospital. However, with the advent of the *Mental Health Act*, the clinical care of each patient in hospital became the responsibility of the particular consultant in charge of his treatment, who was designated 'responsible medical officer' for that patient. The medical superintendent's clinical responsibility was confined to patients for whom he himself was responsible medical officer. At the same time, the medical superintendent's authority, as leader of the hospital, was insidiously eroded by Ministry policy, which transferred more and more of his responsibilities to senior non-medical officers of the hospital. It was not surprising, therefore, that many previously enthusiastic, liberal-minded and progressive medical superintendents should feel that they were being allowed to carry out their duties only by courtesy of these other senior officers, and that 'medical superintendent' had become a 'dirty word'. The blame, in the author's view, for their failure to give leadership subsequently, lies as heavily on those who have contributed to the policy of abolition of the post of medical superintendent as on the much-criticised holders of these posts themselves. It has yet to be seen whether the arrangements for medical administration in the reorganised health service achieve as much as did the best medical superintendents in the past.

Reference has already been made to the questioning of professional roles within the mental handicap service, and the future role of nurses in this field was considered in the report of the Briggs Committee on Nursing, published in 1972. The report envisaged, in the long run, fundamental changes taking place in the care of the mentally handicapped, with implications for the staff employed. The Committee had considered the idea of creating a new professional group of 'care staff' to undertake all but purely physical or mental nursing functions for the mentally handicapped, and believed 'that much of the most successful nursing care being given at present in this field embraces the wider functions envisaged for care staff and that ultimately a new profession probably will and should emerge'. They considered, however, that such a change should proceed by evolution and not by revolution, as part of a broader group of changes, with residential care staff of the kind employed by local authorities working alongside nurses in mental handicap hospitals.

During Spring 1973, the King's Fund Centre held two residential seminars and two one-day seminars on an invitational basis, and one major day conference on an open basis, 'to explore the perspectives of the Briggs Report as it applies to mental handicap nursing'. The number of mental handicap nurses present varied from 50 per cent to 70 per cent, and the remainder were psychiatrists, psychologists and social workers. The discussions resulted in 'Perspectives of the Briggs Report'—a discussion paper on the future role and training of subnormality nurses, and their relationship with residential care staff—published by the King's Fund in December 1973. It suggested that a Mental Handicap Staff Training Board might emerge to achieve compatibility of training between nurses and social workers by collaboration between the two existing Training Councils—the General Nursing Council and the Central Council for Education and Training in Social Work (C.C.E.T.S.W.). It proposed a syllabus for training hospital and social services staff to meet the needs of the mentally handicapped for residential care, which contained sections or modules of training which could be common, not only to nurses and social service staff, but to those staff whose training was about to be transferred from the Training Council for Teachers of the Mentally Handicapped to the C.C.E.T.S.W.

At a Royal College of Nursing Conference at the end of September 1973, a big majority rejected the Briggs proposal for a new caring profession for the mentally handicapped, and opted for retaining the existing distinction between nurses and social workers, but agreed that any new syllabus for nurse training should contain a number of modules common to the training of social workers concerned with residential care, so as to facilitate staff inter- changeability. Shortly afterwards, the Psychiatric Committee of the Royal College of Nursing declared that the parts of the Register and Roll of Nurses for the Mentally Subnormal should continue and be strengthened and improved until such time as a national decision was taken on the future of nurse training. The Committee planned to hold a series of local conferences in various parts of the United Kingdom during 1974 to discuss the Briggs proposals further.

The Royal College of Psychiatrists published its comments on the Briggs Committee recommendations in January 1974. On the specific proposals relating to nursing of the mentally handicapped, the Royal College recognised 'that the formal education of nurses working in the field of mental handicap has lagged behind the pioneering work of those nurses who have already developed successfully the social aspects of care', and that it was right that their basic education should recognise the need for an increased emphasis on the social aspects of care, but it did not seem sensible to the Royal College that this should mean that a new caring profession would be required. Such a proposal would create uncer- tainty within the nursing profession just as its expansion and development was getting under way. The Royal College com- mented that subnormality nurses did not accept that their profes- sion was that of clinical nursing in the strict bedside sense, and had themselves pioneered the change to a greater emphasis on the

social, psychological and educational needs of the mentally handicapped person as an individual or as a member of a group, and
the Royal College pointed out that even that emphasis was a return
to the attitudes previously more widespread in the old colonies '. . .
before the war and its economic aftermath caused a deterioration in
the staffing situation'. The Royal College thought that the Briggs
Committee's proposal that 'residential care staff of the kind now
employed by local authorities' should work alongside nurses in
mental handicap hospitals would cause formidable problems of integration, whether the care staff were running separate units or
were working alongside nurses in the same unit, particularly if the
two groups were administered under different management structures. It seemed sensible 'to encourage, and to accelerate the
development of mental subnormality nursing out from hospitals
into community homes; and to embrace the total residential care of
the mentally handicapped, with greater emphasis on social and
therapeutic needs', as in Belfast, where nurses lived in ordinary
housing estates in ordinary houses with groups of mentally handicapped residents, 'in as normal a situation as it is possible to im-
agine'. The Royal College was in favour of common training
between the nursing and residential care professions regarding
aspects of residential care, with local experiments and development
to utilise whichever type and mixture of staff were considered to be
appropriate, but with administration in one particular situation
under one profession or the other.

The Royal College of Psychiatrists had considered the role of its
own members in March 1973 at a Conference on 'The Responsibilities and Role of the Doctor concerned with the Care of the
Mentally Handicapped', which was chaired by the President of the
College, Sir Martin Roth, and at which the opening address was
given by Sir George Godber, the then Chief Medical Officer,
Department of Health and Social Security. At the end of the day
during which many members spoke, Sir Martin Roth summarised
the discussion as follows:

1. There had been an attempt to attain a consensus on the functions of the doctor in the care of the mentally handicapped.
   There was a role in the community in respect of family dis-
   equilibrium and in the care of those removed from the care of

   the social services.
2. There was a role for a specialist within the hospital setting. The medical role had to be established in the therapeutic community.
3. Within the establishment the doctor's function had to be subordinated to the small group system.
   There seemed to be agreement about role in ascertainment. The specialist in mental handicap should no longer be the recipient of patients for whom nothing could be done.
   For the next 15 to 20 years hospitals would remain. A struggle for resources would continue.
   Of Swedish practices he said these could not be extrapolated to this country and Swedish facilities had not been working for long enough for effective evaluation to be possible.

Sir Martin concluded: 'A more clearly specified meaning of the "subnormality" specialty is needed'. The challenge was to define the skills of specialism. He referred to 'social medicine', optimistically welcomed 20 years ago. But many of its exponents went into genetics and other branches, because social medicine had no skills of its own. Psychiatry was an academic discipline, but in action it was social medicine.

There was a need:

1. To define skills
2. To define training
3. To practise skills
4. To mix with other disciplines

It was agreed that the doctor in mental handicap had clinical skills which could be demonstrated in action. The consultant in mental handicap had a role and responsibility. These needed further definition as far as possible.

The debate has continued since that Conference. Some writers, including the author, see the role of the specialist in mental handicap as that of leader of a multi-disciplinary team of members of other branches of the medical profession and of other non-medical professions, who accept the continuous responsibility for the care and treatment of mentally handicapped people and the related problems in their families. (Heaton-Ward, 1969; Spencer, 1973).

Commenting on the results of his aetiological survey of mental retardation in the Newcastle region (1966–71) Dr. G. McCoull wrote: There is a danger that the care of the retarded person has become one of the many subjects which lend themselves to administrative and social adventurism and that there is a real danger that the medical and nursing burden of care is at present being regarded lightly, and that the retarded in general are now seen sometimes as people who only need educating or who only need social service, and as a corollary to this that they are just the same as other people, only slower, and whose social needs, both inside and outside hospital, are the same as normal people.

> That mental subnormality and severe subnormality is primarily a medical matter is now being largely ignored .... It seems that in spite of figures like these, Medicine is not now the discipline which calls Psychology, Education, Nursing and Social Service to its aid in the overall treatment of the retarded and that there is a considerable danger that, as a result of the many administrative changes that have been made in very recent years and which are still proceeding, these disciplines which should be a coherent whole led by medicine, are now splitting up into their separate parts, leading to a situation where each discipline is acting on its own and in its own right without regard to the need for total integration of effort, and giving an appearance of being more concerned with the rights and privileges and power of the individual discipline and less with the right of the patient to have integrated total treatment.

Others, including Dr. T. L. Pilkington (who in 1967 had written: 'At present far too many people are involved, often duplicating each others work and with none taking continuing responsibility. Subnormality justifies acceptance as a specialty in its own right') were asserting that the concept of mental handicap as a medical speciality in its own right was untenable. (Pilkington, 1973).

The role of psychologists in the Health Service and their relationships with other professional staff, were the terms of reference of a Sub-Committee of the Standing Mental Health Advisory Committee of the Department of Health and Social Security, set up in 1973 under the chairmanship of Professor W. H. Trethowan. These terms of reference included examination of the important contribution of psychologists to the assessment, treatment, education and training of the mentally handicapped. At the time of writing, the Sub-Committee had not yet published their report.

On 26th February 1975, at the Conference on Mental Handicap of the National Society for Mentally Handicapped Children, the Secretary of State for Health and Social Security, Mrs Barbara Castle, made a statement on Government policy on mental handicap. In her statement, Mrs. Castle added to the anxieties of many workers in the health field devoted to the care of the mentally handicapped by referring to the need to look afresh at the question of how far mental handicap should be regarded as a social or educational service responsibility rather than a health one. In this connection, the remarks of Mr. James Elliott, Associate Director, the King Edwards Hospital Fund, who spoke immediately before Mrs. Castle, are worthy of note—Mr. Elliott said that it should be realised that those working in hospital were just as conscious as anyone else of the shortcomings of the service they were providing and were just as anxious as those outside to improve it. He urged the critics of the existing service not to throw the baby out with the bath water and commented on how easy it was to ride into town with banners flying and to fire a couple of shots and then to retire from the scene without any sense of responsibility for the disruption one had caused.

Mrs. Castle said she felt that after the recent reorganisation, further reorganisation, in the form of establishing a National Service for the Mentally Handicapped, financed by Central Government (as suggested in the Labour Party Green Paper 'Health Care', and strongly advocated also by Lord Davidson in 1971) would produce many more problems than it would solve. Again, she did not feel that overall progress could be speeded up by handing existing mental handicap hospitals to local authority social service departments. Mrs. Castle did, however, announce four specific measures:

1. The establishment of a National Development Group for the Mentally Handicapped to advise the Secretary of State and to play an active role in the development of policy and the strategy for its implementation. The Group was to include people from each of the main disciplines involved—medicine, nursing, social services and administration, and was to be

under the Chairmanship of Professor Peter Mittler, of the Hester Adrian Research Centre at Manchester University.

2. The establishment of one or more multidisciplinary Development Teams to work closely with the Group and to provide specialist information about the current state of development of mental handicap services in the National Health Service and Personal Social Services. Consequently, the Hospital Advisory Service would not reconstitute a mental handicap advisory team. Mrs. Castle stressed that the Development Teams would be independent and would 'not be sucked into the machine'.

3. The establishment of an inquiry under the Chairmanship of Mrs. Peggy Jay, a member of the Central Health Services Council, into mental handicap nursing and care, to follow up in greater detail the ideas which were tentatively mentioned in the Briggs Report on Nursing.

4. Continuation of the detailed consultations already in progress about the future role of the medical specialist in mental handicap. As an interim measure, Mrs. Castle proposed to ask Health Authorities to consider in future making new consultant appointments in mental handicap to the Health Area or District rather than to a particular hospital, while recognising the 'very real and continuing need to give a medical lead on the therapeutic needs within the hospital'.

Accepted in good faith, the Secretary of State's proposals ·seem to offer a very positive hope of healing some of the wounds in the mental handicap service which diverse legislation has caused in recent years, and of restoring some of the sense of unity and purpose among sincere people whose morale has been steadily falling during this period.

No account of the changing attitudes towards the care of the mentally handicapped would be complete without acknowledgement of the contribution of the press, television and radio. Undoubtedly, publicity through the mass media concerning the deficiences of the services for the mentally handicapped is painful to many people with statutory responsibilities at all levels in the health and social services, and to those who have been struggling for many years to provide day to day care for the mentally handicapped with grossly inadequate resources and often in appalling surroundings, and also to some relatives of the mentally handicapped. However, in the author's opinion, based on ten years experience of enlisting the help of the mass media, on balance far more is to be gained by frank admission of shortcomings than by adopting defensive attitudes towards any criticism, which is apt to result in distorted and often apparently biased reporting based on inadequate facts (Heaton-Ward, 1972).

REFERENCES

The development of care of the mentally subnormal

The past to the twentieth century

Barr, M. W. *Mental Defectives, Their History, Treatment and Training.* Rebman Ltd., London. 1904.

Bonaterre. *Historique sur le Sauvage de L'Aveyron.* Paris, 1799.

Conolly, J. *British and Foreign Medico-Chirurgical Review.* London, 1847.

Gaskell. 'Idiocy'. Chamber's Edinburgh Journal. 1847. Jan–Feb.

Guggenbuhl. *Europe's First Colony for the Cure of Cretinism.* Jena, 1840.

Itard. *Rapport sur le Sauvage de L'Aveyron.* Paris, 1801.

MacGillivray, R. C. *Mental Deficiency Retrospect and Prospect.* Scottish Association for Mental Health, Edinburgh, 1962.

Saegert. *The Cure of Imbecility by Intellectual Means.* Berlin, 1856.

Schenker. *The Aetiology and Therapeutics of Idiocy.* 1899.

Seguin, E. *Théorie et Pratique de l'Education des Idiots. Leçons aux Jeunes Idiots de L'Hospice des Incurables.* Premiere partie. Paris, 1842.

Seguin, E. *idem,* Seconde partie. Paris, 1843.

Twining, W. *Some account of cretinism and the institution for its cure on the Abendberg.* London, 1843.

The twentieth century

Association of Hospital Management Committees. *Observations on 'Better services for the Mentally Handicapped'.* Command Paper 4863. Assoc. hosp. management committees, May, 1972.

Bavin, J. 'Subnormality in the seventies: Priority in Resources'. Lancet, 1970, *i*, 285.

Beach, Fletcher. 'The Presidential Address delivered at the Fifty-ninth Annual Meeting of the Medico-Psychological Association held on 26.7.1900.' J. ment. Sci., 1900. *XLVI*, No. 195, 623–653.

Better Services for the Mentally Handicapped. Cmnd. 4683. H.M.S.O., London, 1971.

British Medical Journal. 'Institutions for the subnormal.' Leading article, Brit. Med. J. 1960, *2*, 1217–1218.

British Medical Journal. 'Subnormal Hospitals.' Leading article. Brit. Med. J. 1969, *2*, 426.

British Medical Journal, 'Environment for Mental Patients.' Leading article, Brit. Med. J. 1972, *2*, 366.

Burrowes, H. P. 'Care of the Mentally Handicapped.' Lancet, 1969, *ii*, 1004.

CARE. *Nowhere Else to Go.* CARE, London, 1969.

Coldharbour Hospital. Report of the Committee of Inquiry into the Fire at Coldharbour Hospital, Sherborne, Dorset. Cmnd. 5170, H.M.S.O., London, 1972.

'Declaration of General and Special Rights of the Mentally Retarded.' Proc. 4th Congr. Int. Soc. Ment. Ret. 1968.

Department of Health and Social Security. *Consultative Document on National Health Service Reorganisation.* H.M.S.O., London, May, 1971.

Department of Health and Social Security. *The Management of Violent or Potentially Violent Hospital Patients.* HC(76)11. H.M.S.O. London, March 1976.

Education (Handicapped Children) Act 1970. H.M.S.O., London, 1970.

Elliott, J. 'Service for the Mentally Handicapped.' Lancet, 1971, *2*, 92.

Elliott, J. 'Eight Propositions for Mental Handicap.' Brit. J. ment. Sub. 1972; *XXVII*, Part I, No. 34, 24.

Ely Hospital. Report of the Committee of Inquiry into Allegations of Ill Treatment of Patients and other Irregularities at Ely Hospital, Cardiff. Cmnd. 3975, H.M.S.O., London, 1969.

Farleigh Hospital. *Report on Farleigh Hospital Committee of Inquiry.* Cmnd. 4557, H.M.S.O., London, 1971.

Francklin, S. 'Lesson of the Coldharbour Tragedy.' *The Daily Telegraph,* London, 1972.

Francklin, S. and Shearer, A. *Future Services for the Mentally Handicapped.* Campaign for the Mentally Handicapped, London, 1971.

Freeman, H. L. 'The Portsmouth Mental Health Service, 1926–1952.' Med. Off. 1962, *1*, 149.

Goffman, E. *Asylums.* Doubleday & Co., New York, 1961.

Gibson, J. 'The Needs of Mentally Handicapped Children.' J. ment. Subnorm. 1963. *IX*, Part 2, No. 17, 95.

Gibson, J. 'Hospital Services for the Mentally Subnormal.' Lancet, 1963, *2*, 1116.

Hansard. 'Community Care of the Handicapped.' Hansard, 1972, Vol. 330, No. 71, 1923.

Heaton-Ward, W. A. 'Mental Health.' Brit. med. J. 1960, *2*, 1237.

Heaton-Ward, W. A. 'Treatment of the Mentally Subnormal in Hospital.' Proc. Ann. Conf. N.A.M.H., 1961, 53–57.

Heaton-Ward, W. A. 'The National Health Service'. *The Times*, 9th February, 1966, p. 13.

Heaton-Ward, W. A. 'Coldharbour Farm: the First Five Years.' Brit.
   med. Chir. J. 1969. *84*, (ii) No. 310, 46.
Heaton-Ward, W. A. *The Demand for Psychiatrists in the Mental Sub-
   normality Field.'* Conference on post-graduate psychiatric education,
   University of Dundee, March, 1969.
Heaton-Ward, W. A. 'Environment for Mental Patients.' Brit. med. J.
   1972, *2*, 700.
Heaton-Ward, W. A. 'Subnormality.' The Listener, 1972, *87*, No. 2254,
   745.
Heaton-Ward, W. A. 'Staffing our Asylums.' Brit. med. J. 1972, *1*, 750.
Heaton-Ward, W. A. 'Services for the Mentally Handicapped after
   Reorganisation of the National Health Service.' North West
   Somerset Society for the Mentally Handicapped, Year Book
   1973–4. p. 30.
Hoejenbos, E. 'The Needs of Mentally Handicapped Children.' J. Ment.
   Subnorm, 1963, *IX*, Part. I. No. 16, 42.
Hunt, A. *Caring for the Severely Subnormal.* Spastics Society, London,
   1969.
Jones, K. *A Long Look*. MIND/National Association for Mental Health
   Annual Conference, London, March, 1973.
King's Fund Centre. *Perspectives of the Briggs Report*. Mental Handicap
   Papers 4. King Edward's Hospital Fund for London. London, 1973.
Kirman, B. 'Treatment of the Mentally Subnormal.' Lancet *2*, 1962,
   1265–1268.
Kratter, F. E. 'The Future Role of the Modern Hospital for the Mentally
   Subnormal.' Nursing Mirror, 6th August, IX–XI and 13th August,
   VII–IX, XVI, 1965.
Kushlick, A. 'Community Care for the Mentally Subnormal.' Proc. Royal
   Soc. Med., 1965, *58*, 374–379.
Lee, G. *The Daily Telegraph*, 4th May, 1972.
Leys, D. G. 'The Needs of Mentally Handicapped Children.' J. ment. Sub-
   norm. 1963, *IX*, Part I, No. 16, 45.
Local Authority Social Services Act 1970.
Liaison Committee, Royal College of Nursing and Royal College of
   Psychiatrists. 'The Care of the Violent Patient.' R.C.N. and R.C.
   Psych., London, 1972.
Loring, J. 'The Director Writes.' *Spastics News*, May, 1968, p. 4.
McCoull, G. 'Hospitals for Subnormal Patients.' Brit. med. J. 1965, *1*,
   191.
McCoull, G. *Report on the Newcastle upon Tyne Regional Aetiological
   Survey (Mental Retardation), 1966–71.*
MacKeith, R. 'The Needs of Mentally Handicapped Children.' J. ment.
   Subnorm. 1963, *IX*, Part II, No. 17, 96.
McKenzie, M. E. S., Bavin, J. T. R., Finn, G. I. and Shepherd, Eric W.
   'Hospital Services for the Mentally Subnormal.' Lancet *2*, 1963, 1116.
Macmillan, D. 'Mental Health Services in Nottingham.' Int. J. Soc.
   Psychiat. 1958, *IV*, 5.

Macmillan, D. 'Community Mental Health Services.' World ment. health, 1961, *13*, 46.

Macmillan, D. *Personal Communication*, 1967.

Mental Health Act 1959. 7 & 8 Eliz. 2 Ch. 72, H.M.S.O., London.

Ministry of Health. 'Memorandum on the Size of Mental Deficiency Hospitals.' Building Note No. 30. H.M.S.O., London, 1963.

Ministry of Health. *Improving the Effectiveness of the Hospital Service for the Mentally Subnormal.* H.M. (65) 104. H.M.S.O., London, 1965.

Mittler, P. 'The Needs of Mentally Handicapped Children.' J. ment. Subnorm. 1963. *IX*, Part II, No. 17, 96.

Morris, P. *Put Away. A Sociological Study of Institutions for the Mentally Retarded.* Routledge and Kegan Paul, London, 1969.

National Association for Mental Health. *First Priorities in reaching a Policy for Hospitals for the Mentally Handicapped.* N.A.M.H., London, 1969.

National Association for Mental Health. *Guidelines for the Care of Patients who exhibit violent behaviour in Mental and Mental Subnormality Hospitals.* N.A.M.H., London, 1971.

National Association for Mental Health. Mind Report No. 5. *Community Provisions for Mentally Handicapped Men and Women.* N.A.M.H., London, December 1971.

National Association for Mental Health. Mind Report No. 11. *Community Care Provisions for Mentally Ill and Mentally Handicapped Men and Women.* N.A.M.H., London, October 1973.

National Health Service Advisory Service. *Annual Report for 1969–70*, H.M.S.O., London, 1971.

National Health Service. *Annual Report of the Hospital Advisory Service for the year 1971.* H.M.S.O., London, 1972.

National Health Service. *Annual Report of the Hospital Advisory Service for the year 1972.* H.M.S.O., London, 1973.

National Health Service Reorganisation, England. Cmnd. 5055, H.M.S.O., London, August 1972.

National Society for Mentally Handicapped Children. 'The Residential Needs of the Mentally Handicapped.' Parents' Voice, December 1971.

North West Metropolitan Regional Hospital Board. *Report of Mental Deficiency Sub-Committee of the Psychiatric Advisory Committee, 1965.*

Nursing Standard. 'Mental Handicap Nurses Set New Course.' Nursing Standard, Nov.–Dec. 1973.

Nursing Times. 'R.C.N. backs M.S. Nurses qualification.' Nursing Times, December, 1973.

O'Brien, J. 'The Needs of Mentally Handicapped Children.' J. ment. Subnorm, 1964, *X*, Part I, No. 18, 16.

Paediatric Society South East Metropolitan Regional Hospital Board. *The Needs of Mentally Handicapped Children.* 1962.

Payne, R. 'The Needs of Mentally Handicapped Children.' J. ment. Subnorm, 1963, *IX*, No. 16, 44.

Pilkington, T. L. 'Hospital Services for the Mentally Subnormal.' Lancet, 1963, *I*, 992–993.

Pilkington, T. L. 'The Needs of Mentally Handicapped Children.' J. ment. Subnorm. 1963. *IX*, Part I, No. 16, 42.

Pilkington, T. L. 'The Changing Subnormality Hospital.' Brit. Hosp. J. 1967, *LXXVII*, 209.

Pilkington, T. L. 'Is Mental Handicap a Specialty?' World med. 1973, *9*, No. 5, 78.

Raynes, N. V. and King, R. D. 'The Measurement of Child Management in Residential Institutions for the Retarded.' Proc. first Congr. of the Int. Assoc. for Scientific Study of Mental Deficiency, 1967, p. 637.

Report of the Committee on Hospital Complaints Procedure, H.M.S.O., London, 1973.

Report of the Committee on Nursing. Cmnd. 5115, H.M.S.O., London, 1972.

Report of the Briggs Committee on Nursing. The College's Comments. News and Notes, Royal College of Psychiatrists, January 1974, p. 8.

Report of the Royal Commission on Local Authority and Allied Personal Social Services. Cmnd. 3703, H.M.S.O., London, 1969.

Royal College of Psychiatrists. 'Memorandum on the White Paper on N.H.S. Reorganisation and on the Management Study Steering Committee's Report.' News and Notes, March, 1973, p. 5.

Royal College of Psychiatrists. 'Conference on the Responsibility and Role of the Doctor concerned with the Care of the Mentally Handicapped.' News and Notes, Royal College of Psychiatrists, December, 1973, p. 8.

Royal Commission on the Care and Control of the Feebleminded. 1904–1908.

Royal Commission on the Law Relating to Mental Illness and Mental Deficiency. Cmnd. 169, H.M.S.O., London, 1954–1957.

Royal Medico-Psychological Association. 'Future Patterns of Care for the Mentally Subnormal.' Brit. J. Psychiat. 1971, *119*, 95.

Sampson, G. 'The Needs of Mentally Handicapped Children.' J. ment, Subnorm. 1963, *IX*, Part I, No. 16, 43.

Sampson, G. 'The Needs of Mentally Handicapped Children.' J. ment. Subnorm. 1964, *X*, Part I, No. 18, 66–67.

Shapiro, A. 'Hospital Services for the Mentally Subnormal.' Lancet, 1963, *2*, 1165–1166.

Shapiro, A. 'The Needs of Mentally Handicapped Children.' J. ment. Subnorm. 1962, *VIII*, Part 2, No. 15, 101–102.

Shapiro, A. 'The Needs of Mentally Handicapped Children.' J. ment. Subnorm. 1963, *IX*, Part 2, No. 17, 96–97.

Shapiro, A. 'Care of the Mentally Subnormal.' Lancet, 1969, *ii*, 957.

Shapiro, A. 'Care of the Mentally Handicapped.' Brit. med. J. 1972, *1*, 308.

Social Work. 'Residential Work is part of Social Work.' Paper No. 3, C.C.E.T.S.W., London, November, 1973.

South Ockendon Hospital. Report of the Committee of Inquiry into South Ockendon Hospital. H.M.S.O., London, May, 1974.

Spastics Society. 'Mental Subnormality Policy.' Spastics Society, London, 1969.

Spencer, D. A. 'Caring for the Subnormal.' Med. Trib. 23rd October, 1969.

Sykes, P. 'Yes, but what about the Asylum Principle?' MIND/National Association for Mental Health, Annual Conference, London, March 1973.

Tizard, J. *'Residential Care of Mentally Handicapped Children.'* Brit. med. J. 1960, *I*, 1041–1046.

Tizard, J. *'Research into Services for the Mentally Handicapped: Science and Policy Issues.'* Brit. J. Ment. Sub. 1972, *XVIII*, Part I, No. 34, 24, 6.

Tripartite Committee. *'The Mental Health Service after Reorganisation.'* London, June, 1972.

Turner, E. D. 'Mental Deficiency.' J. ment. Sci. 1933, *LXXIX*, No. 327, 563–577.

Whittingham Hospital. Report of the Committee of Inquiry into Whittingham Hospital. Cmnd. 4861, H.M.S.O., London, 1972.

7 Existing facilities for the care of the mentally subnormal

At present, care of the mentally subnormal in the community is the responsibility of the local authority in which each person lives, while hospital care, whether as an out-patient or in-patient, is the responsibility of the National Health Service. In addition to these statutory provisions, community and residential care is provided by a number of voluntary organisations, and private homes and lodgings run for profit.

Supervision of mentally subnormal people living at home, and advisory support for their families, is provided by the staff of local authority social services departments. A recent book by the parent of a severely handicapped mongol child has shown the breakdown in communications that may occur between caring parents and professional workers in this field (Hannam, 1975). A number of studies have shown differing parental reactions to the care of a mentally handicapped child, but all the studies agree that the families are faced with many problems, including those of management, finance, accommodation, and opportunities for rest and leisure (Gath, 1972). Tizard and Grad (1961) concluded that families with a subnormal child at home were dominated by the 'burden of care', while those with a child in an institution were able to lead nearly normal lives. Carr (1975) reached the same general conclusions in her study of 54 babies with Down's Syndrome born during the year 1963–64; 45 of them were looked after at home and 9 of them were boarded out in various foster homes or institutions. On the other hand, Caldwell and Guze (1960) found no significant difference between the mothers of institutionalised and non-institutionalised children.

There is no doubt that the stability of the family may be threatened by the presence of a mentally subnormal member and that, in some cases, marriages may break up because of this. Farber and Jenne (1963) found that subnormal boys, particularly over the age of 9 years, were more disruptive than girls to the marital relationship, this difference being more marked in the lower social classes.

> 'The factors that make the burden of a subnormal child intolerable are unlikely to be the same for families at the extremes of the social ladder. Social class I families esteem highly those standards of education and behaviour that have enabled them to succeed. Therefore, for such families, the value crisis is most poignant and they are deeply distressed by the fact that their child can never aspire to what they themselves hold dear.
>
> In contrast, the value crisis is less threatening to those whose attainments are modest. Instead, they find themselves over-burdened by the necessary extra expenditure caused by the heavy wear and tear on clothes or household decorations by a subnormal child (Younghusband et al., 1970). They are also unable to pay for help which can make the reality crisis less formidable for much more affluent families.'
>
> (Gath, 1972.)

The reactions of siblings to the presence of a mentally subnormal brother or sister vary, as do those of their parents. In a survey of 430 siblings, Holt found that 65 (15 per cent) were said to be adversely affected. Twenty-four (5·6 per cent) were afraid of being physically attacked, and 18 (4·2 per cent) expressed resentment of their parents' attitude towards the mentally subnormal child. Six (1·4 per cent) admitted feeling ashamed at the stigma of mental subnormality and 9 (2·1 per cent) were over-burdened with domestic chores (Holt, 1957). Fowle found significant differences in adjustment between siblings of mentally subnormal children cared for at home and siblings of similar children placed in an institution. Older sisters were particularly likely to benefit from the mentally subnormal child being away from home (Fowle, 1969). This increased incidence of emotional disturbance among the siblings of mentally subnormal children has not been found by other authors (Graliker *et al.*, 1962).

The social worker has a vital role in providing support to relatives through personal counselling and advising them of help available through other agencies, both statutory and non-statutory. Many of these agencies, both local and national, are listed in an excellent publication by the Bristol Campaign for the Mentally Handicapped—*Mental Handicap in Bristol—A Review*—which was born out of the realisation that 'In the experience of many parents this period (the early years), perhaps the time when help and advice is most needed, is the time when the least help and advice is offered'.

Unfortunately, the authors of the second edition (1975) decided to confine themselves mainly to community facilities for the mentally handicapped. They published later a separate document concerning hospital provisions, thus perpetuating the 'apartheid of disability' which they so strongly condemn.

In March 1974, the King Edward's Hospital Fund made a grant of £20,000, over a period of three years, towards the cost of setting up an experimental centre at Toynbee Hall to collate and make available information about all the services available for the mentally handicapped.

In December 1971, a tax-free 'attendance allowance' was introduced by the Department of Health and Social Security, which may be claimed by disabled people living at home, and by parents with severely disabled children between the ages of 2 and 16. To become eligible for payment the person who is the subject of the claim has to be:

1. So severely disabled physically or mentally that he requires from another person, in connection with his bodily functions, frequent attention throughout the day, and prolonged or repeated attention during the night, or
2. So severely disabled physically or mentally that he requires continual supervision from another person in order to avoid substantial danger to himself or others, and . . .
   It can be shown that one or other of the above conditions has existed for at least six months prior to the claim.

Eligibility for an allowance is decided by a doctor appointed by the Attendance Allowance Board, but the claimant has the right to apply for a review within three months if an allowance is not awarded.

The families of children with I.Q.s below 50 due to congenital handicap, not permanently cared for in a residential establishment, may be entitled to financial assistance from the Family Fund, administered on behalf of the Government by the Joseph Rowntree Memorial Trust.

Local education authorities may give grants to enable mentally handicapped children to attend independent schools approved by those authorities, if they are satisfied that they themselves are unable to provide the same form of education.

The *Charities Digest* and *Municipal Charities* contain information of various charities offering help to handicapped children and the conditions of entitlement.

Mentally handicapped people aged 16 and over, not in employment, are entitled as of right to social security benefit. They may also qualify for discretionary benefits to cover items such as clothing and bedding.

The income tax child allowance, or the dependent relative allowance, may be claimed where the child or dependent relative is living at home or in temporary or permanent residential care away from home.

Mentally handicapped children under five may first come to the notice of the statutory services through the health visitors who are able to arrange for the provision of such important items as plastic pants, rubber sheeting and incontinence laundry services. Home help services are available to the mentally handicapped and are provided free by some authorities. Some mentally handicapped people may be entitled to the meals-on-wheels service, in which a main meal is provided daily at a set price. Some mentally handicapped children may be accepted with children of normal intelligence in day nurseries, staffed by nursery nurses, and others may be accepted, at the discretion of the head teacher, in nursery classes in schools run by the local authority education department. There are a number of opportunity classes and play groups, run by voluntary groups or organisations, to assist the social education of both mentally handicapped and non-handicapped children from the age of six months, until they are accepted for full-time education. In the Bristol opportunity group, activities include painting, water and sand play and use of the climbing frame. A very valuable feature of the Bristol group is the mothers' group at which experiences of caring for mentally handicapped children at home are discussed. A branch of the Toy Libraries Association loans parents toys free of charge to enable them to assess their suitability for their children, before deciding whether the expense of purchase is justified.

Play groups usually have one or more paid play-leaders, whose efforts are supplemented by those of the mothers of the children involved, who often help on a rota basis.

In Bristol, medical and other students provide a free but invaluable sitting-in service to enable relatives of the mentally handicapped to take well deserved breaks from their care. A wide range of other services by volunteers in Bristol is offered by 'The Link', the liaison section of the Social Services Department. These services include home bathing, hairdressing and shaving for the housebound, laundry help, shopping and car rides.

Education for mentally handicapped children is provided statutorily in special classes in ordinary schools and in special schools for the educationally subnormal (E.S.N.). For those who are too severely mentally or physically handicapped to attend such schools, there are special-care day centres run as joint ventures by local authority education and social service departments, and involving other services such as physiotherapy (Finnie, 1968; Morgenstern et al., 1966).

Education for mentally handicapped children is provided also by various independent schools such as the Montessori schools, which cater for a very wide range of intelligence, and the various schools based on the Rudolph Steiner method, such as St. Christopher's School in Bristol, and the Sheiling schools at Thornbury in Avon County. At St. Christopher's School, further education beyond the age of 16 is provided, where required. The Sheiling schools are run as therapeutic communities, in which staff and their own children live in family groups with the handicapped pupils. The Meldreth School at Meldreth in Cambridgeshire is run by the Spastics Society for spastics of both normal and subnormal intelligence. Ravenswood Village in Berkshire, run by a Jewish foundation, has a school for severely handicapped children (Segal, 1974).

Although the normal school leaving age is 16, head teachers have the discretion to offer to keep mentally handicapped pupils at school up to the age of 19 if they are capable of benefiting from this further education, and some mentally handicapped people attend adult education classes after this age.

Careers officers of the Youth Employment Service of the Department of Employment have a responsibility to help handicapped young people find employment suitable to their particular abilities and aptitudes. Disablement Resettlement officers have similar responsibilities with handicapped adults, including the arrangement, in suitable cases, of their attendance at Industrial Rehabilitation Units for the purposes of assessing the sort of employment for which they are most suited. Such assessment may be followed by training at a Government Training Centre or their employment by Remploy Ltd.

For those mentally handicapped people found to be permanently or temporarily unsuitable for open or sheltered employment, local authority social service departments provide occupation and further social training in adult training centres. Apart from kitchen and laundry work, trainees are occupied at craft work of various kinds and contract work, such as assembling ball-point pens, making cardboard boxes or packing crayons for private firms, and are remunerated on a piece-work basis. Trainees are allowed to earn up to £9.00, plus fare, per week without their sickness or invalidity payments being affected (Contribution to Maintenance by Hospital Patients Going out to Paid Work', HC (76) 53). A similar range of activities, as well as a drive-in car wash service, is provided for both mentally ill and mentally handicapped people by the Bristol Industrial Therapy Organisation (I.T.O.) founded by Dr. D. F. M. Early (Early et al., 1968).

Recreational facilities for the mentally handicapped are provided in the community by statutory and non-statutory organisations. Many local authorities provide youth clubs with a full range of usual activities such as dancing, films, billiards, darts, table tennis and a variety of handicrafts. Some hospitals such as Stoke Park Hospital, Bristol, run clubs for in-patients, which are also open to any mentally handicapped person in the Bristol area. The National Society for Mentally Handicapped Children started the National Federation of Gateway Clubs about 6½ years ago and now has over 250 Gateway Clubs, with thousands of members throughout the country.

Various voluntary organisation run holiday homes for mentally handicapped children and adults. These include Colwall Court in Bexhill-on-Sea, Sussex, run by the Spastics Society, the Buckets and Spades holiday home in St. Leonards-on-Sea, Sussex, and Pengwern Hall, near Rhyl, run by the National Society for Mentally Handicapped Children. In addition, the National Society for Mentally Handicapped Children run holidays in rented premises, such as special schools and guest houses, and also run adventure and caravan holidays. Their current plans include holidays for severely handicapped children who require special care. Financial help with holidays may be given under the *Chronically Sick and Disabled Persons' Act* 1970 subject to a financial assessment of need. Some local authorities provide holidays for the mentally handicapped without charge.

The National Society for Mentally Handicapped Children can provide information about holiday bungalows, flats and caravans, holiday camps and hotels which welcome families with mentally handicapped children, and the Society also organises holidays to enable mothers of mentally handicapped children to have a rest from looking after their families.

Short-term care for mentally handicapped children or adults living at home is provided during family crises in local authority hostels or in National Health Service hospitals without charge or, by some local authorities, in various private homes for the mentally handicapped.

The bulk of long-term residential care for the mentally handicapped is provided in National Health Service hospitals. In the past, many patients were admitted without having been seen previously by a member of the hospital's staff, but fortunately this practice is becoming less common, with the development of outpatient and in-patient facilities for assessing the needs of mentally handicapped and their families, and domiciliary visits by consultants at the request of general practitioners. It is not always possible to complete assessment on an out-patient basis, and in such cases, the mentally handicapped person is admitted to hospital for a period of about a month for investigation and observation by a multi-disciplinary team. In the case of small children, this will usually be carried out in a children's hospital or in a children's ward in a general hospital, with the paediatrician acting as co-ordinator of the team. A purpose-built assessment centre for children with any handicap, including mental handicap, from birth to school age, was opened at the Bristol Homoeopathic Hospital in 1973. In the case of older children and adults, the assessment is more likely to take place in a mental subnormality hospital, with the consultant psychiatrist acting as co-ordinator, as in the assessment unit opened at Stoke Park Hospital, Bristol in 1971 (Jancar, 1971). Other members of the multi-disciplinary team include child psychiatrists, clinical and educational psychologists, nurses, teachers, occupational therapists, speech and physiotherapists, radiographers, dieticians, social workers, dental surgeons and specialists in other branches of medicine, such as pathologists, geneticists, E.N.T. surgeons, ophthalmologists and orthopaedic surgeons. The purpose of the assessment is to evaluate each individual's abilities and disabilities and treatment needs, and to plan a therapeutic programme and to decide where best this can be provided. The results of the assessment are sent to the patients' general practitioner. Ideally, no mentally handicapped person should ever be admitted to hospital for long-term care unless it is generally agreed that this is the best place for him but, unfortunately, the present lack of suitable alternative residential provision makes hospital admission inevitable in a number of cases, when a crisis occurs in a family. Even so, many mental subnormality hospitals have long waiting-lists for those for whom hospital has been agreed as the most suitable form of care. Some mental subnormality hospitals provide day-care for patients who are unsuitable for the various forms of day-time community care, but who can be cared for at home at night.

The purpose of long-term care in a mental subnormality hospital is to enable each mentally handicapped person to develop to the maximum of his potential and, wherever possible, to leave hospital in due course and return to live in the community as independently as possible. For those in whom the severity of their disability prevents the attainment of this objective, the hospital aims to provide as full and free a life as is compatible with the safety of each individual, in small homely residential units, preferably single storey, to facilitate the movement in and out of those with additional physical handicaps, and their evacuation in case of fire. Unfortunately, there is insufficient ground floor accommodation in most hospitals to meet the needs of these and the increasing proportion of geriatric patients. Some hospitals, such as Princess Marina Hospital, Northampton and Balderton Hospital, Newark, provide phased care, in which a patient spends fixed periods at home and in hospital, *e.g.* one month at home and two months in hospital. At Princess Marina Hospital, the mother is sometimes admitted to hospital at the same time as her child and assists in caring for other children as well as her own, and is given instruction in particular exercises or methods of social training which need to be continued during the home phase of programmed care. This is supplemented by advice from domiciliary nurses from the hospital. Members of the same multidisciplinary team who carried out the initial assessment are available as required to give treatment throughout the patient's stay in hospital, and a number of them meet regularly at case conferences to review the patient's progress and to modify treatment or training programmes as necessary.

A most important aspect of care of the mentally handicapped is their dental hygiene. Very often it has not proved possible to arrange adequate dental care for them before they are admitted to a mental subnormality hospital. To meet this deficiency locally, regular dental surgery sessions under general anaesthesia are being developed for mentally subnormal people living at home, in addition to similar services already provided for in-patients at Stoke Park Hospital, Bristol (Flower, 1974).

For patients admitted as small children, usually the first phase of their care is concerned with habit training, which involves following a routine of toiletting before and after meals and at other set periods—on rising, during the day and before going to bed. In general, mongols are the most easily trained. Starting between the ages of 2 and 3 years, this takes another 3 years, apart from occasional lapses, and by between 7 and 9 they take themselves to the lavatory without being told. Toilet training is accompanied by training in washing and bathing, teeth cleaning and dressing. Recognition of individual face flannels and tooth brushes is facilitated by marking them with a picture of a familiar object or animal. The transition from the relative security of the pot, with the feet on the ground, to the elevated insecurity of the lavatory seat, with the legs dangling, may cause a regression in toilet training, which may be avoided by the use of an armchair attachment to the lavatory seat, which provides support and a greater feeling of security.

More severely subnormal children take progressively longer to toilet train, but with adequate nursing staff freed from ward domestic chores, this may be achieved even in cases in which it has proved impossible prior to admission, because of the numerous other demands on the mother's time in caring for her home and other members of the family.

Habit training is continued in the hospital school concurrently with sense training, which is directed at the full development of each of the senses individually and their co-ordinated use. To achieve the former, the child is taught to sort articles according to their colour and their shape and texture, first with the eyes open and then, in the last two cases, with the eyes closed. Similarly, he is taught to recognise the sounds of common articles, such as a watch ticking or the ring of a coin or glass, and various tastes and smells, with the eyes both open and closed. Co-ordination of the senses is helped, for example, by singing in unison, playing in a percussion band, by physical training, dancing, and playing games to music.

Hospital schools for the more severely mentally handicapped children are arranged as a series of nursery play groups in which Montessori principles of learning by active participation rather than by passive absorption of knowledge are followed, and in which the stress in general is on the practical rather than the academic. Subjects are taught largely for their utilitarian value and as a contribution to the maximum development of independence as the child grows up. Gunzburg has criticised the disproportionate amount of time spent in the past on teaching children to read in a purely mechanical way, without any real understanding of the subject matter or any of the pleasure derived from reading by children of higher intelligence. He has suggested that the time would be better divided between teaching a child to recognise key words with obvious practical applications, such as 'ladies' or 'gentlemen', 'bus stop' or 'cafe', and to do simple calculations necessary for checking change for small purchases (Gunzburg, 1968).

A variety of handicrafts are provided in hospital schools to cater for the wide range of different abilities shown by mentally handicapped children of apparently similar levels of intelligence in terms of I.Q. Children are encouraged in useful domestic tasks such as dusting, tidying drawers and filling water jugs. The imagination is stimulated by encouraging children to use a dressing-up box.

Social training is widened by taking children on outings into town by public transport, on which they are taught to buy their own tickets and to check their change. Visits to the shops enable them to see various foods in their natural state or as normally marketed, rather than as part of a meal mass-produced in the hospital kitchen. Birthday parties, to which children contribute by helping to lay the table and spread the butter, help their understanding of this. Television, outings to the zoo, wild life parks, pantomimes and museums help to broaden their horizons and to overcome the isolation which many people still unfortunately equate with long-term care in hospital. Some hospitals have their own swimming and hydrotherapy pools, which serve the dual purpose of providing facilities for those physically able to learn to swim and for the physically handicapped to receive physiotherapy under ideal conditions. In addition, parties of children attend public swimming baths, and a number obtain certificates of proficiency in swimming.

In the author's view, the long school holidays which are enjoyed by children of normal intelligence are inappropriate for many children of subnormal intelligence, particularly those in hospital. Unfortunately, teachers' holidays are not always staggered to enable the school to remain open during holiday periods and, as a result, the children often have to remain in the wards at these times and become an additional problem for already over-burdened nursing staff. However, in some hospitals this problem has been partially relieved with the help of volunteers who take the children on outings or on holidays. Many parents of over-active mentally handicapped children living at home also experience difficulties during school holidays, particularly if they have other children on holiday at the same time, and request temporary hospital care for the former, which is not always available. Parents' problems would be reduced if education authorities arranged holidays for such mentally handicapped children at times different from those of other children.

On leaving school, all children who are capable of benefiting from it are given vocational training for employment, first within the hospital and, in due course, in the community. At the same time, some continue their education in classes in hospital or in further education departments in the community run by local education authorities. Social training continues within the hospital and on outings. There are hairdressing salons for male and female patients and the latter are taught the use of make-up. For girls, training is mainly for domestic or laundry work. Domestic training is carried out on the wards and in domestic science units in occupational therapy departments, where cookery is also taught. A small flat, equipped like a normal home, helps patients make the transition from large-scale institution-type housework to the smaller scale type they are likely to meet in the average home. It is not usually difficult to find domestic employment for patients outside of hospital, either in private houses or in schools, hotels or other hospitals, although the increasing severity of the mental handicap of most hospital patients means that fewer are likely to be suitable for such outside employment in future. Similarly, the increasing mechanisation and speed of commercial laundries excludes many patients who are capable of working very satisfactorily in the hospital laundry at a more leisurely pace under the supervision of staff who understand their limitations.

Boys, too, are trained in domestic work which may lead to their employment as cleaners in factories or as porters in hotels and schools. Others may do a variety of unskilled jobs in open industry, or for local authorities as road sweepers or in their parks and gardens. Farming in mental subnormality hospitals has been discontinued, as a matter of policy, except where its continuance can be justified on therapeutic grounds. In the past, a graduated two-year farm training programme prepared male patients in the Stoke Park Hospital Group for unskilled employment on outside farms, where they were paid the normal wage, less a proportion agreed by the Agricultural Wages Board according to each individual's degree of disability. Again, unfortunately, increasing mechanisation of farming has made it almost impossible to find such employment nowadays for such patients. However, many patients enjoy working on the hospital farm and there is no doubt that this provides a socially acceptable outlet for the energies of some of the more aggressive patients, which might otherwise be expressed in more antisocial activities.

It is not uncommon for patients who are incapable of living without a great deal of supervision to earn on daily employment more than the nursing staff who look after them in hospital! Patients retain the balance of their earnings after deductions for essential outgoings, which include income tax, employees' social security contributions, travelling expenses, the cost of meals and any other charges arising from their employment, and a contribution for their maintenance in hospital calculated as follows: after the other deductions listed, the patient is allocated £9·00 and a quarter of the balance and the other three-quarters goes to the hospital, subject to a maximum of £16·00 per week (any excess going to the patient) (HC (76) 53).

At present, local authority provisions of hostels for the mentally subnormal is not sufficient in all parts of the British Isles to accommodate all patients who require residential accommodation outside of hospital after completing treatment and training there. Some hospitals themselves provide 'halfway houses' outside the hospital grounds in which patients, who are capable of learning their living are helped to make the transition from large scale institutional care to small group domestic type of living. Some patients are discharged from hospital to lodgings with sympathetic landladies, who receive payment from social security departments. However, it is not easy to find suitable landladies in all parts of the British Isles. A very successful boarding out scheme has been operated in North Wales by the North Wales Guardianship Scheme, which has found places outside of hospital for more than 200 mentally subnormal people from Bryn-y-Neuadd mental subnormality hospital since the scheme was founded in 1961. Landladies taking part in this scheme receive an additional 'extra care allowance' for each patient paid by his home local authority, and the patient himself receives pocket money (Vaughan, 1972).

A survey in January 1973, showed that there were at that time in England and Wales 16 'group homes' for mentally handicapped adults who were capable of living without resident staff, but with some support and supervision from outside sources, such as a warden nearby or a visiting social worker. Most of the residents had come from mental subnormality hospitals. Their ages ranged from 20 to 60 years and the majority had I.Q.s in the 50 to 70 range. All 16 homes were for residents of one sex only. Some residents went back each day to hospital to work, and a number had been sent back to hospitals or hostels during periods of disturbed behaviour (Rosen, 1973).

An increasing proportion of mentally subnormal patients in hospital are incapable, because of the severity of their mental handicap or associated disability, of employment or residence outside of hospital. A number, however, benefit from industrial therapy within the hospital, in which they are taught assembly tasks of various degrees of complexity and for which they are paid by the firms concerned on a piece-work basis. It may take several months' painstaking effort on the part of the staff to teach the patient the basic skill of any process, but once acquired the skill is usually retained and facilitates the learning of more complicated skills. It is sometimes questioned whether such work should correctly be called therapy, but the author has no doubt that it is rightly so described, provided ever-increasing output does not become an end in itself, and that it has valuable socialising effects on patients. In working as members of production teams rather than in isolation as in more traditional craft work, patients become aware of their relationship with other members of the team, and this awareness extends into other social situations, in which they become more considerate of other patients' needs. They show greater care for clothing they have bought with their earnings, and this respect for their own property extends to that of other patients and of the hospital. In some cases, the improvement in patients' appearance and behaviour is remarkable—patients who had previously been considered incapable of any useful occupation and had just sat in the wards every day deteriorating mentally, or had indulged in difficult behaviour because of boredom, show obvious pride in their achievements and a marked improvement in their behaviour (Nicoll et al., 1961; Heaton-Ward, 1966).

Craft work is provided in occupational therapy departments or on the wards for patients who prefer this to industrial therapy and covers a wide range of activities such as knitting, rug-making, painting and pottery, basket making, carpentry and metal work. Male patients may be employed on heavier industrial work, such as making breeze blocks. It is sometimes possible for patients to attend units of the Industrial Therapy Organisation or Spastics Workshops outside of hospital. On such occasions, patients may, in fact, be employed on the same type of work as is provided in hospital, but the fact of leaving the hospital each day to go to work outside is itself valuable in overcoming the patient's isolation from the community and as representing the usual practice for most employed persons.

In the past, hospitals for the mentally subnormal have depended heavily on patient labour as domestics on the wards and in the service departments such as the boot shop, laundry and serving room. However, nowadays when it is generally accepted that all patients who are capable of outside employment should not be denied the opportunity of this merely in order to staff these departments, relatively few suitable long-stay younger patients are available to the hospital for this purpose.

With the departure from hospital of the more capable patients, increasing attention is being paid to the needs of the most severely handicapped and disturbed patients, for whom it was thought, in the past, nothing could be done. Satisfying these needs involves the help of a number of skilled staff, who are, unfortunately, in very short supply, such as clinical psychologists, speech therapists, physiotherapists and remedial gymnasts, occupational therapists and chiropodists. However, the gap may be partially filled with the help of nursing staff who are willing to continue the treatment required between visits of the therapist concerned, and under her guidance.

Behaviour modification or operant conditioning programmes have been developed to help particularly children who are unable to communicate, or to assist habit training or to modify disturbed behaviour in mentally subnormal children and adults. Briefly, the principle underlying such programmes is that achievement and desirable behaviour is rewarded, and so reinforced, while the converse results in withholding of rewards (Ball, 1969). It is obviously important that the patient should learn to relate the reward to his action which has earned it and initially, in children, this involves praising the child and giving it a sweet immediately. Later, it may be possible to substitute a token, which may itself be exchanged at the hospital shop for an article of the child's choice, or kept until enough have been saved to 'buy' a more expensive article (Ayllon et al., 1968). The success of such programmes depends on the awareness of the principles involved by all the staff in contact with the patient and their consistent application of them. It is tempting, for example, in a busy ward, to give a child a sweet to stop him crying rather than when he stops—however, by the former action, the undesirable behaviour is reinforced and, therefore, its repetition is encouraged.

Considerable claims have been made for the benefits of music therapy in assisting communication with autistic children and in improving concentration, increasing the vocabulary and emotional stability of other severely mentally handicapped children (Alvin, 1965). Music also plays an important part in movement education of severely subnormal children, in which movement is used in a one to one relationship within a class as a means of communicating with children and of developing their self-awareness through their improving body awareness (Sherborne, 1969).

Animals often provide a valuable aid to communication with children and some hospitals have introduced pony riding with this in view, as well as for its considerable value in improving balance, muscle control and self confidence, particularly of children with cerebral palsy. It is remarkable how closely some severely handi-capped children, who seem quite unable to relate to adults, are able to relate to ponies and other animals. Some hospitals have links with the Riding for the Disabled Association, and the Diamond Riding Centre for the Disabled was opened in 1974 at Queen Mary's Hospital, Carshalton, Surrey by H.R.H. the Princess Anne, Patron of the Association.

In the Stoke Park Group of hospitals, valuable links with the community have been established through the gymkhanas held each year, which are open to riders from the surrounding areas. In this way, not only is entertainment provided for the patients, but, equally important, young riders are persuaded to enter the hospital and to learn more about the mentally handicapped and to lose any fear of them they may have had (Heaton-Ward, 1972).

Moral and character training is implicit in the aims of hospital care, but it is provided more explicitly in church services and in formal religious instruction and preparation for confirmation where a patient wishes this. In some hospitals for the mentally handicapped, this provision has become ecumenical (and, incidentally, economical as well!) by the willingness of priests of different denominations to take it in turns to conduct services attended by members of other denominations as well as their own. This recent economy had been anticipated by some years in at least one mental subnormality hospital in which the recreation hall was used also as a chapel, offering a choice of C. of E. at one end and T.V. at the other!

The range of recreational activities available in mental subnormality hospitals has inevitably changed as the type of patient has changed. (The author was responsible for starting the only *admittedly* mentally subnormal rugby team, now sadly defunct, when he was on the staff of Brentry Hospital in Bristol.) Gone are the days when most such hospitals were noted for their football and cricket teams, and one of the main qualifications for employment on the nursing staff was sporting ability. Nowadays, matches are less formal, but inter-hospital games are still much enjoyed by participants and spectators. Athletic sports meetings are still held annually between patient teams from hospitals of the South Western Regional Health Authority. An increasing number of hospitals now have swimming pools, which sometimes include hydrotherapy facilities for physically handicapped patients.

Television has almost completely replaced the weekly cinema shows which were a routine feature of most mental subnormality hospitals. The introduction of colour television has captured the interest of many severely subnormal patients who showed no interest in programmes in black and white. However, patients still enjoy live shows provided by visiting artistes, and outings to the pantomime or concerts, and many delight in buying transistor radios, which they carry around with them and on which they listen mostly to pop music. Dances, also, are still very popular as opportunities for patients to meet their boy-friends and girl-friends (often in their fifties and sixties!).

Patients' clubs in hospitals have already been referred to. In the Stoke Park Group of hospitals, recreational activities in the evenings and at weekends are organised by the Recreations Officer, who is a member of the nursing staff. A recent innovation has been the establishment of a branch of the Women's Institute within the group of hospitals. Its committee includes patients and it has a number of severely mentally handicapped patients among its general membership. All members take part in usual W.I. activities, and attend talks and demonstrations, visit other W.I.s in the vicinity and have annual outings which include the Ice Pantomime at Wembley.

Many mental subnormality hospitals provide holiday facilities for their long-stay patients in holiday homes and camps in the British Isles and sometimes abroad.

Voluntary organisations are making an increasing contribution to the care of the mentally handicapped in hospital. Main credit for pioneering this is due to the Leagues of Hospital Friends, who were active in this field many years before it became the fashionable object of voluntary effort. However, as the result of the widespread publicity of recent years, and the appointment of full-time Organisers of Voluntary Service to hospitals for the mentally handicapped, the pool of volunteers has been extended to include a wide range of ages and abilities, from senior pupils at school, through university and other students to older members of religious, political and other organisations. Volunteers do much to overcome the isolation of hospital patients from the wider community outside of hospital, by visiting them regularly, helping to feed the more handicapped ones, playing games with others and sharing their activities, taking them for walks or on outings from the hospital, or on holidays in their own homes or, with the help of nursing staff, to camps under canvas. At one such camp for children from the Stoke Park Group of hospitals, the camping equipment was provided and erected by members of the R.A.F. who voluntarily gave up part of their annual leave to help run the camp. For several years, children from the Stoke Park Group have helped man a float in the annual Bristol University Rag procession.

Work in selected mental subnormality hospitals has been included in the list of social work options offered by New Careers to young offenders on conviction, as an alternative to Borstal training or a prison sentence. Those opting for such work appear genuinely to enjoy it, and often show an obvious aptitude for caring for severely mentally handicapped children.

The general trend in recent years has been to divide up the large wards of mental subnormality hospitals and to create, wherever possible, mixed sex, small group care within the hospital. Mixed child and adult units have been successfully created at St. Lawrence's Hospital, Caterham, Surrey (Gibson, 1971) and at Leavesden Hospital, St. Albans, Herts. (Wertheimer, 1972), among others. In 'Greenacres', the unit at St. Lawrence's, 12 men, 12 women and 12 children share living accommodation, but have separate sleeping quarters and toilet facilities. Such an arrangement means that adult patients provide constancy of presence which is not possible with nursing staff. The children have been able to relate to a few people who have helped to put them to bed and seen to their needs, and certain affectionate bonds between children and adults have developed (Sylvester, 1973).

Unsuitable buildings frequently make the provision of small group care difficult, and a report of a multidisciplinary working party at Monyhull Hospital, Birmingham stressed the importance of 'a realistic and consistently applied training scheme' to help institutionalised patients to make best use of more homely accommodation. Provision for small group care has been the main consideration in planning new purpose-built accommodation for the mentally handicapped on a general hospital site in Sheffield. The functional unit in this provision has 24 beds, divided, in the case of children requiring substantial medical and nursing care, into three separate 'family' groups, sharing some common services with the whole unit. Each family group has 1 room with 4 beds, 1 with 2 beds and 2 single rooms. The unit for adults with similar needs has 4 rooms with 4 beds, 3 with 2 beds and 2 single rooms. Residential accommodation for children who require some continuing medical and nursing care also allows for family group care, in this case, in 3 rooms with 2 beds and in 2 single rooms. Accommodation for adults with similar needs will follow the same plan. It is intended that, wherever possible, children in the latter category should attend local authority special schools, and adults local authority adult training centres, and that both should use local recreational and other community facilities. For children and adults who are incapable of this, day care units are provided within the hospital—25 places for children and 115 places for adults. Both day care units will accept some heavily handicapped children and adults who are living at home.

The Sheffield plan includes designs for mentally handicapped people who require no continuing medical and nursing care and who could be cared for within a normal home, if such were available to them (Bartholomew, 1971).

Princess Marina Hospital, Duston, Northamptonshire, opened in

1970, was designed as a village community in which everyone could live as normal a life as possible, and to provide an integrated community service for persons with mental handicap living in the Borough of Northampton and County of Northamptonshire. An important feature of this service is the emphasis on the role of the hospital based domiciliary nurse, who attends every clinic and may assess the nursing problem at the home of the handicapped person.

The Department of Health and Social Security have published a series of Design Bulletins under the title 'Hospital Building for the Mentally Handicapped', and a Centre on Environment for the Handicapped has been established at the Hospital Centre in London, financed jointly by grants from the D.H.S.S., the King Edward's Fund for London and the Spastics Society, to give 'advice and information on the design of the environment for the handicapped' (the mentally handicapped, the mentally ill, the emotionally disturbed, the deaf, the chronic sick, the elderly and the physically disabled).

Long term residential care is provided by a number of voluntary organisations. The National Society for Mentally Handicapped Children has three training centres—Lufton Manor Rural Training Unit in Somerset, where residents receive instruction in horticulture, agriculture and animal husbandry, and Dilston Hall in Northumberland and Pengwern Hall in North Wales, where a socialisation programme for retarded men and women is followed (Lee, 1973). The National Society is currently advocating village farming communities for mentally handicapped people unable to live in open society (Grenfell, 1972). Such village communities have already been established by the CARE (Cottage and Rural Enterprises) organisation at Blackerton, near Tiverton, Devon and at Shangton in Leicestershire, and a third is planned at Norsted, near Orpington in Kent (Forbes, 1973).

The CARE villages were established to provide lifelong care for mentally handicapped children whose parents did not wish them to enter mental subnormality hospitals. Residents are cared for in cottages run on the family group principle, with 12 residents and 2 living-in staff in each cottage. Few of the staff have any formal training in the care of the mentally handicapped and a high degree of selection is applied in the choice of residents, a choice denied the hospitals criticised by the CARE organisation.

It is intended that these villages will grow by the addition of more cottages as finances allow this, so that, ultimately, they may develop virtually into the old fashioned colonies they were intended to replace! It will be interesting to see whether they are able, as they develop, to avoid the staffing problems of the statutory institutions for the mentally handicapped, and how they will be able to care, in due course, for the inevitable geriatric problems of their residents.

Ravenswood Village in Berkshire caters for lifelong care of residents with a wider range of mental handicap than the CARE villages, including severely handicapped children, who are cared for in the John F. Kennedy wing. The Camphill Villages, run by the Rudolph Steiner organisation in Yorkshire and Gloucestershire, provide long-term care for a wide range of handicaps, including mental handicap. Long-term residential care on a smaller scale is provided by various local voluntary organisations, such as the Home Farm Trust, at Frocester Manor, and Old Quarries in Gloucestershire and at Fairthorn near Sheffield. Residential training and care, initially for a period of two years, with the prospect of longer term care in suitable cases, is provided for mentally retarded boys over school age by the Molesey Venture, East Molesey, Surrey, which is described as a non-denominational home-hostel for 'exceptional' teen-age boys, and is run by the Sons of Divine Providence.

The creation of mixed sex residential units for mentally handicapped people creates problems which are, in general, in inverse proportion to the age and severity of the handicap of the residents. While all mentally handicapped men and women may have a right to love and to sexual fulfilment (Shearer, 1972), not all are capable of undertaking the responsibilities of parenthood, nor, unfortunately, can they always be relied on to make proper use of contraceptives. Under such circumstances, it may be considered justifiable to fit girls of child-bearing age with intrauterine contraceptive devices. Mattinson carried out a survey on the outcome of marriages between 64 spouses, who had all been patients at Starcross Hospital, Devon for periods from 3 to 42 years. In 12 the I.Q. was under 49 (1 between 30 and 39 and 11 between 40 and 49), in 23 it was between 50 and 59 and in 21 between 60 and 69. The I.Q. was not recorded in 8 cases. Of the 40 children of these couples, 34 were being cared for by the parents themselves. Of the 13 who were of school age, 10 were at primary school, 1 was at a secondary modern school and 2 were at a junior training centre (Mattinson, 1970). Craft, on the other hand, believes that the responsibility of parenthood is better avoided and that one or other of the partners should be sterilised.

REFERENCES

Existing facilities for the care of the mentally subnormal

Alvin, J. *Music for the Handicapped Child.* Oxford University Press, 1965.

Ayllon, T. and Azrin, N. H. *The token economy: a motivational system for therapy and rehabilitation.* Appleton-Century-Crofts, 1968.

Ball, T. S. (ed.). *The Establishment and Administration of Operant Conditioning Programs in a State Hospital for the Retarded.* State of California Department of Mental Hygiene Research Symposium No. 4, 1969.

Bartholomew, L. 'First Class Citizenship.' Mind and Mental Health, Winter 1971, 40.

Caldwell, B. M. and Guze, S. B. 'A Study of the Adjustment of Patients and Siblings of Institutionalised and non-Institutionalised Retarded Children.' Amer. J. Ment. Defic. 1960, *64*, 845.

Cameron, F. and Nicoll, S. *Industrial and Social Therapy—an Experiment.* Nursing Times Feb. 3, 1961.

Carr, J. *Young Children with Down's Syndrome.* Butterworth, 1975.

Camphill Village Trust. The Cresset (Journal of the Movement).

Charities Digest. Family Welfare Association, London.

Department of Health and Social Security. *Attendance Allowance for Adults.* Leaflet N1 181, H.M.S.O., London, 1971.

Department of Health and Social Security. *Attendance Allowance for Children.* Leaflet N1 182, H.M.S.O., London, 1971.

Department of Health and Social Security and the Welsh Office. *Help for Handicapped People.* H.M.S.O., Cardiff, 1972.

Department of Health and Social Security. *Hospital Building for the Mentally Handicapped.* Design Bulletins 1 and 2. H.M.S.O., London.

Department of Health and Social Security. 'Contribution to Maintenance by Hospital Patients going out to Paid Work.' HC (76) 53. H.M.S.O., London, March 1976.

Early, D. F. and Magnus, R. V. 'The Industrial Therapy Organisation (Bristol) 1960–1965.' Brit. J. Psychiat. 1968, *114*, 335.

Elliott, J. and Bayes, K. *Room for Improvement: a Better Environment for the Mentally Handicapped.* King Edward's Hospital Fund for London, 1972.

Farber, B. and Jenne, W. C. *Monographs of the Society for Research in Child Development.* 1963, 28, No. 7.

Finnie, N. *Handling the Cerebral Palsied Child at Home.* William Heinemann Medical Books, Ltd., London, 1968.

Flower, A. 'Dental Care in Subnormality Hospitals—A Team Approach.' Apex 1974, 2, 3, 30; 1975, 2, 4, 25.

Forbes, P. Comment. Care for the Mentally Handicapped Magazine 1973/4, 2.

Fowle, C. M. 'The Effect of the Severely Retarded Child on his Family.' Amer. J. ment. Defic. 1969, *73*, 468.

Gath, A. 'The effects of Mental Subnormality on the Family.' Brit. J. hosp. med. 1972, 147.

Gibson, J. 'Greenacres.' Brit. hosp. J. & Soc. Serv. Rev. 1971, 2028.

Graliker, B. V., Fishler, K. and Koch, R. 'Teenage Reactions to Mentally Retarded Sibling.' Amer. J. ment. Defic. 1962, *66*, 838.

Grenfell, Lord. 'Community Care of the Handicapped.' Hansard, 1972, *330*, No. 71, 1023.

Gunzburg, H. *Social Competence and Mental Handicap.* Balliere, Tindall and Cassell, London, 1968.

Hannam, C. *Parents and Mentally Handicapped Children.* Penguin Books Ltd., Harmondsworth, 1975.

Heaton-Ward, W. A. 'Activities of Benefit to the Mentally Handicapped.' Prov. Nat. Conf. Riding for the Disabled Assoc. November, 1972, p. 72.

Heaton-Ward, W. A. 'Industrial Therapy for Severely Subnormal Patients in Hospital.' Proc. IVth Int. Congr. World Fed. Occ. Therapists. July 1966, p. 95.

Holt, K. S. *The Impact of Mentally Retarded Children on their Families.* M.D. Thesis. University of Manchester, 1957.

Jancar, J. 'Assessment Unit for the Mentally Retarded.' Brist. med. chir. J. 1971, *86*, 27.

Lee, G. 'The N.S.M.H.C.'s Role in the next 25 Years.' Outreach. 1973, *3*, No. 3, 7.

Mattinson, J. *Marriage and Mental Handicap.* Duckworth, London 1970.

Mental Handicap in Bristol. A Review. Bristol Campaign for the Mentally Handicapped, Bristol, 1973. Second edition, 1975.

Morgenstern, M., Low-Beer, H. and Morgenstern, F. *Practical Training for the Severely Handicapped Child.* Spastics Society Medical Education and Information Unit in Association with William Heinemann Books Ltd. London, 1966.

Physical Environment of the Mentally Handicapped. V-Ward Design and Ward Programme. Brit. J. ment. Sub. 1972.

Princess Marina Hospital. *Serving the Mentally Handicapped in Northamptonshire. The Work of Princess Marina Hospital.* Oxford Regional Hospital Board, October, 1973.

Ravenswood Centre of Special Education. First Lecture Series in Cooperation with College of Special Education, 85 Newman Street, London W.1.

Rosen, A. 'Adult Group Homes.' Apex 1973, *1*, No. 3, 10.

Segal, S. *No Child is Ineducable.* 2nd Ed. Pergamon Press, Oxford, 1974.

Shearer, A. 'A Right to Love.' Mind and Mental Health Magazine, Summer 1972, 14.

Sherborne, V. 'Movement Education for Brian.' Special Education, 1969, *58*, No. 4.

Stevens, M. *The Educational Needs of Severely Subnormal Children.* Edward Arnold, London.

Sylvester, P. E. 'The Long-Stay Hospital—a Modern Concept.' Nursing Mirror, 1973, 136, No. 20, 34.

Tizard, J. and Grad, J. C. *The Mentally Handicapped and their Families.* Maudsley Monograph No. 7. London, 1961.

Vaughan, P. 'A Job for the Seaside Landlady.' World Medicine, 1972, March 22, 26.

'Ward Design and Ward Programme. Multidisciplinary Working Party, Monyhull Hospital, Birmingham.' Brit. J. ment. Sub. 1972, *XVIII*. Part I. Nos. 34, 48.

Wertheimer, A. 'Combating Social Handicaps.' Mind and Mental Health Magazine, Autumn 1972, 39.

Younghusband, E., Birchall, D., Davie, R. and Kelmer Pringle, M. L. (editors). *Living with Handicap.* The National Bureau for Cooperation in Child Care, London, 1970.

8 The statistics of mental subnormality

Because of the difficulty in making a definite diagnosis of mental subnormality early in a child's life in all but a small number of cases, such as Down's Syndrome (mongolism), it is not possible to state accurately its incidence (i.e. the number of new cases occurring in any population in any period, such as a year). For similar reasons, neither is it possible at a comparable age to make an accurate assessment of the prevalence (i.e. the total number of cases present in any population at any time) of mental subnormality. However, it has been generally accepted that most cases of severe subnormality should have come to light by the ages of 15–19 and that their total number then closely approximates to the true prevalence of that condition. Three recent surveys in England suggest that the prevalence rate of severe subnormality is about 4 per 1,000 (*see* Table II).

Because the severely subnormal do not live as long as the population as a whole, the prevalence of severe subnormality falls as age increases and its overall prevalence at all ages is estimated at between 2 and 3 per thousand.

Estimates of the prevalence of all degrees of mental subnormality in different parts of the British Isles have varied very much more widely over the years, reflecting, possibly, the different criteria and the difficulty of accurate assessment of all those with less severe

TABLE II
Prevalence of Severe Subnormality in the Population

Survey	Age-group	I.Q. under 50 Rate/1,000
Middlesex (Goodman and Tizard, 1962) 1960	10–14	3·61
Salford (Kushlick, 1961) 1961	15–19	3·64
Wessex (Kushlick, 1964) 1963	15–19	3·75

degrees of subnormality. However, with the exception of that for South West Scotland, those in recent years have shown much closer agreement (*see* Table III).

TABLE III
Prevalence of Mental Subnormality of all Degrees in the Population

Survey	Rate/1,000
Royal Commission on Care and Control of the Feeble-Minded (1908)	4·6
E. O. Lewis (1929)	8·57
Bristol (M.O.H. Report, 1958)	4·10
South East Metropolitan Region, 1962	3·48
London (Tizard, 1964)	4·12
Salford (Tizard, 1964)	4·44
South West Scotland (Primrose, 1966)	8·97
West Sussex (Bussey and Wild, 1969)	3·07
City and County of Bristol (Midwinter, 1972)	3·70

Surveys have tended to show a higher prevalence among the male population than among the female, *e.g.* 9·21 per 1,000 males, 7·97 per 1,000 females (Tredgold and Soddy, 1963); 10·72 per 1,000 males, 7·48 per 1,000 females (Primrose, 1966).

The only clear-cut diagnostic category possible in most of these surveys was Down's Syndrome (mongolism). The incidence rate of Down's Syndrome for the country as a whole is 1·8 per 1,000 total births, but only 55 per cent survived the neonatal period, and only

0·7 per 1,000 survived until the age of seven years (Butler and Alberman, 1969). However, the surveys in Middlesex, Salford and Wessex indicate a prevalence of Down's Syndrome of about 1 per 1,000 population (Table IV) and that in these surveys this condition accounts for between a quarter and one-third of all cases of severe subnormality.

TABLE IV
Prevalence of Down's Syndrome in the Population

Survey	Age-group	I.Q. under 50 Rate/1,000
Middlesex (Goodman and Tizard, 1962) 1960	7–14	1·14
Salford (Kushlick, 1961) 1961	15–19	0·90
Wessex (Kushlick, 1964) 1964	15–19	1·17

McCoull, in his Newcastle survey, found a prevalence rate for Down's Syndrome of 0·53 per 1,000 population and that they constituted 8·5 per cent of all retarded people (McCoull, 1971). Tredgold and Soddy (1956) had earlier reported that 5 per cent of all aments of all ages were mongols.

Estimates of cases of Down's Syndrome in mental subnormality hospitals, as a percentage of total hospital population, have ranged in recent years from 5·6 per cent to 13 per cent in different surveys (*see* Table V).

TABLE V
Cases of Down's Syndrome as Percentage of Total Hospital Population

Survey	Percentage of Cases of Down's Syndrome
Hilliard and Kirman, 1957	13
McCoull, 1964	10·01
Heaton-Ward, 1964	9·4
Primrose, 1964	5·6
Richards, 1967	9·1

A directory published by the National Society for Mentally Handi-capped Children (N.S.M.H.C., 1971) stated that there were about 10,000 hostel places for the mentally handicapped in the British Isles, equally divided between local authorities and the private sector.

At 31st December 1969, 96,024 mentally handicapped people were receiving mental health services provided by local health authorities in England. Of these, 28,428 were under the age of 16 and 67,596 were 16 and over. 42,320 (19,849 under 16; 22,471 aged 16 and over) were receiving training in local health authority training centres, and another 574 (of whom 50 were under 16) were receiving training at home. 3,932 (945 under 16; 2,987 aged 16 and over) were receiving residential care from local authorities in homes or residential training centres owned by local health authorities. 12,190 (606 under 16; 1,584 aged 16 and over) were receiving residential care from local health authorities in other homes or private households.

The Report of the Wood Mental Deficiency Committee (1929), based on E. O. Lewis's survey, estimated that 2–3 per 1,000 pop-ulation would require hospital care. The Hospital Plan for England and Wales (1962) gave a figure of 1·3 per 1,000 population. This figure corresponds closely with the figure of 1·2 mental subnor-mality hospital beds per 1,000 population in England and Wales reported by the author in 1970 (*see* Table VI).

It will be seen, however, that in some parts of the country the dis-tribution of beds is very uneven with high concentrations in the South West Metropolitan Region (1·8 beds per 1,000) and in the South Western Region (1·9 beds per 1,000), and a low concentra-tion in the Liverpool Region (0·7 beds per 1,000). For both Scotland and Northern Ireland the figures were 1·4 beds per 1,000 population and there are not the same extreme regional variations in Scotland as in England.

The Department of Health and Social Security's Statistical and Research Report Series No. 12 (1976) showed that during 1973 there had been a total of 11,501 admissions to hospitals and units for the mentally handicapped under Regional Hospital Boards in England (*see* Table VII).

The age distribution of the 2,881 male and 2,158 female long-term admissions is shown in Table VIII.

TABLE VI

Hospital Beds for the Mentally Subnormal

Regional Hospital Board	Population of Region	Mental Subnormality Beds at 31.12.70	Beds per 1,000 Population at 31.12.70
Newcastle	3,039,153	3,815	1·2
Leeds	3,221,630	3,855	1·2
Sheffield	4,681,620	5,108	1·1
East Anglian	1,747,000	1,711	1·0
N.W. Metropolitan	4,169,870	5,757	1·4
N.E. Metropolitan	3,365,700	3,536	1·1
S.E. Metropolitan	3,499,951	4,145	1·2
S.W. Metropolitan	3,679,340	6,753	1·8
Oxford	1,936,790	2,229	1·2
South Western	3,160,140	6,081	1·9
Welsh	2,733,870	2,652	1·0
Birmingham	5,104,653	5,751	1·1
Manchester	4,571,910	6,289	1·4
Liverpool	2,218,000	1,632	0·7
Wessex	2,010,000	1,862	0·9
TOTAL	49,139,627	61,176	1·2
Scotland (mental deficiency)			
Eastern	420,000	634	1·5
Northern	197,657	229	1·2
North Eastern	475,000	659	1·4
South Eastern	1,182,098	1,458	1·2
Western	2,950,000	4,388	1·5
TOTAL	5,224,755	7,368	1·4
Northern Ireland (special care)	1,425,462	2,024	1·4

Of the 11,501 total admissions, 10,949 (95·2 per cent) were informal, and the remainder subject to detention under various sections of the Mental Health Act 1959.

3,455 admissions were as the result of referral by Social Services Departments, 2,657 by a psychiatrist, 1,148 by a general practitioner and only 303 by the Courts. The source of referral in the remaining 3,938 (34·2 per cent) of cases was listed as 'other persons and authorities'.

TABLE VII
Admissions During 1973 (all ages) England

	All		First		Readmissions	
	Male	*Female*	*Male*	*Female*	*Male*	*Female*
Total admissions	6,460	5,041	913	634	5,547	4,407
Short-term admissions	3,579	2,883	424	366	3,155	2,517
Long-term admissions	2,881	2,158	489	268	2,392	1,890

Of the 3,579 male short term admissions, 78·4 per cent were placed in the severely subnormal category, 21·2 per cent in the subnormal category and 0·4 per cent in 'other mental categories'.

For the 2,881 long term admissions the figures were: severely sub-

TABLE VIII
Long-term Admissions During 1973

Age group, years	Number of Admissions					
	All		First		Readmissions	
	Male	*Female*	*Male*	*Female*	*Male*	*Female*
	England					
All ages	2,881	2,158	489	268	2,392	1,890
0–1	36	18	15	5	21	13
2–4	132	99	38	27	94	72
5–9	420	259	80	42	340	217
10–14	392	268	79	42	313	226
15–19	485	309	116	45	369	264
20–24	329	207	41	24	288	183
25–34	423	364	49	29	374	335
35–44	241	219	23	17	218	202
45–54	227	204	29	18	198	186
55–64	126	139	17	13	109	126
65–74	59	59	2	3	57	56
75 and over	11	13		3	11	10

normal 51·1 per cent, subnormal 35·3 per cent and 'other mental categories' 13·6 per cent.

Of the 2,883 female short term admissions, 74·8 per cent were placed in the severely subnormal category, 24·8 per cent in the subnormal category and 0·4 per cent in 'other mental categories'.

For the 2,158 female long term admissions, the figures were: severely subnormal 51·5 per cent, subnormal 36·4 per cent and 'other mental categories' 12·1 per cent.

Of the 6,234 male and 5,086 female patients discharged from hospital during 1973, 70·5 per cent and 69·8 per cent, respectively, had been in hospital under 3 months, but 2·1 per cent of males and 3·0 per cent of females had been there for 30 years or more.

McCoull analysed the reasons for admission to hospital in the Newcastle Hospital Region of 4,806 cases of mental retardation during 1966–1971 (*see* Table IX). Primrose analysed 502 consecutive admissions to the Royal Scottish National Hospital from 1st January 1968 to 31st December 1970 (*see* Table X).

At the end of the period under review, 324 (64·5 per cent) of patients remained in hospital (*see* Table XI).

Primrose commented that half of the patients in the Social Group had an I.Q. over 50 and could fit into hostel-type accommodation in the community. On the other hand, judging from the reasons why the hospital was being asked to admit mental defectives, he did not think that the further provision of community facilities was likely to make much difference to the demand for ad-

TABLE IX
Admissions to Hospitals in the Newcastle Region 1966–1971

Reason for Admission	Percentage
Rejection by parents	2·2
Inability of parents to cope	41·3
Illness or death of parents	19·1
Difficulties with sibs. other than illness	0·5
Unsuitable housing	0·4
No day facilities or other accommodation	0·2
Needing continuous medical or nursing care	15·4
For temporary care	3·0
Disturbed behaviour	17·8

TABLE X
Admissions to the Royal Scottish National Hospital 1.1.68 to 31.12.70

| | Age on admission (years) | | | | |
Reason for admission	0·5	5–16	Over 16	Total	Percentage
Antisocial behaviour	7	93	151	251	50
Severe physical disability	50	20	17	87	17
Psychiatric*	7	18	15	40	8
Social	2	7	30	39	8
Temporary	16	28	31	75	15
Transfers from other hospitals	—	2	8	10	2
Total	82	168	252	502	100
Percentage	16	34	50	100	

* including 18 patients with hyperkinetic behaviour.

TABLE XI
Proportion of Admissions remaining in the Royal Scottish National Hospital at 31.12.70

| | Admissions | Discharges inc. Deaths | Remaining | |
Reason for Admission	No.	No.	No.	Percentage of group
Antisocial behaviour				
(a) High grade	209	70	139	66·5
(b) Low grade	42	5	37	88·1
Severe physical disability	87	25	62	71·2
Psychiatric	40	7	33	82·5
Social	39	4	35	90·0
Temporary	75	67	8	10·7
Transfers from other hospitals	10	—	10	100
Total	502	178	324	64·5

mission, however much it might help to alleviate the strain on those families who continued to look after their handicapped relatives.

A census of mentally handicapped patients in hospitals in England and Wales, carried out by the Department of Health and Social Security at the end of 1970, revealed the following figures (*see* Table XII).

TABLE XII

Census of Mentally Handicapped Patients in Hospitals in England and Wales at the end of 1970

Age	Mental Category			
	Subnormality and Severe Subnormality	Severe Subnormality	Subnormality	Percentage Severe Subnormality
All ages	64,173	47,294	16,879	74
Under 2	44	43	1	98
2–4	407	371	36	91
5–9	2,310	2,171	139	94
10–14	3,583	3,253	330	91
15–19	4,919	4,038	881	82
20–24	6,048	4,839	1,209	80
25–34	10,243	8,166	2,077	80
35–44	9,518	7,076	2,442	74
45–54	10,453	7,374	3,079	71
55–64	9,552	6,081	3,471	64
65+	7,096	3,882	3,214	55

(It should be noted that these figures include mentally subnormal patients resident in hospitals for the mentally ill rather than for the mentally handicapped.)

By December 31st, 1973 the total number of patients in hospitals and units for the mentally handicapped in England had fallen to 51,797 and there had been a corresponding fall in Wales.

The overall figure of 26 per cent subnormality reflects the fall in the numbers of patients in hospital with this degree of handicap revealed in surveys carried out in England and Wales over the past twenty years (*see* Table XIII).

A survey carried out by Primrose in 1964 in Lennox Castle and associated hospitals in Scotland showed a less dramatic fall in the proportion of feeble-minded (subnormal) patients—from 44 per cent in 1939 to 32·8 per cent in 1964. Although the percentage of idiots (I.Q. less than about 25) was considerably lower than that in the other recent surveys already referred to, it had increased from 2·9 per cent to 11·9 per cent since 1939, and the increase in the proportion of imbeciles (I.Q. approximately 25 to 50), from 53·2 per cent to 55·1 per cent, corresponded closely to the upward trend in the other surveys.

The changing pattern of admissions under 16 years of age

TABLE XIII
Patients in Hospital

Source	I.Q. 52–85	I.Q. 20–51	I.Q. <20
O'Connor and Tizard, 1950	52·3	41·7	5·9
McCoull and Slupinski, 1954	25·3	50·3	24·3
McCoull, 1966	19·5	51·6	28·9
	>50	25–50	<25
Heaton-Ward, 1964	14·4	52·9	32·6
Heaton-Ward, 1971	9·4	53·7	36·9

suggests that the percentages in all I.Q. ranges may correspond more closely in future with those in the surveys in England and Wales, viz. the percentage of idiots increased from 3 per cent to 45 per cent, of imbeciles from 17·8 per cent to 36 per cent, while that of feeble-minded decreased from 79·3 per cent to 18·75 per cent between 1940–44 and 1960–64.

The average ages of patients of different degrees of mental sub-normality resident in Lennox Castle, St. Lawrence's and Stoke Park Hospital are shown in Table XIV.

It will be seen from Table XII that, while about 7,000 of the patients were children under the age of 16, over 16,500 were aged 55 and over. (The latter figure had risen from 5,000 in 1954 to 13,000 in 1968).

TABLE XIV
Average Age of Resident Population of Three Hospitals in England and Scotland

		Grade of Patient		
Survey		Idiot	Imbecile	Feeble-minded
Lennox Castle, 1964 (Primrose)	Males	13·85	37·84	36·04
	Females	17·64	40·43	39·66
St. Lawrence's, 1966 (Richards)	Males	30·7	36·1	48·9
	Females	26·7	43·2	45·2
		I.Q. < 25	I.Q. 26–50	I.Q. 50+
Stoke Park Hospital, 1964 (Heaton-Ward)	Males	29·0	39·5	33·5
	Females	32·0	45·2	46·0

Table XV shows that there had been an increase in the number of patients over the age of 60 in the Stoke Park Hospital Group between 1964 and 1971, in all I.Q. ranges, with the exception of females with I.Q.s over 50. These increases reflect the increase in the life expectation of the mentally subnormal as a result of improved medical care, which has been reported by a number of writers, including the author (see Table XVI).

TABLE XV
Stoke Park Hospital Group—Patients over Age 60

		31.7.64	31.1.71
I.Q. < 25	Males	5	18
	Females	10	18
I.Q. 25–50	Males	23	65
	Females	80	138
I.Q. > 50	Males	2	11
	Females	30	29
	Total	150	279

TABLE XVI
Life Expectation of Mentally Subnormal in Hospital in Different I.Q.
Ranges

Survey	I.Q. 50+		I.Q. 25–50		I.Q. < 25	
	M.	F.	M.	F.	M.	F.
Primrose (1966)	45·1	47·5	45·1	46·2	25·2	25·0
Heaton-Ward (1967)	—	—	40·0	49·8	28·8	29·3
McCurley, et al. (1972)	58·1	49·8	37·1	40·8	17·3	14·0

A later survey in the Stoke Park Hospital Group suggested that the life expectation of severely subnormal patients in hospital was continuing to rise (*see* Table XVII).

TABLE XVII
Average Age of Mentally Subnormal Patients at Death

		Males	Females
I.Q. < 25	1.8.54–31.7.64	28·8	29·3
	1.8.64–31.1.71	27·5	35·5
I.Q. 25–50	1.8.54–31.7.64	40·0	49·8
	1.8.64–31.1.71	54·4	56·7
I.Q. > 50	1.8.54–31.7.64	37·9	56·8
	1.8.64–31.1.71	46·2	61·2

The lower average age of death of males with I.Q.s over 50 compared with females in the same I.Q. range, and of both males and females in the I.Q. 25 to 50 range may, in fact, represent a true lower expectation of life for male patients in hospital in this group, as those males who are physically fit are likely to have been discharged before reaching this age, whereas females of similar I.Q., and both male and females in the lower I.Q. range tend to remain in hospital.

As in surveys of incidence and prevalence of mental subnormality, the only clear-cut major diagnostic category in which life expectancy has been consistently estimated is Down's Syndrome. The age distribution of cases of Down's Syndrome resident in hospital in two surveys is shown in Tables XVIII and XIX.

TABLE XVIII
Age Distribution of Cases of Down's Syndrome Resident in Hospital I.Q.
Unspecified

Survey	Age in Years							
	0–10	11–20	21–25	26–35	36–45	46–55	56–65	Total
Primrose, 1964								
Males	10	15	2	9	11	4	2	53
Females	13	7	1	8	8	3	4	44

[Journal of Mental Deficiency Research]

The average of all cases in Primrose's survey was 26·6 years and of those in a survey by Richards at St. Lawrence's Hospital in 1967, 28·2 years. In the author's survey, the average age of the 42 males with I.Q.s below 25 was 25·3 years, and that of the 46 females, 29·3 years. For the I.Q. range 25 to 50 the average was 28·3 years for both males and females. Thus, there was not the striking difference in average age between the two I.Q. ranges noted in the Stoke Park patients as a whole (*see* Table XV).

Primrose (1966) found that the average age at death of patients in hospital with Down's Syndrome was 31·7 years. McCurley, Mackay and Scally (1972) reported figures of 25·6 years for males

TABLE XIX
Age Distribution of Cases of Down's Syndrome Resident in Hospital

Survey	Age in Years						
	⩽10	11–20	21–30	31–40	41–50	51–60	Total
			I.Q. < 25				
Heaton-Ward, 1964							
Males	5	9	12	10	5	1	42
Females	6	7	8	12	10	3	46
			I.Q. 25–50				
Heaton-Ward, 1964							
Males	6	4	4	15	2	3	34
Females	2	7	8	10	2	2	41

[British Journal of Psychiatry]

TABLE XX
Deaths—Causes of Death (Primrose)

Causes	Feeble-minded		Imbecile		Idiot		Total	
	Male	Female	Male	Female	Male	Female	Male	Female
Cardio-Vascular	20	36	43	49	1	1	64	86
Cerebro-Vascular	2	8	15	13	1	—	18	21
Pulmonary Infection (Non T.B.)	18	22	44	54	18	26	80	102
Tuberculosis	14	7	21	13	2	3	37	23
Neoplasm	15	21	17	22	2	2	34	45
Nephritis	8	3	5	19	—	1	13	23
'Surgical Abdomen'	5	3	13	13	3	—	21	16
Miscellaneous Infection	6	5	11	12	1	4	18	21
Status Epilepticus	9	6	11	1	6	2	26	9
Known Brain Disease	4	4	5	4	6	12	15	20
'Organic Brain Disease'	3	6	5	5	4	2	12	13
Diabetes Mellitus	—	1	1	2	—	—	1	3
Accident	—	—	7	1	—	—	7	1
Senility	2	2	5	2	—	1	7	5
Marasmus	—	—	2	1	2	—	4	3
Miscellaneous	1	2	5	6	—	2	6	10
TOTAL	107	128	210	217	46	56	363	401

and 30·5 years for females. Commenting on a survey covering the period 1955–1967, Richards observed that the mongol death rate was lower than that of non-mongols of comparable mental grade up to the age of 50 years. In the 50–59 year age group the mongol rate rose sharply to nearly four times that of non-mongols, and no mongol in his survey had reached the age of 70 years.

In his Wessex survey, Kushlick found that 1 in 3 severely mentally handicapped children in hospital also suffered from epilepsy, that 1 in 5 had defects of vision or hearing and that 1 in 20 was blind. Of the severely mentally handicapped adults in hospital, 1 in 5 suffered from epilepsy, 1 in 5 had defects of vision or hearing and almost 1 in 3 had speech defects. McCoull, in his Newcastle survey, quotes a figure of 32·1 per cent prevalence of epilepsy among mentally subnormal patients of all ages in hospital and a prevalence of 24·3 per cent of visual and hearing defects, either occurring singly or in combination in the 6,258 mentally subnormal people

TABLE XXI
Causes of Death (McCurley *et al.*)

Cause of death	Feeble-minded	Imbecile	Idiot	Total
Cardiovascular	26	48	5	79
Cerebrovascular	11	12	4	27
Congenital heart disease	—	3	1	4
Rheumatic heart disease	—	1	—	1
Respiratory infections	7	57	61	125
Other infections	2	4	5	11
Status epilepticus	2	21	7	30
Cerebral (hydrocephalus, micro-cephalus, cerebral degeneration)	1	2	18	21
Neoplasms	10	6	1	17
Leukaemia	—	2	—	2
Trauma	1	4	—	5
Asphyxia	—	3	—	3
'Surgical Abdomen' (peritonitis, intestinal obstruction)	1	4	1	6
Miscellaneous	6	16	4	26
Unknown	1	1	—	2
TOTAL	68	184	107	359

[Journal of Mental Deficiency Research]

surveyed (including 1,321 E.S.N. pupils). Primrose found that one third of all patients surveyed had suffered from epilepsy.

It will be seen from Tables XX and XXI that cardiovascular, cerebrovascular and pulmonary infection accounted for between 48·5 per cent (Primrose) and 66 per cent (McCurley *et al.*) of all deaths. It will also be seen that status epilepticus accounted for 4·6 per cent and 8·3 per cent, respectively, of deaths in the two surveys despite modern treatment.

Comparative costs of patient care in acute hospitals and mental subnormality hospitals
Table XXII shows the average net cost per in-patient week in acute

TABLE XXII
Costs of Acute Hospitals per In-Patient Week

| Region | Average Net Cost per In-patient per Week | | | |
	1970–1 (£)	1971–2 (£)	1972–3 (£)	1973–4 (£)
English Regions (Teaching Hospitals excluded)				
Newcastle	59·73	76·49	88·05	—*
Leeds	63·97	75·80	87·70	103·94
Sheffield	68·33	80·24	96·25	113·17
East Anglian	73·79	86·89	99·55	114·27
N.W. Metropolitan	65·62	76·57	88·50	111·33
N.E. Metropolitan	70·03	82·07	92·89	—*
S.E. Metropolitan	67·83	80·33	93·50	111·85
S.W. Metropolitan	71·68	81·73	94·80	111·24
Oxford	72·23	85·79	98·71	116·95
South Western	69·88	82·03	97·04	115·29
Birmingham	66·48	77·83	91·03	—*
Manchester	60·95	71·59	85·12	96·25
Liverpool	59·01	70·95	81·06	90·88
Wessex	71·68	81·82	94·71	—*
National Average for Regions (England)	66·70	78·58	91·54	108·19
Wales	67·44	80·78	92·72	110·00
London Teaching Hospitals	96·74	112·25	129·14	154·22
Provincial Teaching Hospitals	87·84	99·53	115·66	131·50

* Figures not available

hospitals in each region of England and in Wales for the years
1970–71, 1971–72, 1972–73 and 1973–74.

Table XXIII gives similar information for mental subnormality
hospitals for the years 1970–71, 1972–72 and 1972–73.

It will be seen that, while the average weekly cost in acute, non-
teaching hospitals in 1973–4 was £75·51 higher in England,
£71·99 higher in Wales and £97·82 higher in provincial teaching
hospitals than that in mental subnormality hospitals, the percentage

TABLE XXIII

Costs of Mental Handicap Hospitals per In-patient Week

Region	1970–71		1971–72		1972–73	
	Cater-ing	Total	Cater-ing	Total	Cater-ing	Total
Newcastle	2·62	18·52	3·03	23·30	3·43	26·08
Leeds	2·80	18·99	3·35	24·21	3·82	28·75
Sheffield	2·69	19·16	3·21	24·18	3·75	28·62
East Anglian	2·99	20·85	3·66	27·62	4·19	32·67
N.W. Metropolitan	2·70	18·31	3·08	22·88	3·55	27·18
N.E. Metropolitan	2·87	20·55	3·30	26·36	3·77	30·98
S.E. Metropolitan	2·64	17·47	3·05	22·70	3·43	28·65
S.W. Metropolitan	2·59	18·82	2·98	24·11	3·38	27·04
Oxford	3·03	23·42	3·54.	28·82	4·11	33·55
South Western	2·71	17·66	3·32	22·45	3·69	26·28
Birmingham	2·43	17·93	2·93	22·94	3·34	26·90
Manchester	2·73	18·23	3·16	23·03	3·46	26·66
Liverpool	2·42	23·65	2·98	28·65	3·41	32·51
Wessex	2·63	18·71	3·08	22·97	3·46	27·28
Average for England	2·68	18·86	3·15	23·39	3·58	28·02
Wales	2·94	21·49	3·72	28·34	4·01	31·94
Provincial Teaching Hospitals	—	—	4·20	29·04	4·47	32·63

rise over the year 1972–3 was 18·19 per cent for acute, non-
teaching hospitals, compared with 20·2 per cent for mental subnormality hospitals in England and 18·6 per cent, compared with 19·0
per cent in Wales (see Table XXIV).

It will also be seen that average weekly catering costs in mental

TABLE XXIV
Average Net Cost per In-patient per Week

	Acute Non-teaching Hospitals (£)	Mental Handicap Hospitals (£)
ENGLAND		
1973–1974	108·19	33·68
1972–1973	91·54	28·02
Increase	16·65	5·66
% Increase	18·19%	20·2%
1972–1973	91·54	28·02
1971–1972	78·58	23·39
Increase	12·96	4·63
% Increase	16·5%	19·8%
1971–1972	78·58	23·39
1970–1971	66·70	18·86
Increase	11·88	4·53
% Increase	17·8%	24·0%
WALES		
1973–1974	110·00	38·01
1972–1973	92·72	31·94
Increase	17·28	6·07
% Increase	18·6%	19·0%
1972–1973	92·72	31·94
1971–1972	80·78	28·34
Increase	11·94	3·60
% Increase	14·8%	12·7%
1971–1972	80·78	28·34
1970–1971	67·44	21·49
Increase	13·34	6·85
% Increase	19·8%	31·9%

subnormality hospitals rose by 13·6 per cent in England, but by only 7·8 per cent in Wales between 1971–2 and 1972–3. However, it should be noted that there had been major percentage rises in Wales between 1970–71 and 1971–72, both in average weekly costs and in catering costs—31·9 per cent and 26·5 per cent respectively—over the figures for the year 1970–71. There are no comparable figures for 1973–4 due to a revised method of calculation.

REFERENCES

The statistics of mental subnormality

Bristol. *The Health in Bristol*, M.O.H. Report. H.M.S.O., London, 1958.

Bussey, A. and Wild, D. 'Mental Subnormality in West Sussex.' Med. Office., 1969, *122*, 26, 331.

Butler, N. R. and Alberman, E. D. *British Perinatal Mortality Survey, 1958. Perinatal Problems, Second report*. Livingstone, Edinburgh & London, 1969.

Directory of Residential Accommodation for the Mentally Handicapped in England, Wales and N. Ireland. National Society for Mentally Handicapped Children, London, 1971.

Goodman, N. and Tizard, J. 'Prevalence of Imbecility and Idiocy among Children.' Brit. med. J. 1962, *1*, 216–219.

Heaton-Ward, W. A. 'The Life Expectation of Mentally Subnormal Patients in Hospital.' Brit. J. Psychiat. 1968, *114*, No. 517, 1591–1592.

Hilliard, L. T. and Kirman, B. H. *Mental Deficiency*. Churchill, London, 1957.

Hospital Costing Returns, 1971–2, H.M.S.O., London, 1973.

Hospital Costing Returns, 1972–3, H.M.S.O., London, 1974.

Kushlick, A. *Subnormality in Salford*, pp. 18–48 in Susser, M. W. and Kushlick, A. *A Report on the Mental Health Services of the City of Salford for the year 1960*. Salford Health Department, 1961.

Kushlick, A. 'The Prevalence of Recognised Mental Subnormality of I.Q. under 50 among Children in the South of England with Reference to the Demand for Places for Residential Care.' Proc. Conf. I.S.S.M.D., Copenhagen, 1964.

Lewis, E. O. *Report on an Investigation into the Incidence of Mental Deficiency in Six Areas, 1925–1927*. Report of the Mental Deficiency Commission, Part IV. H.M.S.O., London, 1929.

McCoull, G. M. *Report on the Newcastle upon Tyne Regional Aetiological Survey (Mental Retardation) 1966–71*.

McCoull, G. M. and Slupinsky, L. 'Assessment of 1011 Patients in a Mental Deficiency Hospital.' Brit. med. J. 1954, *2*, 341.

McCurley, R., Mackay, D. N. and Scally, B. G. 'The Life Expectation of the Mentally Subnormal under Community and Hospital Care.' J. ment. Defic. Res. 1972, *16*, 57.

Midwinter, R. E. 'Mental Subnormality in Bristol.' J. ment. Defic. Res. 1972, *16*, 48–56.

National Health Service. A Hospital Plan for England and Wales. H.M.S.O., London, 1962.

O'Connor, N. and Tizard, J. 'A Survey of Patients in Twelve Mental Deficiency Institutions.' Brit. med. J. 1954, *1*, 16.

Primrose, D. A. A. 'Natural History of Mental deficiency in a Hospital Group and in the Community it Serves.' J. ment. Defic. Res., 1966, *10*, Part 3, 159–189.

Report of the Royal Commission on Care and Control of the Feeble Minded, 1908, Vol. VIII, Part VI. H.M.S.O., London.

Richards, B. W. 'Age Trends in Mental Deficiency Institutions.' J. ment. Defic. Res. 1969, *13*, Part 3, 171–183.

Richards, B. W. and Sylvester, P. E. 'Mortality Trends in Mental Deficiency Institutions.' J. ment. Defic. Res. 1969, *13*, Part 4, 276–292.

Statistical Report Series. No. 12. *In-Patient Statistics from the Mental Health Enquiry for the Year 1969*. H.M.S.O., London, 1971.

The Needs of Mentally Handicapped Children. Report of a Working Party Set up by the Paediatric Society of the South East Metropolitan Region 1962. Millbrook Press, London.

Tizard, J. *Community Services for the Mentally Handicapped*. Oxford University Press, 1964.

Tredgold, R. F. and Soddy, K. *Textbook of Mental Deficiency*, 9th Edition. Balliere, Tindal and Cox, London.

Tredgold, R. F. and Soddy, K. *Mental Retardation*, p. 17. Balliere, Tindall and Cassell, London, 1963.

9 Educational establishments and institutes for research into mental subnormality

There is at present no University Chair in Mental Subnormality in any medical school in the British Isles, and the importance attached to teaching the subject to undergraduates varies greatly according to the interest of the Professor of Psychiatry or Mental Health. However, the present Director of the Institute of Mental Subnormality in Birmingham is a consultant psychiatrist—Dr. G. B. Simon. The objects of this Institute, founded in 1972, are to promote and advance study and research into all matters relating to mental subnormality ... 'The Institute is very active in promoting courses and seminars on a wide range of subjects related to mental subnormality for members of various professions working in the field'. The Institute for Research into Mental Retardation in London was founded in 1966 on the initiative of the Research Advisory Panel of the National Society for Mentally Handicapped Children, for the 'scientific study of the causes of mental retardation; of methods of prevention; of the education and training of the mentally retarded; and to improve the care and provisions for the mentally retarded in society'. In 1973, the Institute was renamed the Institute for Research into Mental and Multiple Handicap, and is now run by mutual agreement with the Spastics Society, who have given considerable financial support. The present Executive Director of the Institute is Dr. Peter Woodford, a biochemist.

In 1968, the Hester Adrian Research Centre for the Study of Learning Processes in the Mentally Handicapped was established within the University of Manchester and, in 1973, its Director, Peter Mittler, a psychologist, was appointed to the newly established Chair of the Education of the Mentally Handicapped at that University.

There are a number of research projects in the Mental Handicap field financed by the Medical Research Council in various parts of the country. However, such financial support constitutes only a small fraction of the mere 8 per cent of the total financial budget allocated by the Council for research in all fields of mental disorder.

The National Association for Mental Health (now MIND) pioneered training courses for teachers of the mentally handicapped before these became the responsibility of the Training Council. Such courses are now run by teacher training colleges. However, MIND is still active in organising courses for a wide range of professional and voluntary workers in the field of mental handicap.

The King Edward's Fund for London makes an invaluable contribution by providing a forum at the Hospital Centre in London, at which many professions can meet to discuss mutual problems in the care of the mentally handicapped. Such meetings led to the formation in 1973 of A.P.M.H.—the Association of Professions for the Mentally Handicapped. The same year saw the foundation of the British Association for the Retarded with a rather wider membership as reflected in its following objectives:

> To promote the interest of the mentally handicapped of all ages through increasing understanding of the personal, family, social, educational, training, vocational, and medical aspects of the problem and to unite in a sense of common purpose, parents, professional workers, politicians and all those who, in any capacity lay or otherwise, are involved in the well-being of mentally handicapped people.

REFERENCES

Educational establishments and institutes for research into mental subnormality

Mittler, P. (Ed.). 'Hester Adrian Research Centre—A Report for Teachers'. Suppl. Teaching and Training, Summer, 1970.

10 Legal aspects of the care of the mentally subnormal

A. ENGLAND AND WALES

THE MENTAL HEALTH ACT 1959

The Mental Health Act 1959, for all practical purposes, is applicable only to England and Wales, and all references to sections of that Act apply to all types of mental disorder except where specifically stated.

The Mental Health (Scotland) Act 1960, will be outlined in the following chapter, in which reference will be made also to the *Mental Health Act (Northern Ireland)* 1961.

Various sections of these Acts have been repealed or amended by subsequent legislation. These sections are marked below with an asterisk and the effect of the subsequent legislation is stated at the end of the first relevant section.

PART I

Section 2 effects the dissolution of the *Board of Control*.
Section 3 establishes in place of the Board of Control:

MENTAL HEALTH REVIEW TRIBUNALS

Under the *Mental Health Act* 1959, there is one Mental Health Review Tribunal for each Regional Hospital Board Area (now Regional Health Authority).

Each Tribunal consists of *legal members* approved by the Lord Chancellor, *medical members* appointed by the Lord Chancellor after consultation with the Minister of Health, and a *number of other persons* appointed by the Lord Chancellor, after consultation with the Minister, as having such experience in administration, such knowledge of social services, or such other qualifications or experience as the Lord Chancellor considers suitable.

The *Chairman* of the Tribunal is appointed by the Lord Chancellor, and must be *a legal member.*

For the purposes of any proceedings under the *Mental Health Act* 1959, a Mental Health Review Tribunal must consist of a *minimum of three persons* appointed by the Chairman—one from the legal members, one from the medical members, and one from the members who are neither legal nor medical members. If the Chairman is unable himself for any reason to appoint the members, this function is carried out by another member appointed by the Chairman for this purpose and, in the absence of the Chairman, one of the other legal members nominated by him acts as President of the Tribunal.

A member of a Mental Health Review Tribunal for one area may be appointed to serve on a Mental Health Review Tribunal for any other area as though he were a member of the other Tribunal.

PART II

LOCAL AUTHORITY SERVICES

Functions of Local Health Authority

* Section 6. This section confirms local health authorities' functions, under Section 28 of the *National Health Service Act* 1946, to provide residential accommodation for the care and after-care of

---

* These sections were repealed by the *Health Services and Public Health Act* 1968 and local health authorities' responsibilities were later transferred from local authorities' Health Departments to their Social Service Departments by the *Local Authority Social Services Act* 1970.

mentally disordered persons, to provide occupation and training facilities for them, and to undertake their guardianship under the *Mental Health Act* 1959. It also authorises the local health authority to appoint officers to act as *mental welfare officers* for the purpose of the Act.

* Section 10. This section requires the local health authority to visit, in hospital or nursing home, mentally disordered children or young persons, where parental rights have been assumed by the Children's Department of the local authority, mentally disordered persons subject to their guardianship, and those whose nearest relatives' rights have been transferred to the local health authority.

Duty of Local Education Authority

Sections 11, 12 and 13. These sections were repealed by the *Education (Handicapped Children) Act* 1970, which made local education authorities responsible for providing education for all children of school age, *irrespective of their level of intelligence.*

PART III

MENTAL NURSING HOMES AND RESIDENTIAL HOMES

Sections 14–17. These sections impose on the local health authorities responsibility for the registration and inspection of '*mental nursing homes*' in their area to ensure that conditions imposed by the local health authority itself or by the Minister are being fulfilled.

The local authority is authorised (Section 22) also to inspect premises registered under the *National Assistance Act* 1948 as a residential home for mentally disordered persons, if at any time it has reasonable cause to believe that any mentally disordered patient therein is not under proper care.

HOSPITAL CARE AND GUARDIANSHIP

Informal Admission of Patients to Hospital

Section 5. This section *permits* the informal admission to any hospital or mental nursing home of any patient who requires treatment for mental disorder. By inference from subsection 2 of this section, a patient informally admitted may be detained in hospital at his parents' or guardian's request until the age of 16 years, whatever his own wishes in the matter may be. However, there is no provision in the Act for the detention in hospital of an informally admitted severely subnormal person (who is by definition incapable of living an independent life or of guarding himself against serious exploitation) over the age of 16 years for even a few hours pending the making of alternative arrangements for his care outside hospital. This, in the author's submission, is a real defect of the Act, which could lead to charges of wrongful detention if this section were strictly interpreted. Experience in the past has suggested that strict legal interpretations are often considered to be more important than a patient's welfare.

PART IV

COMPULSORY ADMISSION TO HOSPITAL AND RECEPTION INTO GUARDIANSHIP

Admission for Observation

Section 25. This section *authorises the detention in hospital for observation* (with or without other medical treatment) *for a period not exceeding twenty-eight days*, of any patient suffering from a mental disorder, *provided* it can be shown that his mental disorder warrants this and that it is in the interests of his own health or safety or of the protection of others.

Section 27. An *application for admission for observation* may be made to the managers of the hospital, either *by the nearest relative* or *by a mental welfare officer*, who must have seen the patient personally within a period of fourteen days ending with the date of the application.

Section 28. The application has to be founded on the *written recommendations* in the prescribed form, signed on or before the date of application, *of two medical practitioners* who have personally examined the patient together or at an interval of not more than seven days. One of these medical recommendations must be given by a practitioner approved by the local health authority as having special experience in the diagnosis or treatment of mental disorder. Unless this practitioner has himself previous acquaintance with the patient the other recommendation must, if practicable, be given by a medical practitioner with such acquaintance. The recommendations may be given either separately or as a joint recommendation signed by both practitioners (Section 27).

The patient must be admitted to hospital within a period of fourteen days, beginning with the date on which he was last examined by a practitioner before giving his medical recommendation (Section 31).

Except where the application is for admission to a mental nursing home or to private beds in a hospital, one of the medical recommendations may be given by a practitioner on the staff of the hospital to which the patient is to be admitted. In addition to these limitations a medical recommendation may not be given by any of the following persons:

a. The applicant.
b. A partner of the applicant or of a practitioner by whom another medical recommendation is given for the purposes of the same application.
c. A person employed as an assistant by the applicant or by any such practitioner as aforesaid.
d. A person who receives or has an interest in the receipt of any payments made on account of the maintenance of the patient, or by the husband, wife, father, father-in-law, mother, mother-in-law, son, son-in-law, daughter, daughter-in-law, brother, brother-in-law, sister, sister-in-law of the patient or of any such person as aforesaid, or of a practitioner by whom another medical recommendation is given for purposes of the same application.

ADMISSION FOR TREATMENT

Section 26. This section *authorises the detention in hospital for treatment* (in the first instance, *for a period not exceeding one year* (Section 43)), of a patient of *any* age suffering from mental illness or *severe* subnormality; or from *psychopathic disorder* or *subnormality if under the age of 21 years, provided* that it can be shown that his mental state warrants this and that it is in the interests of his own health or safety or of the protection of others.

Section 27. An *application for admission for treatment* under Section 26 may be made either *by the nearest relative* (as defined by Section 49) of the patient or *by a mental welfare officer* after consultation with the nearest relative (and *not against his expressed objection*), unless consultation is not reasonably practicable or would involve unreasonable delay. The applicant must have seen the patient personally within a period of fourteen days ending with the date of the application and must, if the patient is suffering from psychopathic disorder or subnormality, state his age or that he is believed to be under the age of 21 years, if his exact age is not known.

Section 28. In addition to the general requirements as to *medical recommendations* under the application for observation procedure, described above, the following requirements apply specifically in the case of the application for admission for treatment procedure under Section 26:

The recommendation must state whether other methods of dealing with the patient are available, and, if so, why they are not appropriate. Both recommendations must describe the patient as suffering from the *same* form of mental disorder, although either or both may describe him as suffering from other forms, in addition.

The patient must be admitted to hospital within a period of fourteen days, beginning with the date on which he was last examined by a practitioner before giving his medical recommendation (Section 31).

The patient may apply to a *Mental Health Review Tribunal* within a period of six months, beginning with the day of his admission or with the day on which he attains the age of 16 years, whichever is the later (Section 31).

ADMISSION FOR OBSERVATION IN CASE OF EMERGENCY

Section 29. This section authorises the *mental welfare officer* or *any relative of the patient*, in any case of urgent necessity, to apply for the patient's detention in hospital for observation under Section 25 if full compliance with the provisions of that section would involve unreasonable delay. The applicant must have seen the patient personally within a period of three days ending with the date of application.

The application may be founded on *one* medical recommendation only, given, if practicable, by a practitioner with previous acquaintance with the patient and signed on or before the date of the application.

The patient must be admitted to hospital within a period of three days beginning with the date on which he was examined by the medical practitioner giving the medical recommendation or with the date of the application, whichever is earliest (Section 31).

Under this emergency procedure a patient may be detained for seventy-two hours only, unless a second medical recommendation (subject to the limitations defined in Section 28 as regards the practitioner's relationship with the applicant or the practitioner giving the other recommendation) is given and received by the managers within that period.

APPLICATION IN RESPECT OF PATIENTS ALREADY IN HOSPITAL

Section 30. This section *authorises the detention in hospital for a period of three days of an informal admission*, on the written report to the managers of the hospital by the *responsible medical officer* (the medical practitioner in charge of the case), that it appears to him that an application should be made for the patient's admission to hospital under one of the compulsory procedures in earlier sections.

GUARDIANSHIP

* Section 33. This section *authorises the reception into the guardianship* of either a local health authority or of any other person, including the applicant himself, approved by the local health authority, of any person suffering from mental disorder which warrants his reception into guardianship, *provided* that it is in the interests of the patient or for the protection of other persons. The same age limits apply in psychopathic disorder or subnormality as in the case of applications for admission for hospital treatment under Section 26 and also the same general provisions as to applications and medical recommendations. However, in the case of guardianship the application is made to the local health authority named as guardian or to the local health authority for the area in which the person named resides, with a statement that he is willing to act as guardian.

* Section 34. The *application* has to be forwarded to the local health authority within a period of fourteen days beginning with the

* See footnote on page 162.

date on which the patient was last examined by a medical practitioner before giving a medical recommendation. If accepted by the local health authority the application immediately confers on the authority or person named as guardian the same powers over the patient as would be the case if they or he were the father of the patient and the patient were under the age of 14 years.

The patient may apply to a *Mental Health Review Tribunal* within a period of six months beginning with the day on which the application is accepted, or with the day on which he attains the age of 16 years, whichever is the later.

PATIENTS' CORRESPONDENCE

Section 36. Authorises the responsible medical officer (*and no one else*) to withhold from a patient detained in hospital any postal packet addressed to him if it is calculated to interfere with the patient's treatment or to cause him unnecessary distress.

The responsible medical officer is required to return the packet to the sender if he can be identified.

The section also authorises the responsible medical officer to withhold from the Post Office any postal packet addressed by a patient in hospital either if the addressee has specifically requested this in writing to the managers of the hospital or to the responsible medical officer, or if it appears to the responsible medical officer that the packet would be unreasonably offensive to the addressee, or is defamatory of other persons (*other than persons on the staff of the hospital*), or would be likely to prejudice the interests of the patient. No one, apart from the responsible medical officer, has any authority to open and examine a postal packet from a patient detained in hospital, and he may do so only if, in his opinion, the patient's mental disorder is calculated to lead him to send a communication of the type referred to. However, *no one* has any authority to open, examine, or withhold from the Post Office a postal packet addressed to any of the following:

1. The Minister.
2. Any Member of the Commons House of Parliament.
3. The Master or Deputy Master or any other officer of the Court of Protection.
4. The managers of the hospital.

5. Any other authority or person having power to discharge the patient (apart from authorities or persons with powers of discharge of patients concerned in criminal proceedings only).

6. A Mental Health Review Tribunal: at any time the patient is entitled to apply to that Tribunal, and to any other class of persons as the Minister may prescribe by regulations.

The provisions of this section apply similarly to *patients undergoing treatment informally* in hospital or in a mental nursing home (Section 134) and to *patients subject to guardianship*, with the substitution of 'guardian' for 'managers of the hospital' and 'guardian or any other person authorised by the guardian' for 'responsible medical officer'.

LEAVE OF ABSENCE FROM HOSPITAL

Section 39. The section *authorises the responsible medical officer to grant, for any period, leave of absence* to a patient liable to be detained in hospital, subject to any condition he considers necessary in the interests of the patient or for the protection of other persons, including the requirement that the patient shall remain during his absence in the custody of any person authorised in writing by the managers of the hospital.

A patient may not be recalled to hospital from leave of absence after he has ceased to be liable to be detained in hospital or *after the expiration of the period of six months* beginning with the first day of his absence on leave, *provided* he has not returned to hospital, or been transferred to another hospital under the provisions of the Mental Health Act during this period and *provided* he is not absent without leave at the expiration of this period.

ABSENCE WITHOUT LEAVE

* Section 40. This section *authorises the taking into custody and the return to hospital* by any mental welfare officer or any officer on the staff of the hospital, by any constable, or by any person authorised in writing by the managers of the hospital, of any patient absent without leave from the hospital or failing to return to the hospital at the expiration of a period of authorised leave or if recalled

* See footnote on page 162.

from leave or absenting himself without permission from any place where he is required to reside as a condition of leave.

Similarly, this section *authorises the taking into custody and return to his required place of residence* by any officer on the staff of a local health authority, by any constable, or by any person authorised in writing by the guardian or a local health authority, of any patient subject to guardianship who absents himself without the leave of his guardian from his required place of residence.

Psychopathic and subnormal patients *over the age of twenty-one* on the first day of absence without leave may be dealt with in this way at any time *within a period of six months* beginning with that day, but *in any other case* this period is limited to *twenty-eight days*. After these periods have expired the patient ceases to be liable to be detained or subject to guardianship.

TRANSFER OF PATIENTS

* Section 41. This section *authorises the continued detention of patients liable to detention when they are transferred from one hospital to another*, the *transfer to the guardianship of another local health authority* (or of any person approved by such an authority) *of any person subject to guardianship*, or the *transfer into guardianship of a patient liable to detention in hospital, or vice versa*.

A patient who has attained the age of 16 years, transferred from guardianship to hospital in this way, may apply to a *Mental Health Review Tribunal* within the period of six months beginning with the day on which he is transferred.

If a guardian dies or is unwilling to continue as guardian, the guardianship of the patient thereupon rests in the local authority pending the appointment of another guardian. The functions of a guardian, temporarily incapacitated by illness or any other cause, may be transferred during his incapacity to the local health authority or any other person approved by that authority.

A County Court, on application by a mental welfare officer, may order that the guardianship of a patient be transferred to a local health authority or to any other person approved by that authority,

* See footnote on page 162.

if it appears that the current guardian has performed his functions negligently or in a manner contrary to the interests of the patient (Section 42).

DURATION OF AUTHORITY FOR DETENTION OR GUARDIANSHIP AND DISCHARGE OF PATIENTS

* Section 43. This section *limits the authority for detention in hospital or under guardianship to a period not exceeding one year*, beginning with the day the patient was admitted to hospital or the guardianship application accepted. However, it authorises the detention or guardianship for a *further period of one year* and, *subsequently, for periods of two years* at a time if, within a period of two months ending with the last day of these periods, the responsible medical officer reports to the managers of the hospital, or if the nominated medical attendant of a patient under guardianship reports to the responsible local health authority in the prescribed form, that continued detention is necessary in the interests of the patient's health or safety or for the protection of others or that guardianship is necessary in the interests of the patient or for the protection of other persons.

The managers or local health authority are required to notify patients over the age of 16 years of each renewal of authority and the patient may apply to a *Mental Health Review Tribunal* within the period for which the authority is renewed.

SPECIAL PROVISIONS AS TO PSYCHOPATHIC AND SUBNORMAL PATIENTS

Section 44. This section *terminates the authority for detention or guardianship* of a psychopathic or subnormal patient upon his attaining the age of 25 years, *unless*, in the case of a patient detained in hospital, the responsible medical officer, within the period of two months ending on the patient's twenty-fifth birthday, furnishes to the managers a report in the prescribed form, that it appears to him that the *patient would be likely to act in a manner dangerous to other persons or to himself* if released from hospital.

* See footnote on page 162.

The managers are required to inform the patient and nearest relative of this report, and both have the right within a period of twenty-eight days beginning with the patient's twenty-fifth birthday to apply to the *Mental Health Review Tribunal.*

DISCHARGE OF PATIENTS

* Section 47. This section *authorises the following persons to make an order discharging a patient from detention or guardianship*:

The *responsible medical officer* or the managers of the hospital in the case of a patient detained in hospital for *observation*
The responsible medical officer, the managers of the hospital, or the *nearest relative* in the case of a patient detained for treatment
The *responsible medical officer,* the *responsible local health authority,* or the *nearest relative* in the case of a patient subject to guardianship
The *registration authority* in the case of a patient liable to be detained in a *mental nursing home* for *observation* or *treatment* or the *Regional Hospital Board*** if the patient is maintained there under a contract with that Board.

All these powers may be exercised by *any three or more members* of the authorities authorised to act on their behalf.

RESTRICTIONS ON DISCHARGE BY THE NEAREST RELATIVE

Section 48. This section *requires the nearest relative to give not less than seventy-two hours' notice in writing* to the managers of the hospital *of an order to discharge a patient liable to detention in hospital* and *authorises the continued detention of the patient, against the nearest relative's wishes,* if the responsible medical officer reports to the managers, *within the period of notice,* that in his opinion the patient would be *likely to act in a manner dangerous to others or himself if discharged.* It also denies the relative the right to order discharge again *during a period of six*

---

* See footnote on page 162.
** The Regional Hospital Board's powers under this section were transferred to the Regional Health Authority in April, 1974.

months beginning with the date of the responsible medical officer's report, but requires the relative to be informed of the report and confers on him the right to apply to a *Mental Health Review Tribunal* within the period of twenty-eight days beginning with the day on which he was informed.

Section 52. This section *authorises a County Court*, upon application, *to order that the functions of the nearest relative be transferred*, under circumstances defined in the section, to any other person specified in the application, who, in the opinion of the Court, is a proper person to act as the patient's nearest relative.

Such an application may be made by *any* relative of the patient, by any other person with whom the patient is residing or was last residing before admission to hospital, or by a mental welfare officer.

This section *confers on the nearest relative* of a patient liable to detention or subject to guardianship the *right to apply to a Mental Health Review Tribunal* within the period of twelve months beginning with the date of the order under this section and in any subsequent period of twelve months.

PART V

ADMISSION OF PATIENTS CONCERNED IN CRIMINAL
PROCEEDINGS AND TRANSFER OF PATIENTS UNDER SENTENCE

* Section 60. This section *authorises a Court of Assize or Quarter Sessions*** (in the case of a person convicted of an offence other than one for which the sentence is fixed by law), or a *Magistrates' Court* (in the case of a person convicted of an offence punishable on summary conviction) *to order that person's admission to, and detention in, a specified hospital or to place him under the guardianship of a local health authority* or of any other specified person approved by a local health authority, provided that the Court is satisfied on the written or oral evidence of *two* medical practitioners that the offender is suffering from mental illness, psychopathic disorder, subnormality or severe subnormality which

* See footnote on page 162.
*** As a result of the *Courts Act* 1971, the powers of the Courts of Assize and Quarter Sessions were transferred to Crown Courts.

warrants this, and that, having regard to all the circumstances, this is the most suitable method of dealing with the case. The Court must also be satisfied that the hospital specified will be able to admit the patient within a period of twenty-eight days beginning with the date of the making of the order, or that the local health authority or other person specified is willing to receive the offender into guardianship.

A *Magistrates' Court* may make an order under this section of the Act *without convicting a person* suffering from mental illness or *severe* subnormality provided the Court is satisfied he did the act.

**** Section 61. This section *authorises a Juvenile Court* (in the case of a child or young person brought before the Court under Section 62 or Section 64 of the *Children and Young Persons Act 1938) to make a hospital order or guardianship order, provided* that the Court is satisfied that the child or young person is in need of care or protection, or that his parent or guardian is unable to control him and that the conditions which are required under Section 60 for the making of a hospital order or guardianship order are, so far as is applicable, satisfied in the case of the child or young person.

The Court must also be satisfied that the *parent or guardian understands* the results which will follow from the order and *consents* to its being made.

Section 63. This section *cancels the power of the nearest relative to order discharge of a patient admitted to hospital as a result of a Court order* and *removes the age limits to the detention of psychopathic and subnormal patients in hospital or under guardianship.* However, it *authorises the patient to apply to a Mental Health Review Tribunal* within the period of six months beginning with the date of the order or with the day on which he attains the age of 16 years, whichever is the later, and authorises the nearest relative to make a similar application within the period of twelve months beginning with the date of the order and in any subsequent period of twelve months.

Section 64. This section *authorises the patient's detention in a place of safety pending his admission to hospital within a period of*

**** This section was repealed by the *Children's and Young Persons Act* 1969 and the Juvenile Courts' power to make a hospital or guardianship order is now conferred by Section 1(3) of that Act.

twenty-eight days beginning with the day on which the hospital order was made by the Court.

*** Section 65. This section *authorises a Crown Court or County Court to impose an order restricting the patient's discharge and any of the following special restrictions,* either indefinitely or for a specified period, where this is considered necessary for the protection of the public, *provided* that the medical evidence of *at least one* of the medical practitioners was given orally in Court:

> During the period that discharge is restricted, the normal limit to the duration of the authority for detention does not apply and *no application can be made to the Mental Health Review Tribunal.* The *consent of the Secretary of State is necessary* before the patient can be transferred to another hospital or to guardianship or vice versa or before he can be granted leave, and he can be recalled from leave at any time while the order restricting discharge is in force. The Secretary of State's consent is also necessary before the patient may be discharged by any of the persons who normally have this power.

Unfortunately, Courts do not always ascertain, before making an order under Section 65, that the receiving hospital is able to implement its requirements. *These restrictions are, in the author's view, quite inappropriate in an open hospital, which is trying to follow a therapeutic rather than custodial role.*

Section 66. *Authorises the Secretary of State to terminate the order restricting discharge* if he is satisfied that it is no longer required for the protection of the public. It also authorises him, during the period of an order restricting discharge, to discharge the patient either absolutely or subject to conditions and, in the latter case, to recall him to hospital at any time while the order restricting discharge is still in force.

Under this section the *Secretary of State is required to refer to a Mental Health Review Tribunal for their advice* within two months of receiving a written request to do so from a patient subject to an order restricting his discharge, which has been in force for a year or more. The patient may subsequently request this once during each period during which he could have applied to a Mental Health Review Tribunal had the order restricting his discharge not been in

*** See footnote on Section 60.

force. However, a patient recalled to hospital after being conditionally discharged may, in addition, make a request to the Secretary of State six months after the date of his recall to hospital.

*** Section 67. *Authorises a Magistrates' Court*, on conviction of a person over the age of 14 years of an offence punishable on summary conviction with imprisonment, *to commit him in custody to Quarter Sessions to be dealt with if it appears to the Court that an order restricting discharge should be made.* The Court of Quarter Sessions may make a hospital order with or without an order restricting discharge or may deal with the offender in any other manner the Magistrates' Court might have dealt with him.

*** Section 68. *Authorises the Magistrates' Court to order the patient's admission to hospital* (with the hospital's consent) *instead of committing him in custody, pending his appearance at Quarter Sessions.* Such an order has the same effect as if the patient had been admitted to hospital subject to an order restricting his discharge.

Section 69. *Authorises a patient*, subject to an order restricting his discharge made by a Court of Quarter Sessions or under Section 67, *to appeal against the order to the Court of Criminal Appeal*, who may deal with the appeal as though it were also an appeal against the hospital order itself.

This section was repealed by the *Criminal Justice Act* 1967.

*** Section 70. *Authorises a patient* subject to a hospital order or guardianship order made by a Magistrates' Court without convicting him *to appeal against the order to Quarter Sessions*; it also *authorises a child or young person* brought before a Juvenile Court as in need of care or protection or as beyond the control of his parent or guardian *to appeal to Quarter Sessions* against such hospital or guardianship order as the Court may make. His parent or guardian may similarly appeal.

The right of appeal of a child or a young person is now conferred by Section 2(12) of the *Children and Young Persons Act* 1969.

Section 72. *Authorises the Secretary of State to direct the transfer of a person serving a sentence of imprisonment to a hospital* (*not* a mental nursing home) *if* he is satisfied on the reports of at least two medical practitioners that the person is suffering

*** See footnote on Section 60.

from mental illness, psychopathic disorder, subnormality, or severe subnormality, which warrants the detention of the patient in hospital for medical treatment and that this is in the public interest. *At least one* of the medical practitioners giving reports must be approved by the local health authority as having special experience in the diagnosis or treatment of mental disorders. Each medical practitioner must describe the patient as suffering from the same one form of mental disorder, although either or both may describe him as suffering from other forms as well. A direction under this section is valid for a period of fourteen days beginning with the date on which it was given.

Section 73. *Authorises the Secretary of State*, if he is satisfied on similar reports to those required under Section 72 that a person is suffering from mental illness or severe subnormality, which warrants the detention of the patient in hospital for medical treatment, *to order that person's transfer to hospital* from the various types of custody specified in the section or from civil imprisonment or from detention in prison as an alien. Except where the patient falls within the last two categories the restrictions of Section 65 apply to him (after his transfer to hospital) (Section 74).

Section 75. *Authorises the Secretary of State to direct the transfer back to prison of any patient* subject to an order restricting his discharge on notification by the responsible medical officer that he no longer requires treatment for mental disorder, *provided the period of his prison sentence has not expired.*

Section 76. *Similarly authorises the Secretary of State* to take this step under similar circumstances *in the case of patients transferred to hospital under Section 73.* This section also *authorises a Court to make a hospital order* (with or without an order restricting discharge) in the case of a patient specified under Section 73 if it appears impracticable or inappropriate to bring him before the Court, *provided* the Court is satisfied on the oral evidence of *at least two medical practitioners* (one approved by the local health authority) that the person is suffering from mental illness or severe subnormality which warrants his detention in hospital for medical treatment and that it is proper to make such an order.

* Section 79. *Authorises the Secretary of State to direct that a*

* See footnote on page 162.

child or young person detained in an approved school should *be placed under the guardianship of a local health authority* or of any such other person approved by a local health authority *if* he is satisfied on the reports required under Section 72 that the child or young person is suffering from mental illness, psychopathic disorder, subnormality or severe subnormality, which warrants the reception of the patient into guardianship under this Act and that this is in the public interest.

As a result of the *Children and Young Persons Act* 1969, *the Secretary of State no longer has powers to make guardianship orders under this section.* However, he has power under Section 27 (3) of the 1969 Act to require a local authority to comply with his directions in relation to a particular child *provided* that, in his opinion, the protection of members of the public makes it necessary. (Approved schools are now known as Community Homes.)

PART VI

REMOVAL AND RETURN OF PATIENTS WITHIN UNITED KINGDOM, ETC.

These matters are dealt with in Sections 81 to 96, subject to a number of consequential amendments resulting from the later *Mental Health (Scotland) Act* 1960, and the *Mental Health Act (Northern Ireland)* 1961.

PART VII

SPECIAL HOSPITALS

Section 97. *Authorises the Minister of Health to provide special hospitals* under his control and management (Section 98) for persons subject to detention who, in the opinion of the Minister, require treatment under conditions of special security on account of their dangerous, violent, or criminal propensities.

Section 99. *Authorises the Minister to direct the transfer of any patient from a special hospital to any other type of hospital.*

PART VIII

MANAGEMENT OF PROPERTY AND AFFAIRS OF PATIENTS

This is dealt with in Sections 100 to 121, which are principally concerned with the appointment by the Lord Chancellor of *'nominated judges'*, the *Master and Deputy Master of the Court of Protection* and *Medical* and *Legal Lord Chancellor's Visitors* and the appointment by any of the foregoing of a receiver and the functions and powers of each in the management of the property and affairs of patients while they are mentally disordered.

There have been minor consequential amendments of this part of the Act as a result of the *Administration of Justice Act* 1969 and the *Courts Act* 1971.

PART IX

MISCELLANEOUS AND GENERAL

Powers and Proceedings of Mental Health Review Tribunals

Section 122. *Requires all applications to Mental Health Review Tribunals to be made in writing* to the appropriate Tribunal for the area in which the hospital or nursing home in which the patient is detained is situated or in which the patient is residing under guardianship.

Section 123. *Authorises a Mental Health Review Tribunal to order a patient's discharge from detention* if they are satisfied that the patient is not suffering from mental illness, psychopathic disorder, subnormality, or severe subnormality and that it is not necessary, in the interests of his health or safety or for the protection of others, for him to be detained and that he is not likely to act in a manner dangerous to other persons or himself. Similarly, a *Mental Health Review Tribunal may direct a patient's discharge from guardianship* if they are satisfied that it is not necessary in his interests or for the protection of others for him to remain under guardianship.

If they do not order discharge, a Mental Health Review Tribunal may direct that the form of mental disorder specified in the application order or direction be amended to a more appropriate form if they are satisfied that the patient is suffering from this.

ILL-TREATMENT OF PATIENTS

Section 126. *Renders it an offence* for any officer on the staff of a hospital or mental nursing home, for anyone otherwise employed there, or for any of the managers *to ill-treat or wilfully neglect a patient receiving treatment* for mental disorder *as an in-patient*, or on the premises of the hospital or home while the patient is attending there for treatment for mental disorder *as an out-patient*. It is also an offence for any individual to ill-treat or wilfully neglect a mentally disordered person while he is subject to his *guardianship* under the Act or in his custody or care.

The *penalties* for the above offences are, *on summary conviction*, a term of imprisonment not exceeding six months, or a fine not exceeding £100·00, or both, or, *on conviction on indictment*, a term of imprisonment not exceeding two years, or a fine, or both.

Amendment of Sexual Offences Act 1956

Section 127. *Amends the Sexual Offences Act 1956*, in that it makes it an offence for a man to have unlawful sexual intercourse with a woman suffering from severe subnormality (but not with a subnormal woman, except under Section 128), *provided* he knows or has reason to suspect her to be severely subnormal.

SEXUAL INTERCOURSE WITH PATIENTS

Section 128. *Renders it an offence* for an officer on the staff of a hospital or mental nursing home, for anyone otherwise employed there, or for any of the managers, *to have unlawful sexual intercourse on hospital premises* with a woman receiving treatment for mental disorder there *either as an in-patient* or *as an out-patient*.

It is also an offence for a man to have unlawful sexual intercourse with a mentally disordered woman subject to his guardianship or otherwise in his custody or care under this Act or as a resident in a residential home for mentally disordered persons.

In each case under this section it must be shown that the man knew or had reason to suspect that the woman was a mentally disordered person.

No action may be taken under this section without the consent of the Director of Public Prosecutions.

The penalty for this offence on *conviction or indictment* is a term of imprisonment not exceeding two years.

ASSISTING PATIENTS TO ABSENT THEMSELVES WITHOUT LEAVE

Section 129. *Renders it an offence to induce or knowingly assist a patient detained in hospital or subject to guardianship under this Act to absent himself without leave* or to escape from legal custody or knowingly to harbour a patient absent without leave or to assist him to prevent, hinder, or interfere with his being taken into custody or returned to hospital or where he should be under guardianship.

The *penalties* for the above offences are, *on summary conviction*, a term of imprisonment not exceeding six months or a fine not exceeding £100·00, or both, or *on conviction on indictment*, a term of imprisonment not exceeding two years, or a fine, or both.

AUTHORITY TO SEARCH AND REMOVE PATIENTS

Section 135. *Authorises a Justice of the Peace to issue a warrant authorising a constable to enter*, if need be by force, any premises within his jurisprudence specified in the warrant, and, if thought fit, *to remove from there to a place of safety*, pending arrangements for his treatment or care, any person (who need not be named in the warrant) whom the magistrate has, on information sworn by a mental welfare officer, reasonable cause to suspect to be suffering from mental disorder and to have been or to be ill-treated, neglected, or not kept under proper control or to be living alone and unable to care for himself. *The constable must be accompanied* in the execution of the warrant by a *mental welfare officer* and by a *medical practitioner*.

This section also *authorises a Justice of the Peace*, on the sworn evidence of any constable or any other person authorised under this Act to take a patient to any place or to take into custody or retake a patient, *to issue a warrant authorising any named constable to enter any premises*, if need be by force, and *to remove from there any patient liable to be taken or retaken, provided* admission to the premises has been refused or if such a refusal is apprehended. The constable *may* be accompanied in the execution of the warrant by a *medical practitioner* or by *any person authorised* under the Act to take or retake the patient.

A patient removed to a '*place of safety*' under this section may be detained there for a period not exceeding seventy-two hours.

A '*place of safety*' is defined as residential accommodation provided by a local authority under Part III of the *National Health Service Act* 1946, or under Part III of the *National Assistance Act*

1948, a hospital as defined in this Act, a police station, a mental nursing home or residential home for mentally disordered persons, or any other suitable place, the occupier of which is willing temporarily to receive the patient.

MENTALLY DISORDERED PERSONS FOUND
IN PUBLIC PLACES

Section 136. *Authorises a constable to remove to a place of safety an apparently mentally disordered person* in immediate need of care or control, found by him in a place to which the public have access, *provided* he considers it necessary in the interests of that person or for the protection of other persons.

A person removed in this way may be detained in the *place of safety* for a period *not exceeding seventy-two hours* so that he may be examined by a medical practitioner and interviewed by a mental welfare officer and any necessary arrangements made for his treatment or care.

CRIMINAL RESPONSIBILITY

The fact that a person is suffering from one of the forms of mental disorder described in the Mental Health Act *1959, whether or not he is subject to a hospital detention order or guardianship, is not of itself a defence to a criminal or civil charge.* However, under the circumstances described in Section 60, a Magistrates' Court may, in the case of a person suffering from mental illness or severe subnormality, order his detention in hospital or reception into guardianship under the Act, without convicting him. In other cases, a mentally disordered person may be found *unfit to plead* because he is incapable of understanding the charge against him, or instructing his counsel, and in this case he is not put on trial but ordered to be detained until Her Majesty's pleasure be known.

If a mentally disordered person is fit to plead to a criminal charge he may be found *legally insane* if it can be shown that his mental disorder was at the time he committed the offence such that he did not know what he was doing, or, if he did, that he did not know that what he was doing was wrong (the so-called M'Naghten Rules). Upon finding a person legally insane the Court orders him to be detained until Her Majesty's pleasure be known.

CONTRACTS

A contract entered into by a subnormal or severely subnormal person is binding upon him and upon the person contracting with him, unless it can be shown that the former person was incapable of understanding the terms of the contract and the other person knew that his mental state was such that he did not understand what he was doing. If both these conditions are fulfilled, the contract entered into becomes voidable at the option of the subnormal or severely subnormal person or of his committee or trustees.

TESTAMENTARY CAPACITY

Legally, *the ability of the subnormal or severely subnormal person to execute a valid will is governed by the same conditions as in the case of the mentally ill.* Briefly, a will is valid only if the testator is able at the time he makes it to recall and keep clearly in his mind the nature and extent of his property and the persons who have claims on his bounty, his judgment and will being so unclouded as to enable him to determine the relative strength of these claims.

MARRIAGE

There is no law to prevent the mentally subnormal from marrying, but a marriage is voidable under the *Matrimonial Causes Act* 1950, if at the time of the marriage either of the parties was suffering from mental disorder within the meaning of the *Mental Health Act* 1959, of such a kind or to such an extent as to be unfitted for marriage and the procreation of children or subject to recurrent attacks of insanity or epilepsy *provided* that the petitioner was at the time of the marriage ignorant of the facts alleged, that the proceedings were instituted within a year from the date of the marriage and that marital intercourse, with the consent of the petitioner, has not taken place since the discovery by the petitioner of the existence of the grounds for a decree. Mental disorder, of course, includes subnormality or severe subnormality.

REPRESENTATION OF THE PEOPLE ACT 1949

The fact that a subnormal or severely subnormal person is detained in hospital under an order does not, of itself, prohibit him from voting provided his name appears on the Register of Voters for the constituency which includes his place of residence immediately *before* his admission to the hospital.

B. SCOTLAND

THE MENTAL HEALTH (SCOTLAND) ACT 1960

The provisions of the *Mental Health (Scotland) Act* 1960 differ from those of the *Mental Health Act* 1959, in the following main respects:

The numbering of sections dealing with similar provisions does not necessarily correspond in the two Acts.

PART I

Section 1 repeals the *Lunacy (Scotland) Acts* 1857 to 1913, and the *Mental Deficiency (Scotland) Acts* 1913 and 1940.

Section 2 establishes in place of the *General Board of Control for Scotland*, whose dissolution is effected by Section 3:

THE MENTAL WELFARE COMMISSION FOR SCOTLAND

The Act requires that the Mental Welfare Commission shall consist of *no fewer than seven and not more than nine commissioners*, including its *Chairman*. It specifies that at least one commissioner shall be a *woman*, at least three shall be *medical practitioners*, and that one shall have been for a period of at least five years either a *Member of the Faculty of Advocates* or a *solicitor*.

The Commissioners are appointed by Her Majesty on the recommendation of the Secretary of State, and *members of the Civil Service are specifically barred* from membership of the Commission.

A *quorum* of the Mental Welfare Commission is defined as *four* Commissioners, including at least' one medical commissioner.

Section 4. This section *defines the functions and duties of the Mental Welfare Commission*, which include many of those formerly undertaken by the General Board of Control. Thus, the Mental Welfare Commission has the general function of protecting the persons and interests of those whose mental disorder prevents their doing so adequately themselves. For this purpose the Commission has *authority to discharge* such patients from detention in hospital or guardianship and a duty to enquire into any case where there may be ill-treatment, deficiency in care or treatment, or improper detention of a mentally disordered person, or a risk of loss or damage to his property. The Commission, represented by at least one medical member, is *required to visit regularly and to grant private interviews on request* to patients detained in hospital or subject to guardianship, and to draw the attention of the hospital board of management or local authority to any apparent shortcomings of the type specified above concerning any patient under their care.

Authority is imposed on the Commission to advise the Secretary of State on any matter arising out of the Act which he may refer to it and to draw his attention to any matter under the Act of which it feels he should be aware.

TYPES OF MENTAL DISORDER

Section 6. This section *defines 'mental disorder'* as 'mental illness or mental deficiency however caused or manifested'. That is to say, the *Mental Health (Scotland) Act* 1960 recognises only two types of mental disorder and retains the term 'mental deficiency' without defining it.

PART II

LOCAL AUTHORITY SERVICES

Functions of Local Health Authority

* Section 7. This section *authorises the provision by local health authorities* of the same services for the mentally disordered as does Section 6 of the *Mental Health Act* 1959, with the *exception* of specific mention of occupation and training facilities and with the *addition* of the *ascertainment of mental defectives* not of school age and the *supervision of mental defectives not subject to guardianship or detention in a hospital*. The description *'mental health officer'* replaces 'mental welfare officer'.

---

* The local health authorities' responsibilities under this section were transferred to the local authorities' social service departments by the *Social Work (Scotland) Act* 1968.

** Section 12. This section *imposes a duty on local health authorities to provide*, or secure the provision of, suitable training and occupation, not only for children under the age of 16 years unsuitable for education or training in a special school, but also for mental defectives over that age, and to arrange the necessary transport.

Local Health Authority's Powers to compel attendance at Training Centres

* Section 13. This section corresponds, in effect, to Section 12, *Mental Health Act* 1959, with the exception that it is the Secretary of State who is required to reach a decision if the parent is aggrieved.

PART III

PRIVATE HOSPITALS AND RESIDENTIAL HOMES

Sections 15–18. These sections differ from Sections 14–17 in the *Mental Health Act* 1959, in that the premises are designated as '*private hospitals*' and not as 'mental nursing homes', and in that the functions of registration, imposition of conditions, and inspection are vested in the Secretary of State and not the local health authority.

PART IV

HOSPITAL CARE AND GUARDIANSHIP

It is in these sections that the *Mental Health (Scotland) Act* 1960 differs most significantly from the *Mental Health Act* 1959.

Section 23. This section, in effect, *excludes from compulsory admission to hospital* (except under the provisions for emergency admission) or *from reception into guardianship, patients over the age of twenty-one years*, who would satisfy the definitions of *subnormality* and *psychopathic disorder* in the *Mental Health Act* 1959. It imposes limitations (with exceptions) on the compulsory detention in hospital, or under guardianship past the age of 25 years, of such patients, similar to the limitations in the 1959 Act.

** The local health authorities' responsibilities under this section for children under 16 were transferred to the local authorities' education departments by the *Education (Handicapped Children) Act* 1970 and, for older mental defectives, to their social services departments by the *Social Work (Scotland) Act* 1968.

* See note on Section 7.

Informal Admission of Patients to Hospital

Section 23 also *permits* the informal admission of mentally dis-ordered patients *without* the mention of parental rights below the age of 16 years implied in Section 5, *Mental Health Act* 1959.

COMPULSORY ADMISSION TO HOSPITAL AND RECEPTION INTO GUARDIANSHIP

Legal authority for detention in hospital or reception into guar-dianship is retained in the *Mental Health (Scotland) Act* 1960 in the person of the *Sheriff*, who has to approve all applications before they become effective.

There is no separate provision in the *Mental Health (Scotland) Act* 1960 for admission for *twenty-eight days' observation*, this, in effect, being incorporated in the procedure for the admission of patients to hospital for treatment.

ADMISSION FOR TREATMENT

Section 24. The *application for admission*, founded on *two medical recommendations*, has to be made by the nearest relative (defined in Section 45) or by the mental health officer, who can act *in spite* of the nearest relative's objections (Section 26), although he must inform him of his *right of appeal* to the Sheriff (Section 28).

Section 27. For the purposes of making their recommendations, the medical practitioners may examine the patient together only when no objection has been made by the patient or his nearest relative.

One of the medical practitioners has to be approved for the pur-poses of this section by the Regional Hospital Board, and not by the local health authority, as in the *Mental Health Act* 1959.

Not more than one of the medical recommendations may be given by a medical officer in the service of a local authority, and neither by a medical practitioner who is making the application. The other exclusions listed in Section 28, *Mental Health Act* 1959, do not apply, although the relationship of either medical prac-titioner to the patient, or any pecuniary interest he may have in the admission of the patient into hospital, has to be stated in his recommendation. Medical practitioners on the staff of a *private* hospital, or other private accommodation to which the patient is to be admitted, are specifically excluded from giving either medical recommendation.

Section 28. The *application for admission* has to be submitted to the Sheriff for his approval *within seven days* of the last date on which the patient was examined for the purposes of any medical recommendation accompanying the application. The Sheriff, in considering the application, may make such enquiries and see such persons (including the patient) as he thinks fit. Where the patient's relative has objected to the application, he must afford that relative, and any witness the latter may call, an opportunity of being heard. At the patient's or applicant's request or the Sheriff's wish these proceedings shall be conducted in private.

Section 29. The *Patient may be admitted* to the hospital named in the application at any time *within a period of seven days* from the date on which the Sheriff approved the application.

The board of management of the hospital are required to send to the Mental Welfare Commission, *within seven days* of the patient's admission, copies of the application and medical recommendations.

The *responsible medical officer* is required to examine the patient himself, or to obtain from another medical practitioner a report on the condition of the patient, *within the period of seven days ending on the twenty-eighth day after his admission.* If the responsible medical officer does not then discharge the patient, he must inform the Mental Welfare Commission, the nearest relative, and the board of management (cf. Section 25, *Mental Health Act* 1959).

ADMISSION IN CASE OF EMERGENCY

Section 31. This section *authorises a medical practitioner*, who has personally examined a mentally disordered person, to make a medical recommendation concerning him *on the same day*, which permits the patient's removal to hospital *within three days* and his detention there *for a period not exceeding seven days* provided the medical practitioner considers the necessity for this is so urgent that compliance with the provisions of Section 24 would involve unreasonable delay.

The medical practitioner is required, when practicable, to seek the consent of a relative or mental health officer to the making of an emergency recommendation, which must be accompanied by a statement that he has done so or of the reason for his failure to obtain that consent.

The board of management of the hospital to which the patient is admitted must, without delay, where practicable, inform the nearest relative and some responsible person residing with the patient of the latter's emergency admission.

APPLICATIONS IN RESPECT OF PATIENTS ALREADY IN HOSPITAL

Section 32. This section *authorises the use of the application for admission and emergency recommendation procedures for patients already in hospital*, and the latter procedure may therefore be used in an emergency to detain informal admissions pending action under Section 24.

GUARDIANSHIP

* Section 25. This section *authorises*, subject to approval by the Sheriff of the application, the *reception into guardianship* of either a local health authority or of any other person (including the applicant himself) approved by that authority, of any person suffering from mental illness or mental deficiency which requires or is susceptible to medical treatment and warrants his reception into guardianship *provided* that this is in the interests of the patient or for the protection of other persons.

The same categories of patients are excluded by Section 23 from liability to reception into guardianship as from liability to detention in hospital, and the same general provisions as to applications, reports to the Mental Welfare Commission and nearest relative, and medical recommendations apply to guardianship cases as to hospital cases.

The effect of a guardianship application, approved by the Sheriff and forwarded to the local health authority within seven days, is to confer on the authority or person named, to the exclusion of any other person, the same powers over the patient as would be the case if they or he were the father of the patient and the patient were a *pupil child*. However, the guardian is given no power with respect to any property of the patient and is prohibited from administering corporal punishment to him (Section 29).

* See footnote on Section 7.

LEAVE OF ABSENCE FROM HOSPITAL

Section 35. There is no *automatic discharge* from hospital detention *after six months' authorised leave of absence* as in the *Mental Health Act* 1959, but the responsible medical officer is required *within fourteen days* to inform the Mental Welfare Commission of the patient's name and address on any leave *exceeding twenty-eight days*, including extensions of this duration of a previous six months' leave period. The responsible medical officer is also required to notify the commission *within fourteen days of the patient's return.*

ABSENCE WITHOUT LEAVE

Section 36. The provisions of this section are similar to those of the *Mental Health Act* 1959, with the important variation in the period during which patients absent without leave, who are liable to detention in hospital or subject to guardianship, may be taken into custody, *i.e.*, in the case of a *mental defective—within three months*, in the case of a *patient subject to an emergency recommendation—within seven days,* and in *any other case—within twenty-eight days*, beginning in each case with the first day of their absence.

TRANSFER OF PATIENTS

* Section 37. A *patient may be transferred* from one hospital to another with the consent of the board of management of the two hospitals or from hospital to the guardianship of a local health authority or someone approved by the authority, with the consent of the board of management and the proposed guardian. A patient subject to guardianship may be transferred by a local health authority to the guardianship of another person with the latter's consent, but the Mental Welfare Commission's consent and that of the hospital board of management are required before a local authority can transfer a patient from guardianship to hospital and, in *all cases*, either the consent of the guardian must be obtained or, if this is refused, the approval of the Sheriff to the transfer must be sought. The board of management of the hospital to which the patient is transferred or the local health authority concerned, as the case may be, are required to notify the nearest relative and the Mental Welfare Commission *within seven days* of the date of transfer.

* See footnote on Section 7.

DURATION OF AUTHORITY FOR DETENTION OR GUARDIANSHIP AND DISCHARGE OF PATIENTS

* Section 39. The *initial duration and period of renewal* specified in this section are similar to those in Section 43, *Mental Health Act* 1959, but in this case the responsible medical officer is required to obtain, *within two months of the expiry of authority*, for detention or guardianship, a report from *another* medical practitioner on the patient's condition, and to consider this report in assessing the need for continued detention or guardianship, having regard to their necessity in the interests of the health or safety of the patient and for the protection of other persons.

In each case where the responsible medical officer considers continued detention or guardianship necessary he is required to furnish a report to that effect, in the prescribed form, with the report of the second medical practitioner to the board of management of the hospital or local health authority, as the case may be, and also to the Mental Welfare Commission.

The board of management or local health authority are required to notify the patient and his nearest relative or guardian when authority for detention or guardianship is renewed.

On *attaining the age of 16 years* a patient may appeal to the Sheriff to order his discharge, within the period for which the authority for his detention or guardianship is renewed.

Section 40. This section *requires the responsible medical officer, board of management, or local health authority* to take action similar to that specified in Section 39, *within two months of the twenty-fifth birthday* of a mental defective who has been continuously detained in hospital or subject to guardianship since attaining the age of 21 years, or of a patient detained in hospital or subject to guardianship who is suffering from mental illness which manifests itself only as persistent abnormally aggressive or seriously irresponsible conduct.

Where the authority for detention or guardianship is continued the patient and his nearest relative have, *within a period of 28 days*, beginning with the patient's twenty-fifth birthday, the right of appeal to the Sheriff for the patient's discharge.

---

* See footnote on Section 7.

DISCHARGE OF PATIENTS

* Section 43. This section *authorises the following persons to make an order discharging a patient from detention or guardianship:*

The *responsible medical officer* or the *Mental Welfare Commission* in the case of a patient detained in hospital or subject to guardianship (but not the responsible medical officer without the consent of the board of management when the patient is detained in a State hospital).

The *Sheriff* when an appeal has been made to him under Sections 39, 40 or 44 of this Act.

The *nearest relative*, the *board of management*, in the case of a detained patient, and the *local health authority*, in the case of a patient subject to guardianship, with the consent in *both* cases of the responsible medical officer who, when he does not consent, is required to furnish a report that, in his opinion, the patient cannot be discharged without being a danger to himself or to others. In the absence of such a report the *discharge order takes effect at the end of a period of seven days after it is made.*

RESTRICTIONS ON DISCHARGE BY NEAREST RELATIVE

Section 44. This section *requires the nearest relative to give not less than seven days' notice in writing* to the board of management or local health authority *of an order to discharge a patient* liable to detention in hospital or subject to guardianship and *authorises the continued detention of the patient, against the nearest relative's wishes,* if the responsible medical officer reports to the appropriate authority, *within the period of notice,* that in his opinion the patient's mental disorder is such as would warrant his admission to hospital or reception into guardianship, or if the patient is already detained in hospital, that he would be likely to act in a manner dangerous to others or to himself, if discharged. It also *denies the relative the right to order discharge again during a period of six months* beginning with the date of the responsible medical officer's report, but requires the relative to be informed of the report and confers on the relative the *right to appeal to the Sheriff within the*

* See footnote on Section 7.

period of twenty-eight days, beginning with the day on which he was informed.

This section also *precludes the nearest relative from making a discharge order in respect of a patient detained in a State hospital.*

PART V

DETENTION OF PATIENTS CONCERNED IN CRIMINAL
PROCEEDINGS AND TRANSFER OF PATIENTS UNDER SENTENCE

Section 54. This section *authorises a court*, when they are satisfied on the written or oral evidence of a medical practitioner, that a person charged with an offence whom they are remanding or committing for trial is suffering from mental disorder, *to commit him to hospital*, instead of remanding him in custody, *provided* the court is also satisfied that that hospital is available for his admission and suitable for his detention.

A person committed to hospital in this way is liable to be detained there for the period for which he is remanded or for the period of committal *unless*, before the expiration of that period, he is liberated in due course of law, or the responsible medical officer reports to the court that the person committed is not suffering from mental disorder of a nature or degree which warrants his admission to hospital under Part IV of the Act. In the latter case, the court may commit him to any prison or other institution to which he might have been committed had he not been committed to hospital, or may otherwise deal with him according to law.

* Section 55. This section *authorises the High Court of Judiciary or the Sheriff Court* (in the case of a person convicted of an offence other than an offence the sentence for which is fixed by law), or a Sheriff Court (in the case of a person remitted to that court by a court of summary jurisdiction other than a Sheriff Court, before which he has been charged with any act or omission constituting an offence punishable with imprisonment), *to order that person's admission to and detention in a specified hospital or to place him under the guardianship* of a local health authority provided that the court is satisfied, on the written or oral evidence of two medical practitioners, that the offender is suffering from mental disorder of

* See footnote on Section 7.

a nature or degree which, in the case of a person *under 21 years of age*, would warrant his admission to a hospital or his reception into guardianship under Part IV of this Act and that, having regard to all the circumstances, this is the most suitable method of dealing with the case. The court must also be satisfied that the hospital specified will be able to admit the patient *within a period of twenty-eight days* beginning with the date of the making of the order, or that the local health authority or other person specified is willing to receive the offender into guardianship.

A *Sheriff Court* may make an order under this section of the Act without convicting a person charged summarily before it *provided* the court is satisfied he did the act.

A *State hospital may not be specified* in a hospital order *unless* the court is satisfied, on the evidence of the medical practitioners, that the offender, on account of his dangerous, violent or criminal propensities, requires treatment under conditions of special security and cannot suitably be cared for in a hospital other than a State hospital.

A *duty is imposed on the prosecutor* to bring before the court evidence of the mental condition of any person charged who appears to him to be suffering from mental disorder.

*** Section 56. This section *authorises a Sheriff Court* (in the case of a child or young person brought before that court—or before a Juvenile Court and remitted to the Sheriff Court—under Section 66 or Section 68 of the *Children and Young Persons (Scotland) Act* 1937) *to make a hospital or guardianship order* provided the court is satisfied that the child or young person is in

---

*** Juvenile Courts have now been abolished in Scotland and the following procedure substituted by Part III of the *Social Work (Scotland) Act* 1968: an official with the title of 'Reporter' considers whether any child referred to him as having committed an offence is in need of compulsory measures of care and, if so, arranges for him to be brought with his parents before a 'Children's Hearing', which is a sitting of a treatment authority for each local authority area. The Children's Hearing has no power to adjudicate on whether or not the child committed the alleged offence and where the facts alleged are disputed, the hearing cannot proceed with the case unless it is referred to the Sheriff and he finds the facts established. The Children's Hearing then has the power to impose (by means of a 'supervision requirement') what compulsory measures of care it considers are required. For the purposes of the Act, 'child' means basically a person under 16 years of age but includes a person aged 16 and over but under 18 if he has a supervision requirement in force in respect of him.

need of care and protection, or that his parent or guardian is unable
to control him, and that the conditions which are required under
Section 55 for the making of a hospital order or guardianship order
are, so far as applicable, satisfied in the case of the child or young
person.

The court must also be satisfied that the *parent or guardian understands* the results which will follow from the order and *consents*
to its being made.

*A duty is imposed on the person bringing the child or young
person before the court* to bring such evidence as may be available
of the mental condition of the child if he appears to that person to
be suffering from mental disorder.

Section 58. This section *cancels the power of the nearest relative
to order discharge* of a patient admitted to hospital as a result of a
court order and *removes the age limits to the detention in hospital
or under guardianship of patients* whose only manifestation of
mental illness is persistent abnormally aggressive or irresponsible
conduct, or whose mental deficiency is not such that they are incapable of living an independent life or of guarding themselves
against serious exploitation.

Section 59. This section *authorises the patient's detention in a
place of safety pending his admission to hospital within a period of
twenty-eight days*, beginning with the day on which the hospital
order was made by the court.

Section 60. This section *authorises a court making a hospital
order to impose an order restricting the patient's discharge and any
of the following special restrictions*, either indefinitely or for a
specified period, where this is considered necessary for the protection of the public *provided* that the evidence of the medical practitioner approved by the Regional Hospital Board was given *orally*
in Court: during the period that discharge is restricted, the normal
limit to the duration of the authority for detention does not apply
and a guardianship order may not be made in respect of the patient.

The *consent of the Secretary of State* is necessary before the
patient can be transferred to another hospital or before he can be
granted leave, and he can be recalled from leave at any time while
the order restricting discharge is in force. The Secretary of State's
consent is also necessary before the patient may be discharged by
any of the persons who normally have this power.

Section 61. This section *authorises the Secretary of State to terminate the order restricting discharge* if he is satisfied that it is no longer required for the protection of the public. It also authorises him, during the period of an order restricting discharge, to discharge the patient either absolutely or subject to conditions and, in the latter case, to recall him to hospital at any time while the order restricting discharge is still in force.

Section 62. This section *gives a patient a right of appeal against a hospital or guardianship order or order restricting discharge made by a court.*

Section 65. This section *authorises the Secretary of State to apply to the Sheriff to direct the transfer of a person in custody, awaiting trial or sentence, to a hospital* (*not* a private hospital), when it appears to the Secretary of State that the person is suffering from mental disorder of a nature or degree which warrants his admission to a hospital under Part IV of the Act. If the Sheriff is satisfied of this, on the reports of *two* medical practitioners, he may make a hospital order, which is *subject to a restriction on discharge of unlimited duration.* At *least one* of the medical practitioners giving reports must be approved by the Regional Hospital Board**** as having special experience in the diagnosis or treatment of mental disorders. Each medical practitioner must describe the patient as suffering from the *same* one form of mental disorder, although either, or both, may describe him as suffering from the other form as well. A detention order under this section is *valid for a period of fourteen days* beginning with the date on which it is given.

The patient remains liable to be detained in hospital, *but not subject to a restriction order*, if the proceedings against him are dropped, or after his case has been disposed of by the Court to which he was committed or by which he was remanded, unless the Court pass a sentence of imprisonment or make a guardianship order concerning him, or the responsible medical officer notifies the Secretary of State that he no longer requires treatment for mental disorder (Section 68).

Section 66. This section *authorises the Secretary of State*, if he is satisfied on similar reports to those required under Section 65 that a person is suffering from mental disorder which warrants his ad-

---

**** Now Regional Health Authority.

mission to hospital, *to direct that person's transfer to hospital from prison* in which he is serving a sentence as a civil prisoner or detained as an alien. This direction is *valid for a period of fourteen days* beginning with the date on which it is given.

A person dealt with in this way may appeal to the Sheriff within three months, and if his transfer order is cancelled the Secretary of State is required to direct his return to prison.

Section 67. This section *authorises the Secretary of State to impose restriction on discharge of prisoners transferred to hospital.*

Section 69. This section *authorises the Secretary of State to direct the transfer back to prison* of any patient subject to a direction restricting his discharge, on notification by the responsible medical officer that he no longer requires treatment for mental disorder *provided the period of his prison sentence has not expired.*

The responsible medical officer is required to assess the need for the continued detention of a patient *after a direction restricting his discharge has ceased to have effect*, on the basis of a report on his condition obtained by the responsible medical officer from *another* medical practitioner *within a period of twenty-eight days of the expiry of that order.* If the responsible medical officer considers that the patient's continued detention in hospital is necessary in the interests of the health or safety of the patient or for the protection of other persons, he is required to furnish a report to this effect, in the prescribed form, with the other medical practitioner's report, to the hospital board of management and Mental Welfare Commission. The patient is then treated as though he had been admitted to hospital on a hospital order *without restriction on his discharge* on the date the previous restriction direction expired, and the patient and his nearest relative must be informed of this by the board of management.

* Section 71. This section *authorises the Secretary of State to direct that a child or young person detained in an approved school be placed under the guardianship of a local health authority*, if he is satisfied on the reports required under Section 65 that the child or young person is suffering from mental disorder of a nature or degree which warrants his reception into guardianship under this Act and that this is in the public interest.

* See footnote on Section 7.

PART VI

REMOVAL AND RETURN OF PATIENTS WITHIN THE UNITED KINGDOM, ETC.

Sections 73–88. These sections, with the amendments they contain to the *Mental Health Act* 1959, *authorise the Secretary of State/Minister of Health to direct the transfer of a patient liable to be detained or subject to guardianship in Scotland, England, Wales or Northern Ireland to any other of these countries if* he considers this to be in the patient's interest.

The sections similarly *authorise the taking into custody* anywhere within Scotland, England, Wales or Northern Ireland of any patient absent without leave.

PART VIII

STATE HOSPITALS

The State hospitals in Scotland correspond to the *special hospitals* in England.

Section 89. This section *requires the Secretary of State to provide State hospitals* for mentally disordered patients subject to detention who require treatment under conditions of special security on account of their dangerous, violent, or criminal propensities.

The Secretary of State is authorised to appoint committees to manage the State hospitals.

Miscellaneous and General

PATIENTS' CORRESPONDENCE

Section 34. This section differs from Section 36, *Mental Health Act* 1959, only in the following list of persons which is substituted for that in the latter Section:

1. The nearest relative of the patient
2. The Secretary of State
3. The Lord Advocate
4. Any Member of the Commons House of Parliament
5. Any Mental Welfare Commission or any Commissioner thereof

6. Any Sheriff or Sheriff Clerk

7. The board of management of the hospital

ILL-TREATMENT OF PATIENTS

Section 95. As Section 126, *Mental Health Act* 1959, except that it specifies the amount of the maximum possible fine as £500 on conviction on indictment.

SEXUAL INTERCOURSE WITH FEMALE DEFECTIVES

Section 96. This section *renders it an offence for a man to have unlawful sexual intercourse with a female defective*, for anyone to procure or encourage a female defective to have unlawful sexual intercourse, or for the owner or occupier of any premises or any person having or assisting in the management or control of the premises to induce a female defective to resort to or be on such premises for the purpose of unlawful sexual intercourse with any man *provided* these persons had reason to know or had reason to suspect that the woman concerned was a defective incapable of living an independent life or of guarding herself against serious exploitation. The penalty for the above offence is, on conviction on indictment, a term of imprisonment not exceeding two years.

Section 97. This section, which *concerns sexual intercourse with patients*, is in all essential respects identical with Section 128, *Mental Health Act* 1959, except that the institution of proceedings is not dependent on the consent of the Director of Public Prosecutions.

ASSISTING PATIENTS TO ABSENT THEMSELVES WITHOUT LEAVE

Section 98. As Section 129, *Mental Health Act* 1959, except that it specifies the amount of the maximum possible fine as £500 on conviction on indictment.

AUTHORITY TO SEARCH FOR AND REMOVE PATIENTS

Section 103. This section *authorises a mental health officer or medical commissioner*, on production of documentary proof of his authority, to demand admission at all reasonable times to inspect any place in which he has reasonable cause to believe that a person suffering from mental disorder is being ill-treated, neglected, or not kept under proper control, or is living alone and unable to care for himself. When a Justice of the Peace, on sworn evidence in writing by either of these officers, is satisfied that he has been refused admission, or such refusal is apprehended, the *Justice may issue a warrant authorising a constable to enter*, if need be by force, any premises specified in the warrant, and, if thought fit, *to remove any person suffering from mental disorder from there to a place of safety*, pending arrangements for his treatment or care. The constable *must* be accompanied in the execution of the warrant by a medical practitioner.

This section also authorises a Justice of the Peace, on the sworn evidence in writing of any constable or any other person authorised under the Act (or under Section 93, *Mental Health Act* 1959) to take a patient to any place or to take into custody or retake a patient, *to issue a warrant authorising any named constable to enter any premises*, if need be by force, and *to remove from there any patient liable to be taken or retaken provided* admission to the premises has been refused or if such a refusal is apprehended. The constable *may* be accompanied in the execution of the warrant by a *medical practitioner* or by *any person authorised* under the Act (or Section 93, *Mental Health Act* 1959) to take or retake the patient.

A patient removed to a place of safety under this section may be detained there for a period *not exceeding seventy-two hours.*

A *place of safety* means a hospital as defined by this Act, a residential home for persons suffering from mental disorder, or any other suitable place, the occupier of which is willing temporarily to receive the patient, but shall *not* include a police station unless by reason of emergency there is no place as aforesaid available for receiving the patient.

MENTALLY DISORDERED PERSONS FOUND IN PUBLIC PLACES

Section 104. As Section 136, *Mental Health Act* 1959, with the omission of the interview by a mental welfare officer, but with the *additional requirement* that the constable inform *without delay* some responsible person residing with the patient and the nearest relative of the patient.

C. NORTHERN IRELAND

THE MENTAL HEALTH ACT
(NORTHERN IRELAND) 1961

The *Mental Health Act (Northern Ireland)* 1961 differs considerably from the *Mental Health Act* 1959 and from the *Mental Health (Scotland) Act* 1960 as regards definitions and the procedures for hospital detention and guardianship.

As a result of the reorganisation of Health and Social Services which took place in Northern Ireland on 1st October 1972, the only fully integrated service for the mentally handicapped in the British Isles was unfortunately destroyed by the abolition of the Northern Ireland Hospitals Authority which had previously been responsible for both hospital and community care. Also abolished were its three special care management committees, whose duties included the ascertainment of persons requiring special care, their supervision, guardianship and training in the community and in residential accommodation, including hospitals. These duties are now the responsibility of four Area Boards for Health and Social Services and references in the following sections of the Act to the Authority or Management Committee should be amended accordingly.

PART I

Sections 1 to 4 define the general duties and powers of the Northern Ireland Hospitals Authority and their specific duty to submit to the Ministry of Health and Local Government schemes for the management and control of special care services, and the Ministry's duty to implement schemes it has approved (with or without modifications).

Section 6. This section *permits* the informal admission to any hospital or private hospital of any person who requires treatment for mental disorder and also permits such a person to make use of any of the services provided under the Act for persons requiring special care. By inference from subsection 2 of this section, a patient informally admitted may be detained in hospital at his parent's or guardian's request until the age of 16, whatever his own wishes in the matter may be, but on reaching the age of 16 years, if he is capable of expressing his own wishes, these override those of his parent or guardian.

Section 7. This section *defines mental disorder as mental illness, arrested or incomplete development of mind and any other disorder or disability of mind.* It *defines* also *a person requiring special care as someone suffering from arrested or incomplete development of mind* (whether arising from inherent causes or induced by disease or injury), *which renders him socially inefficient to such an extent that he requires supervision, training or control in his own interests or in the interests of other persons.* The *criteria of social inefficiency are* defined as *incapability of guarding oneself against physical dangers, managing oneself or one's affairs or, if a child, or being taught to do so or being found unsuitable for education at school, or whether a child or adult, being in need of care for the protection of other persons.*

PART II

PROVISIONS RELATING TO SPECIAL CARE AND
ADMISSION TO HOSPITAL AND GUARDIANSHIP

Notification and Examination of Persons Requiring Special Care

Section 8. This section *imposes a duty* on any medical practitioner, health authority or welfare authority *to notify* to the local education authority any person between the ages of 2 and 16, and to the special care management committee, any other case where it appears that steps should be taken, either in the interests of the person concerned or for the protection of other persons, *to ascertain* whether he is a person requiring special care.

On receiving such a notification, the local education authority or special care management committee, is required to notify the nearest relative where the person is under the age of 16 years, or the person himself and his nearest relative if he is over that age.

Section 9. This section *authorises special care management committees to require,* by notice in writing, *persons notified* under Section 8 of this Act or Sections 32 or 53 of the *Education Act (Northern Ireland) 1947, to submit themselves for examination by a medical practitioner* appointed by the authority for the purposes of Section 19, where such an examination has not taken place or been arranged by the person concerned (or by his nearest relative if he is under the age of 16) after the date of notification.

This section also *gives special care management committees similar powers to require medical examination of persons* ordinarily resident within their area, *who appear to them to require special care*, and entitles the nearest relative to be present at any medical examination of which he has been notified in the case of a person under the age of 16 years.

ATTENDANCE AT TRAINING CENTRES OF CHILDREN REQUIRING SPECIAL CARE

Section 10. This section *gives any special care committee powers*, on giving notice in writing to the parent of a child of compulsory school age, *to compel the parent to cause the child to attend a training centre* provided or approved by the Authority, either by day or as a resident, where it appears to the committee that the child should receive such training and that he is not receiving adequate comparable training elsewhere. Where a notified parent feels aggrieved on the ground that the child is receiving such training, he may require the special care committee to refer the question to the *Review Tribunal*, who may either confirm the notice or direct its amendment or withdrawal.

Section 11. This section lists the following '*reasonable causes*' for exemptions in respect of Section 10:

sickness of the child preventing his attendance at the centre

non-attendance on any day exclusively set apart for religious observance by the religious body to which the person notified belongs

impracticability for the child to make his own way or to be taken to and from the centre, in the absence of suitable arrangements for his transport or residential accommodation at or near the centre, by the special care management committee

the child's lack of a fixed abode, due to the nature of his parents' business, provided the child has attended as regularly as the latter permits

other circumstances which in the opinion of the Authority or the court afford a reasonable excuse.

ADMISSION TO HOSPITAL

Section 12. This section *authorises*, as the result of an application for admission, the *detention in hospital for a period not exceeding twenty-one days*, of any person suffering from mental illness or requiring special care *provided* it can be shown that his mental disorder warrants this and that it is in the interests of his own health or of the protection of others.

The application has to be founded on the *written recommendation* in the prescribed form, signed on or before the date of application, *of one medical practitioner*, who has personally examined the patient not more than two days before the date on which he signs the recommendation, and who, if practicable, shall be the patient's medical practitioner, or by a medical practitioner who has previous acquaintance with the patient (Section 14).

The medical recommendation must confirm that the above conditions concerning the mental disorder are satisfied and state the grounds for that opinion and whether other methods of dealing with the patient are available and, if so, why they are not appropriate.

Section 14 *excludes* the following persons from giving the recommendation:

a. the applicant;
b. a partner of the applicant;
c. a person employed as an assistant by the applicant;
d. a person who receives or has an interest in the receipt of any payments made on account of the maintenance of the patient; or
e. except in the case of an emergency application (as defined in Section 15), a practitioner on the staff of the hospital to which the patient is to be admitted; or by the husband, wife, father, father-in-law, mother, mother-in-law, son, son-in-law, daughter, daughter-in-law, brother, brother-in-law, sister or sister-in-law of the patient.

Section 13. An *application for admission* may be made either *by the nearest relative* (as defined by Section 37) or *by the welfare officer* for the area in which the patient then is, after consultation with the nearest relative (and *not against his expressed objection*), unless consultation is not reasonably practicable or would involve unreasonable delay. The applicant must personally have seen the patient within a period of fourteen days ending with the date of the application.

The patient must be admitted to hospital within a period of fourteen days beginning with the date on which he was examined by the medical practitioner giving the recommendation for admission (Section 17).

The patient may apply to the *Review Tribunal* within the period of six months beginning with the day on which he was admitted to hospital or with the day on which he attains the age of 16 years, whichever is the later (Section 19).

Admission in Case of Emergency

Section 15. This section authorises the *welfare officer* or *any relative of the patient*, in any case of urgent necessity, to apply for the patient's detention in hospital if full compliance with the provisions of Section 12 would involve undesirable delay. The application may be founded on one medical recommendation only.

The patient must be admitted to hospital within a period of three days beginning with the date on which he was examined by the medical practitioner giving the recommendation for admission (Section 17).

Under this emergency procedure, the *patient may be detained for seven days only*, beginning with the day on which he was admitted to hospital, unless the management committee of the hospital receive the medical report mentioned in Section 19 within that period.

APPLICATIONS IN RESPECT OF PATIENTS ALREADY IN HOSPITAL

Section 16. This section *authorises the detention in hospital for a period of three days of an informal admission*, on the written report to the management committee by the *medical practitioner in charge of treatment*, that it appears to him that an application should be made for the patient's admission to hospital and his detention there.

Section 18. This section *requires a medical practitioner on the staff of the hospital to which a patient is admitted for treatment, to examine him immediately after admission* (unless he has been examined before admission by a medical practitioner appointed for the purposes of Section 19) and to report the results in writing to the management committee.

Section 19. This section *extends the authority for detention in hospital* of a patient admitted under Section 12 *for a period of up to six months* beginning with the day on which he was so admitted, *provided a* medical officer appointed by the Authority for the purpose of this section makes a medical report to the management committee in the prescribed form, between the fourteenth and twenty-first day after admission, that, in his opinion, the patient is suffering from mental disorder of a nature or degree which warrants his detention in hospital, and that this is necessary in the interests of his own health or safety or for the protection of other persons, with a statement of the grounds for his opinion and the reasons why other methods of dealing with the patient are not appropriate.

The following are prohibited from giving a medical report under this section—the person making the application for admission of the patient, the medical officer who gave the recommendation for admission, or a person who receives or has an interest in the receipt of payments made on account of the maintenance of the patient, or by the husband, wife, father, father-in-law, mother, mother-in-law, son, son-in-law, daughter, daughter-in-law, brother, brother-in-law, sister or sister-in-law of the patient.

The medical report has no effect unless both it and the recommendation for admission describe the patient as being mentally ill or as requiring special care (whether or not they describe the patient in both those ways).

GUARDIANSHIP

Section 21. This section *authorises the reception into guardianship* of either a local authority, a management committee or any other person including the applicant himself, approved by the management committee, of any person suffering from mental illness or requiring special care, which warrants his reception into guardianship, *provided* that it is necessary in his own interest or for the protection of other persons.

The *guardianship application* is founded on the *written recommendations* in the prescribed form *of two medical practitioners* who have each examined the patient not more than two days before the date on which each signs the recommendation. *One recommendation must be given by a medical practitioner appointed by the Authority for the purposes of Section 19* and the other, if practicable, by the patient's medical practitioner or by a practitioner with previous acquaintance with the patient. The recommendations may be signed separately or given as a joint recommendation signed by both medical practitioners. The recommendations must state the grounds and reasons for the medical practitioners' opinion and include a statement why other methods of dealing with the patient are not appropriate.

Section 22. A guardianship application accepted by a management committee itself or on behalf of another named individual, confers on that committee or person all such powers in relation to the patient as would be exercisable by the father of a child under the age of 14 years.

The guardianship application must be forwarded to the management committee within fourteen days beginning with the date on which the patient was last examined by a medical practitioner before giving a recommendation for guardianship.

A patient placed under guardianship may be kept under guardianship for a period not exceeding six months beginning with the day on which the guardianship application was accepted, but the patient may apply to the *Review Tribunal* within that period or within a period of six months of his 16th birthday, whichever is the later.

Section 23. This section defines the procedure for transfer of guardianship in the event of the death or incapacity of the guardian or of the neglect by him of his duties towards the patient.

Section 24. This section requires the guardian, as far as is practicable, to make arrangements for the occupation, training or employment of the patient and for his recreational and general welfare, including the promotion of his physical and mental health.

PATIENTS' CORRESPONDENCE

Section 25. This section requires the management committee, a person carrying on a private hospital, or a person appointed as a guardian *to forward unopened* all letters addressed by any patient liable to be detained or subject to guardianship to the following:

the Lord Chief Justice

the Minister of Health and Local Government
any Member of Parliament
the Review Tribunal
the Ministry
the Registrar of the Department for the Affairs of Mental
   Patients
the nearest relative of the patient

RIGHTS OF PATIENTS AND NEAREST RELATIVES

Section 27. This section requires management committees to furnish the patient and his nearest relative with a *statement of their respective rights* and powers under the Act, as soon as practicable after the patient is admitted to hospital or placed under guardianship.

RECLASSIFICATION OF MENTAL DISORDER

Section 28. This section authorises the *reclassification of the form of mental disorder*, where the responsible medical officer (as defined in Section 47) reports to the management committee or to the guardian that the patient is suffering from a form of mental disorder other than that specified in the original application, and requires the management committee or guardian to inform the patient himself if he is over the age of 16 and his nearest relative of the report. The patient, or his nearest relative, may apply to the *Review Tribunal* within twenty-eight days beginning with the day on which he was so informed.

LEAVE OF ABSENCE FROM HOSPITAL

Section 29. This section *authorises the responsible medical officer to grant, for any period, leave of absence* to a patient detained in hospital, subject to any condition he considers necessary in the interests of the patient or for the protection of other persons, including the requirement that the patient shall remain during his absence in the custody of any person authorised in writing by the management committee. The responsible medical officer may *revoke the leave* of absence and recall the patient to hospital if it appears necessary to do so in the interests of the patient's health or safety or for the protection of other persons or because the patient is not receiving proper care.

Absence Without Leave

Section 30. This section *authorises the taking into custody and the return to hospital* by any officer on the staff of the hospital, any welfare officer, any constable or any person authorised in writing by the management committee of the hospital, of any patient absent without leave from hospital or failing to return to the hospital at the expiration of a period of authorised leave, or, if recalled from leave or absconding himself without permission from any place where he is required to reside as a condition of leave.

Similarly, this section *authorises the taking into custody and return to his required place of residence* by any officer on the staff of a management committee, by any constable or any person authorised in writing by the guardian or a management committee, of any patient subject to guardianship, who absents himself without the leave of his guardian from his required place of residence.

A *patient may not be taken into custody after the expiration of twenty-eight days beginning with the first day of his absence without leave*, and after this period he ceases to be liable to be detained or subject to guardianship.

TRANSFER OF PATIENTS

Section 31. *This section authorises the continued detention of patients liable to detention, when they are transferred by the Authority from one hospital to another, the transfer of a detained patient from hospital to guardianship of any person by arrangement of the management committee, the transfer of a patient already subject to guardianship to the guardianship of any other person or to a hospital*, in each case by arrangement of the same committee.

A patient who has attained the age of 16 years, transferred from guardianship to hospital in this way, may apply to the *Review Tribunal* within the period of six months beginning with the day on which he is transferred.

RENEWAL OF AUTHORITY FOR DETENTION OR GUARDIANSHIP

Section 32. This section *extends the authority for detention in hospital or guardianship for a further period of one year* from the expiry of the six month period specified in Sections 19 and 22, *if* within a period of one month ending with the last day of that period, the responsible medical officer examines the patient and reports to the responsible management committee in the prescribed form that continued detention or guardianship is necessary in the interests of the patient's health or safety or for the protection of other persons.

The section *extends the same authority for a further period of two years* from the expiry of the first extension of one year, *if* within a period of two months, ending with the last day of that period, two medical practitioners have, by arrangement of the management committee, examined the patient and reported in writing, either separately or jointly, to the responsible management committee in the prescribed form, that in the practitioners' opinion the requirements of Sections 12 and 21 as regards the patient's condition and the inappropriateness of alternative methods of care for him are satisfied. The management committee is required to give the patient and his nearest relative not less than fourteen days' notice in writing of the date of the medical examination. At least one of the medical practitioners appointed to carry out the examination must have made neither the original recommendation for admission or guardianship nor the medical report in connection with the detention of the patient.

The section *extends the same authority subsequently for periods of two years at a time* from the expiry of the preceding period, *if* within a period of two months ending with the last day of each two year period, the responsible medical officer examines the patient and reports to the responsible management committee in the prescribed form that continued detention or guardianship is necessary in the interests of the patient's health or safety or for the protection of other persons.

This section requires the responsible management committee to inform in writing a patient who has attained the age of 16 years, of the renewal of the authority for his detention or guardianship, and the patient may apply to the *Review Tribunal* at any time before the expiry of the period of renewal.

DISCHARGE OF PATIENTS

Section 35. This section *authorises the following persons to make an order in writing discharging a patient from detention or guardianship* (referred to as '*an order for discharge*')—the responsible medical officer, the responsible management committee or the nearest relative—and the responsible medical officer is required to make such an order if he is satisfied that the patient no longer suffers from mental disorder and that, having regard to the care or supervision available if he were discharged, it is not necessary in the interests of his health or safety, or for the protection of other persons, for him to continue to be liable to detention or subject to guardianship. Except where the patient is discharged from hospital other than on the application of his nearest relative, the responsible medical officer is required to notify the appropriate welfare authority to that effect.

The responsible medical officer is prohibited from discharging a patient detained in any special accommodation without the consent of the management committee.

RESTRICTIONS ON DISCHARGE BY THE NEAREST RELATIVE

Section 36. This section *requires the nearest relative to give not less than seventy-two hours notice in writing of an order for discharge* (extended to ninety-six hours if that period includes a Sunday) to the management committee of the hospital and *authorises the continued detention of the patient, against the nearest relative's wishes, if* the responsible medical officer reports in writing to the management committee that, in his opinion, *the patient would be likely to act in a manner dangerous to others or to himself if discharged*, and that he is not satisfied that the patient would receive proper treatment.

The section also *denies the relative the right to order discharge again during* a *period of six months* beginning with the day of the responsible medical officer's report, but require, the relative to be informed of the report and confers on him the right to apply to the *Review Tribunal* within a period of twenty-eight days beginning with the day on which he was informed.

REFERENCE OF CASES TO THE REVIEW TRIBUNAL

Section 45. This section authorises the following persons to refer the case of any patient liable to be detained or subject to guardianship to the Review Tribunal at any time—the Attorney General, the Ministry or, on the direction of the Lord Chief Justice, the Registrar of the Affairs of Mental Patients.

DEFINITION OF RESPONSIBLE MEDICAL OFFICER

Section 47. This section *defines the responsible medical officer* 'as any medical practitioner authorised to act as responsible medical officer by the Authority in the case of a patient detained in hospital, or by the management committee in the case of a patient subject to guardianship'.

PART III

ADMISSION OF PATIENTS CONCERNED IN CRIMINAL PROCEEDINGS AND TRANSFER OF PATIENTS UNDER SENTENCE

Section 48. This section *authorises a Court of Assize or Quarter Sessions* (in the case of a person convicted of an offence other than one for which the sentence is fixed by law) or *a Court of Summary Jurisdiction* (in the case of a person convicted of an offence punishable with imprisonment on summary conviction) *to order that person to be committed to the care of the Authority for admission to hospital or to place him under guardianship of a management committee*, or of any other specified person approved by a management committee, *provided* that the Court is satisfied on the written or oral evidence of the medical practitioners (of whom at least one shall be approved by the Authority for the purposes of Section 19, (Section 50)) that the offender is suffering from mental disorder of a nature or degree which would warrant his detention under Part II, and that having regard to all the circumstances, this is the most suitable method of dealing with the case.

A *Court of Summary Jurisdiction may make an order* under this section *without convicting* a person if the Court is satisfied he did the act and the other requirements of this section are satisfied.

The Court is required to be satisfied that the person to be named in a guardianship order is willing to receive the patient into guardianship.

Section 49. This section *authorises a Juvenile Court* (in the case of a child or young person brought before the Court under Section 63 or Section 65 of the *Children's and Young Persons' Act (Northern Ireland) 1950) to make a hospital order or guardianship order, provided* that the Court is satisfied that the child or young person is in need of care or protection, or that his parent or guardian is unable to control him and that the conditions which are required under Section 48 for the making of a hospital or guardianship order are, so far as is applicable, satisfied in the case of the child or young person.

The Court must also be satisfied that *the parent or guardian understands* the results which will follow from the order and consents to its being made.

Section 50. This section *requires that a copy of any medical report tendered in evidence to the Court* in connection with Sections 48 or 49 *is given to the accused's counsel or solicitor*, or if the accused is not legally represented, requires that the contents of the report shall be disclosed to him, or, if he is a child or young person, to his parents or guardian if present in Court, except in each case where the report has been tendered in evidence on his behalf.

In any case the accused may require that the practitioner by whom the report was signed be called to give oral evidence and rebutting evidence may be called by him or on his behalf.

Section 51. This section *imposes a duty on the Authority to designate a hospital to which a patient subject to a hospital order may be taken* by a constable, welfare officer or any other person directed by the Court, and *imposes a duty on the management committee of that hospital to admit him* within a period of twenty-eight days.

This section also *cancels the powers of the nearest relative* under Section 35 *to order the discharge of a patient admitted to hospital as the result of a Court order.* However, it authorises the patient to apply to the *Review Tribunal* within the period of six months beginning with the date of the order or the day on which he attains the age of 16 years, whichever is the later, and authorises the nearest relative to make a similar application within the period of twelve months beginning with the date of the order, and in any subsequent period of twelve months.

Section 52. This section *authorises the patient's detention in a place of safety pending his admission to hospital* within the period of twenty-eight days beginning with the day on which the hospital order was made by the Court.

POWERS OF COURT TO RESTRICT DISCHARGE FROM HOSPITAL

Section 53. This section *authorises a Court to impose an order restricting the patient's discharge and any of the following restrictions, either indefinitely or for a specified period*, where, having regard to the nature of the offence, this is considered necessary for the protection of the public, *provided* that the medical practitioners appointed by the Authority for the purposes of Section 19 have given evidence orally in Court.

During the period that discharge is restricted, the normal limit to the duration of the authority for detention does not apply and no application can be made to the Review Tribunal.

The consent of the Minister of Home Affairs is necessary before the patient can be transferred to another hospital or to guardianship or vice versa or before he can be granted leave, and he can be recalled from leave by the Minister as well as by the responsible medical officer while the order restricting discharge is in force.

Section 54. This section *authorises the Minister of Home Affairs himself, and no one else, to terminate the order restricting discharge*. While the order restricting discharge is still in force, the Minister may discharge the patient from hospital either absolutely or subject to conditions, with power to recall the patient to hospital if he thinks this necessary.

Under this section, *a patient subject to an order restricting his discharge is entitled*, within the period of six months beginning with the date of the relevant hospital order or with the day on which he attains the age of 16 years, whichever is later, and within each period during which he could himself have made an application to the Review Tribunal if the restriction order had not been in force, *to request the Minister to refer his case to the Review Tribunal for their advice*. The *Minister is required to comply with this request within two months of receiving it*. A patient recalled to hospital after being conditionally discharged may, in addition, make a similar request to the Minister during the period six to twelve months from the date of his return to hospital.

APPEALS

Section 55. This section *authorises a patient subject to a hospital or guardianship order or order restricting his discharge made by a Court of Summary Jurisdiction* (whether or not the Court convicted him), *County Court, or Court of Assize, to appeal against the order* in the same manner as against a conviction.

Transfer to Hospital or Guardianship of Prisoners, etc.

Section 58. This section *authorises the Minister to direct the transfer of a person serving a prison sentence to hospital if* he is satisfied on the reports of at least two medical practitioners that the person is suffering from mental illness or requires special care which warrants his detention in hospital for medical treatment and that this is in the public interest. At least one of the medical practitioners giving reports must be approved for the purposes of Section 19 by the Authority. Each medical practioner must describe the patient as being mentally ill or as requiring special care, although either or both may describe him as suffering from both forms of mental disorder.

Section 59. This section *authorises the Minister*, if he is satisfied on similar reports to those required under Section 58 that a person is suffering from mental illness or requires special care which warrants his detention in hospital for medical treatment, *to order that person's transfer to hospital from the various types of custody specified in the section* or from civil imprisonment or from detention in prison as an alien. The restrictions of Section 53 are applied mandatorily to all but the last two categories of prisoners, to whom they may be applied at the discretion of the Minister (Section 60).

Section 61. This section *authorises the Minister to direct the transfer back to prison or any other institution of detention of any patient subject to an order restricting his discharge*, on notification by the responsible medical officer that he no longer requires treatment for mental disorder, *provided* the period of his prison sentence has not expired. Under this section the Minister may himself exercise, or authorise the managers of a training school to which a patient might have been remitted to exercise, any power of releasing him on licence or discharging him under supervision which would have been exercisable if he had been remitted to a prison or other institution of detention.

Section 62. This section *authorises the Minister to direct that a person on remand, who is subject to a hospital transfer direction, be transferred to a place where he would otherwise have been detained* if he had not been committed to the care of the Authority, *provided* the responsible medical officer notifies the Minister that he no longer requires treatment for mental disorder.

This section also *authorises a Court of Assize or a County Court to make a hospital order* (with or without an order restricting discharge) *concerning a person in his absence, if* the Court is satisfied on the medical evidence of at least two medical practitioners (at least one of whom must be a practitioner appointed by the Authority for the purposes of Section 19) that the person is suffering from mental disorder of a nature or degree which warrants his detention in hospital for medical treatment, and if the Court is satisfied that it is impracticable or inappropriate to bring him before the Court. The Court must be further satisfied after considering any depositions or other documents required to be sent to the proper officer of the Court that it is proper for it to make such an order.

Section 63. This section *gives similar authority to that in Section 62 to a Court of Summary Jurisdiction to make a hospital order* (with or without an order restricting discharge) *concerning a person in custody on remand, in his absence and without convicting* him, *provided* that it appears impracticable or inappropriate to bring him before the Court and that the conditions required by Section 62 concerning medical and other evidence are satisfied.

Section 65. This section *authorises the Minister to direct that a child or young person detained in a training school be placed under the guardianship of a management committee or* any such other person approved by a management committee subject to the willingness of either to accept him, if he is satisfied on the reports required under Section 58 that the child or young person is suffering from mental disorder which warrants his reception into guardianship under this Act and that it is in the public interest and expedient to do so.

PART IV

REGISTRATION OF PRIVATE HOSPITALS

Sections 67 to 72 concern the conditions of registration of private hospitals by the Ministry and the control of private hospitals by those running them and by regular inspection on behalf of the Minister.

PART V

PROPERTY OF PATIENTS

Section 73. This section *requires a* welfare authority to apply to

the Department of Affairs of Mental Patients for the appointment
of a committee in respect of the estate of any person in their area
who is incapable by reason of mental disorder of managing his
affairs.

Section 74. This section *requires management committees,
welfare authorities and persons running private hospitals to notify*
the Department for the Affairs of Mental Patients, of *any person
under their care* whom they have reason to believe is *incapable of
managing his affairs* by reason of mental disorder, within such time
and in such form as the Lord Chief Justice may prescribe.

Section 75. This section *authorises the authority* responsible for
the payment of earnings or pension from the sources referred to in
the section to any person incapable by reason of mental disorder of
managing and administering his property and affairs, *to pay
whatever proportion they think fit to the institution or person
having the care of the patient, to be applied for his benefit.* At their
discretion they may pay all or part of the remainder to members of
the patient's family or other persons for whom the patient might be
expected to provide if he were not mentally disordered, or in reim-
bursement of money applied by any person in payment of the
patient's debts or his maintenance or other benefit or that of his
dependants referred to above, provided in each case that a committee, receiver or guardian has not been appointed in Northern
Ireland in respect of the patient's estate.

PART VI

THE REVIEW TRIBUNAL

There is only one *Review Tribunal* for Northern Ireland with
membership and functions similar to those of the Mental Health
Review Tribunal in England and Wales (Sections 76 to 79 and
Third Schedule).

PART VII

ADMINISTRATIVE PROVISIONS

Section 80. This section *authorises the Authority to provide
special accommodation under its control and management for
persons subject to detention under this Act who,* in the Authority's

opinion, *require treatment under conditions of special security on account of their dangerous, violent or criminal propensities.*

Section 84. This section *authorises the Minister to set up an inquiry* in any case where it appears desirable to do so in connection with any matter arising under this Act.

ANNUAL REPORTS

Section 85. This section *requires the Authority and every hospital management committee to include a report of their respective operations under this Act in their annual reports* and every *special care management committee to make annual reports to the Authority on their operations under this Act*, with a copy to the Ministry each year.

Section 87. This section *requires a management committee, a person carrying on a private hospital and a welfare authority to furnish to the Lord Chief Justice, the Review Tribunal, the Ministry and the Department for the Affairs of Mental Patients such returns*, reports and other information in relation to patients in their care *as are required for the purposes listed in the section.*

PART VIII

FINANCIAL PROVISIONS

Sections 90 to 97 concern various financial matters, including medical practitioners' fares, travelling and subsistence allowances, pocket money for patients and grants to health authorities.

PART IX

Miscellaneous and General

OFFENCES

Section 98. This section *defines offences arising from forgery* or the making of false statements connected with the various processes under the Act which are listed in the section.

The *penalties* for the above offences are, on summary conviction, a term of imprisonment not exceeding six months or a fine not exceeding £100, or both, or, on conviction on indictment, imprisonment for a term not exceeding two years or a fine not exceeding £500, or both.

Ill Treatment of Patients

Section 100. This section *renders it an offence for* any officer on the staff or otherwise employed in a hospital, a private hospital, or for any member of the management committee of a hospital or any person running a private hospital *to ill-treat or wilfully neglect a patient receiving treatment* for mental disorder *as an in-patient or on the premises of the hospital or private hospital* while the patient is attending there for treatment for mental disorder *as an out-patient.*

It is also an offence for any individual to ill-treat or wilfully neglect a mentally disordered person while he is subject to his *guardianship* under this Act or in his custody or care.

The *penalties* for the above offences are similar to those in Section 98.

PROTECTION OF FEMALE PATIENTS

Section 101. This section *renders it an offence* for any person *to have sexual intercourse with, or commit any of the other acts listed involving a woman detained under this Act* or by order of the Lord Chief Justice *or, not liable to be detained, being a person requiring special care, provided the person charged cannot prove that he did not know and had no reason to know that the woman was within either of these categories.*

The *penalty* for this offence on conviction or indictment is a term of imprisonment not exceeding two years.

ASSISTING PATIENTS TO ABSENT THEMSELVES WITHOUT LEAVE

Section 102. This section *renders it an offence to induce or knowingly assist a patient detained in hospital or subject to guardianship under this Act to absent himself without leave*, or to escape from legal custody, or knowingly to harbour a patient absent without leave, or to assist him to prevent, hinder, or interfere with his being taken into custody or returned to hospital or where he should be under guardianship.

The *penalties* for offences under this section are the same as those in Section 98.

WARRANT TO SEARCH FOR AND REMOVE PATIENTS

Section 105. This section *authorises a Justice of the Peace to issue a warrant authorising a constable to enter,* if need be by force, *any premises specified in the warrant,* and, if thought fit, *to remove from there to a place of safety,* pending arrangements for his treatment or care, *any person whom the Justice of the Peace has,* on information sworn by a welfare officer, by an officer authorised by the Authority or by a constable, *reasonable cause to believe to be suffering from mental disorder and to have been or being ill-treated, neglected, or not kept under proper control and to be living alone and unable to care for himself.* The *constable must be accompanied in the execution of the warrant by a medical practitioner.*

This section also *authorises a Justice of the Peace,* on information sworn by a welfare officer, by an officer authorised by the Authority or by a constable, *to issue a warrant authorising any named constable, accompanied by a medical practitioner, to enter any premises, if need be by force, and to remove from there any patient liable to be taken or retaken to any place under this Act, provided admission to the premises has been refused or that such refusal is apprehended.*

A *patient* taken to a place of safety under this section *may be detained there for a period not exceeding seventy-two hours.*

A *'place of safety'* is defined as any hospital the management committee of which are willing temporarily to receive persons taken there under this Act, any Royal Ulster Constabulary station or any other suitable place whose occupier is willing temporarily to receive such persons.

MENTALLY DISORDERED PERSONS FOUND IN PUBLIC PLACES

Section 106. This section *authorises a constable to remove to a place of safety an apparently mentally disordered person in immediate need of care or control, found by him in a place to which the public have access, provided he considers it necessary in the interests of that person or for the protection of other persons.*

A person removed in this way *may be detained in the place of safety for a period not exceeding seventy-two hours,* so that he may be examined by a medical practitioner, interviewed by a welfare officer and any necessary arrangements made for his treatment or care.

Notification of Nearest Relative

Section 109. This section *requires the management committee of a hospital* to which a patient has been admitted, other than on an application of his nearest relative, *to inform that relative of his admission as soon as may be practicable.*

ADMISSION OF PATIENTS TO SPECIFIED HOSPITALS

Section 110. This section *authorises the Authority to order* in writing *a patient's admission*, as the result of any duly completed application under Part II of this Act, *to any hospital specified in the order, and imposes a duty on the management committee of that hospital to admit the patient.*

11 1976 and after

> We trained hard, but it seemed every time we were beginning
> to form teams we would be reorganised. I was to learn later
> in life that we tend to meet every situation by reorganising,
> and a wonderful method it can be for creating the illusion of
> progress while producing confusion, inefficiency and
> demoralisation.
>
> *Petronius Arbiter* c. A.D. 65.

1st April, 1974 was the appointed day for the disorganisation of the
National Health Service, legalised by the *National Health Service
Reorganisation Act* 1970. On that date, all hospital management
committees were abolished and thus those mental subnormality
hospitals which had previously retained their identity and avoided
amalgamation with other types of hospital finally lost their independent representation by lay members with executive authority.
This occurred just at the time when they were beginning to achieve
the improvements in the facilities for the care of the mentally subnormal for which they had struggled for years against a
background of disinterest on the part of both medical and non-
medical members of authorities not directly concerned with the
problem. Their abolition left the general public without any
representation on statutory bodies with executive authority below

the Area Health Authority level, and the membership of that body was numerically restricted, so that there was no guarantee it would always include anyone with particular experience and interest in the field of mental subnormality. The responsibility for the organisation and day-to-day running of the mental subnormality hospitals, as part of the medical services linked with a district general hospital, passed to District Management Teams consisting of a community physician, a lay administrator, a finance officer, a nursing administrator, a general practitioner and a representative of all the hospital consultants in the district. Again, the possible limitations on adequate representation of the mental subnormality field are obvious.

The intention of the Act was that the interests of the consumer at district level were to be represented by Community Health Councils. However, these are entirely advisory and they have no executive authority or control of financial budgets as did the hospital management committees, and it has yet to be seen whether the care of the mentally subnormal will be any better under these new arrangements than it was before their abolition—in the author's view, for the foreseeable future, it may well be worse.

Certainly, 1st July, 1976—twenty-seven months after the appointed day—finds morale in many mental subnormality hospitals at a very low level, with feelings of great uncertainty as to their future, and the sad picture of senior officers, who have given many years devoted service in this field, opting for early retirement rather than serve under those appointed from other fields who have no previous experience and, as yet, no proved interest, in the care of the mentally subnormal. The hospital service for the mentally subnormal gives the impression of slowly bleeding to death as it loses its senior officers in this way, and as other members of staff move to Local Authorities able to offer them far better pay and conditions of service for comparable jobs than can the hospital service. At the same time, hospital social workers who opted to remain hospital-based when they became employees of Local Authorities' social service departments as a result of the *Social Services Act* 1971, continue under conditions and salaries inferior to those of their community-based colleagues!

The staff left in hospital find themselves caring for patients with the most severe mental and physical handicaps, or with disturbed behaviour which has proved unmanageable elsewhere. Against this background, it is not surprising that nurses of the mentally handicapped should have been among the most militant members of the Confederation of Health Service Employees (COHSE) in their industrial action for improved pay and conditions. Meanwhile, following the publication of the Report on the South Ockendon Inquiry, consultants in mental subnormality hospitals are expressing concern that the normal rules of evidence of a court of law do not appear to apply in such inquiries under Section 70 of the *National Health Service Act* 1946 and that, as a result, opinions on identifiable individuals may be expressed by the Committee of Inquiry, based on evidence not always on oath, and subsequently published, with intensely damaging results to those referred to, and with little real opportunity of redress for them. Consultants, too, are particularly concerned at a recommendation in the South Ockendon Report, which appeared to imply that their clinical decisions concerning the care of the patients, for which they have ultimate legal responsibility, may be over-ruled by 'policy decisions of the hospital multidisciplinary team on general principles of care in the villas . . .'.

Looking ahead at a time of economy and financial cuts, it is easier to state what one would like to happen than what is, in fact, likely to happen. As has been stated previously, a comprehensive, integrated service for the mentally subnormal should be sufficiently flexible to provide for their various needs at different times. This will only be possible if the government of the day allocates sufficient money to the service to provide and staff all the extra places in special schools, adult training centres and hostels indicated in the document 'Better Services for the Mentally Handicapped', and to develop day-care facilities in mental subnormality hospitals. More social workers will be needed with, it is to be hoped, the expertise and interest in the problems of the mentally subnormal which their mental welfare officer predecessors showed.

It seems certain that mental subnormality hospitals will be asked in future to care for an increasing number of severely mentally and physically handicapped patients, who will require skilled general nursing care, as well as psychiatric care of their instability due to brain damage or to frank, superimposed mental illness. Such patients will require the services of far more physiotherapists, speech therapists and occupational therapists than are at present working in these hospitals.

Mental subnormality hospitals are at present caring for the majority of patients of limited intelligence with antisocial or psychopathic behaviour, who are not in the maximum security hospitals at Rampton and Moss Side. Many such patients are unsuitable for care in open hospitals and need the sort of security envisaged in the regional units first proposed in 1961, which have not yet materialised, but which have recently been recommended again in the interim report of the Butler Committee on the Care of Mentally Abnormal Offenders.

In a joint publication, Campaign for the Mentally Handicapped, MIND and the Spastics Society (1975) advocated the sale of surplus hospital land and the use of the proceeds to house the patients in the community, claiming that in many cases, hospital care was unnecessary and inappropriate. However, this author still sees a need for mental subnormality hospitals as sheltered communities for a number of mentally handicapped people, who do not need continuous medical or nursing care, but who are unable to live independently in society. I envisage the organisation of such communities as villages, with renaming of hospitals accordingly, and the provision within them of a full range of educational, occupational, recreational, spiritual and therapeutic facilities and the establishment of free communication in both directions between the residents of the village and members of the general public in the area. I believe that, for many mentally subnormal people in the category described, such village communities would offer a much fuller and happier life than their care in small hostels in urban areas, with difficulties of access to the full range of services available in the villages. My experience convinces me that to use for political and doctrinaire purposes estimated percentages of the existing population of mental subnormality hospitals who 'could' be cared for in hostels in the community, if they were available, is both unrealistic and lacking in compassion for those it claims to help, in that it ignores the fact that many of them have been in hospital for 20 or more years, that it is the only real home they have ever known and is where the only friends they have also live. Nevertheless, I am in favour of transferring as many suitable patients from hospitals to hostels as possible, but would suggest consideration of the following criteria in each case before reaching a decision:

1. The patient's own wishes.
2. The location of the hostel in relationship to the place which the patient regards as home and where most of his friends are situated.
3. The availability near the hostel of employment or occupation similar to that at which the patient has proved most suitable during his rehabilitation in hospital.
4. The adequate staffing of hostels, and the level of tolerance of staff and neighbours of behaviour disorders which would be regarded as quite acceptable in hospital.
5. The availability of the services of a consultant psychiatrist from the mental subnormality field to treat any psychiatric disturbance in hostel residents in its early stages and so avoid the necessity for their return to hospital.
6. The reasonable certainty that the patient will be at least no worse off in the hostel than he would be had he remained in hospital.

There are at present not enough trained nurses to provide desirable standards of care for mentally subnormal people who require hospital care, but it is to be hoped that their numbers may increase so as to allow them to become community nurses and to provide a follow-up domiciliary service after patients have been discharged from hospital. There will be an obvious area of overlap here with the social worker's field, and the necessity for definition of roles if possible friction is to be avoided.

At a time of intense general economic gloom and cutback in expenditure in the National Health Service, the prospect of the development of a truly integrated service for the mentally subnormal, in which staff doing comparable work in any of its branches are employed on similar conditions of service and receive the financial rewards they deserve, seems a distant Utopian dream. However, the service can no longer depend on the goodwill of a number of devoted individuals, and the public have no right to criticise the shortcomings of the existing services unless they are prepared to find the money to improve them. Until they do, the responsibility for the conditions which gave rise to the inquiries at

Ely, Farleigh and South Ockendon and others, no doubt yet to come, is ultimately as much theirs as that of the staff who were struggling under impossible conditions long before interest in the mentally subnormal became the currently fashionable and respectable 'in thing'.

REFERENCES

1976 and After

Arbiter, P. *Satyricon,* trans. W. Arrowsmith, Univ. of Michigan Press, Ann Arbor, 1959.

Butler Committee. *Interim Report of the Committee on Mentally Subnormal Offenders*. Cmnd. 5698, H.M.S.O., London, 1974.

Campaign for the Mentally Handicapped, MIND, Spastics Society. Hospital Land—A Resource for the Future?, 1975.

Appendix

SOME ORGANISATIONS CONCERNED WITH THE CARE OF THE MENTALLY HANDICAPPED

Association of Occupational Therapists,
251 Brompton Road, London S.W. 3.
Telephone: 01-589 7458.
Association of Professions for the Mentally Handicapped,
24 Nutford Place, London W1N 6AN.
Telephone: 01-262 2641.
Bristol Campaign for the Mentally Handicapped,
65 Halsbury Road, Bristol BS6 7EG.
Telephone: 0272-422052.
British Association for the Retarded,
17 Pembridge Square, London W2.
Telephone: 01-229 1855.
British Association of Social Workers,
42 Bedford Square, London WC1B 3OP.
Telephone 01-580 9421.
British Society for the Study of Mental Subnormality,
Monyhull Hospital, King's Norton, Birmingham B30 3QB.
Telephone: 021-444 2271.

British Society for Music Therapy,
 48 Lanchester Road, London N6 4TA.
 Telephone: 01-883 1331.

Buckets and Spades,
 Churchwood Road, Hollington, St. Leonard's on Sea, Sussex.
 Telephone: Hastings 51215.

Campaign for the Mentally Handicapped,
 96 Portland Place, London W.1.

Camphill Village Trust,
 Delrow House, Aldenham, Watford, Herts.
 Telephone: 092-766066.

Central Council for Education and Training in Social Work,
 Clifton House, Euston Road, London NW1 2RS.
 Telephone: 01-387 3456.

Chartered Society of Physiotherapists,
 14 Bedford Row, London WC1 4ED.
 Telephone: 01-242 1941.

College of Speech Therapists,
 47 St John's Wood High Street, London.
 Telephone: 01-586 1958.

Cottage and Rural Enterprises,
 Blackerton, East Anstey, Near Tiverton, Devon.
 Telephone: Anstey Mills 252.

Department of Health and Social Security,
 Alexander Fleming House, Elephant and Castle,
 London SE1 6BY.
 Telephone: 01-407 5522.

Family Fund, Joseph Rowntree Memorial Trust,
 Beverley House, Shipton, Yorks YO3 6RB.
 Telephone: 0904-29241.

Hester Adrian Research Centre,
 The University, Manchester M13 9PL.
 Telephone: 061-273 3333.

Home Farm Trust,
 57 Queen Square, Bristol 1.
 Telephone: 0272-292060.

Institute for Research into Mental and Multiple Handicap,
 16 Fitzroy Square, London W1P 5HQ.
 Telephone: 01-387 6066.

Institute of Mental Subnormality,
    Wolverhampton Road, Kidderminster, Worcs. DY10 3PP.
    Telephone: Kidderminster 850251.
King Edward's Hospital Fund for London,
    King's Fund Centre, 24 Nutford Place, London W1H 6AN.
    Telephone: 01-262 2641.
Mental Welfare Commission for Scotland,
    22 Melville Street, Edinburgh EH3 7NS.
    Telephone: 031-225 8338.
MIND/Mental Health,
    22 Harley Street, London W1N 2ED.
    Telephone: 01-637 0741.
Molesey Venture, The Sons of Divine Providence,
    Westminster House, 25 Lower Teddington Road,
    Hampton Wick, Kingston-upon-Thames, Surrey.
    Telephone: 01-977 5130.
National Association of Teachers of the Mentally Handicapped,
    1 Urchfield Avenue, Urmston, Manchester M31 3RT.
National Society for Autistic Children,
    1A Golders Green Road, London NW11 8AE.
    Telephone: 01-458 4375.
National Society for Mentally Handicapped Children,
    17 Pembridge Square, London W2 4EP.
    Telephone: 01-229 8941.
Northern Ireland. Ministry of Health and Social Services,
    Dundonald House, Upper Newtownards Road,
    Belfast BT4 3SF.
    Hospital Authority,
    26 Adelaide Street, Belfast BT2 8FG.
    Telephone: Belfast 27871.
Preschool Playgroups Association,
    Alford House, Aveline Street, London SE11 5DJ.
    Telephone: 01-582 8871.
Ravenswood Foundation,
    18 Seymour Place, London W.1.
    Telephone: 01-723 2213.
Riding for the Disabled Association,
    National Equestrian Centre, Kenilworth, Warwicks CV8 2LR.
    Telephone: Coventry 27192.

Royal College of Nursing,
   Henrietta Place, Cavendish Square, London W1M 0AB.
   Telephone: 01-580 2646.
Royal College of Psychiatrists,
   17 Belgrave Square, London S.W.1.
Scottish Home and Health Department,
   St. Andrew's House, Edinburgh EH1 3DE.
   Telephone: 031-556 8501.
Spastics Society,
   12 Park Crescent, London W1N 4EQ.
   Telephone: 01-636 5020.
Welsh Office, (Health Department),
   Cathay's Park, Cardiff CF1 3NQ.
   Telephone: 0222 28066.

Index